Time Management of Twenty-first Century

Time Management of Twenty-first Century

By

Dr. Ila A. Thanki
(*M.A. Ph.D.*)

ADHYAYAN

ADHYAYAN PUBLISHERS & DISTRIBUTORS
New Delhi-110 002

Published by
ADHYAYAN PUBLISHERS & DISTRIBUTORS
4378/4B, 105, J.M.D. House, Murari Lal Street
Ansari Road Darya Ganj, New Delhi - 110002
Ph.: 011-23263018, 011-23277156, Fax: 011-23280028
Email: adhyayanpublishers@yahoo.com

Time Management of Twenty-First Century

Edition 2010
ISBN 978-81-8435-216-0

Printed in India

Published by Harish Chandra Yadav for Adhyayan Publishers & Distributors, Delhi. Laser Typesetting at V. M. Graphics and Printed at Tarun Offset Printers, Delhi

Dedicated to

God, Parents

&

My Lovely Daughter

Ishita, Khushuli & Chandni

Acknowledgements

My debts are many and I acknowledge them with much pride and delight.

First I feel immense pleasure with a deep sense of reverence my heartfelt gratitude to my learned Principal Shree Dr. Anupam R. Nagar, Dr. V.R. Godhaniya Mahila College, Porbandar for his excessive co-operation and support. I express my gratitude my most Respected President Shree Virambhai Godhaniya and all trustees of Dr. V.R. Godhaniya Mahila College, Porbandar, who are helpful and co-operate me.

I am greatly indebted my elder sister Ilaben Vajariya, Deptt of English, Kalpanaben P. Joshi, Deptt. of Computer, Dr. Sulbha R. Devpurkar, Smita H. Acharya, Dr. Ramila H. Virani. Dr. Jamkuben Sojitra and just like my younger sister Dr. Bhavana R. Keshwala and Nathiben Rajshakha & all my colleagues of Dr. V.R. Godhaniya Mahila College, Porbandar whose all encouraged me their kind co-operation and support.

I express my profound sense of gratitude to my Hon. Professor and Reader Dr. Mahesh V. Joshi and Mrs. Ushaben Joshi Rajkot, under his guidance and constant encouragement, I can do my work.

I never forget that the help of most. Hon. to my esteemed Professor Shri Jyotiben Thanki who always helpful me (Spiritual) and moral support during my life.

I never forget the contribution of my parents. Both of my younger sister Pragna and Jignasa and both of Jijaji in preparation of this work. I never forget my dearest and lovely daughter Chandni. Ishita and Khushali Joshi who always treat me a cup of tea.

I express my gratitude of Adhyayan Publishers and Distributors, New Delhi who pains to bring this book into a beautiful computerise form.

I am also indebted to the contribution of the others though unnamed in giving shape to my ideas and thinking in fast. It is very difficult to acknowledge all the names and nature of help and encouragement.

Finally, I wish to devote a supplication to the Divine spirit without whose blessings this task would not have been accomplished. I bow my head in utter humility and complete dedication.

Dr. Ila A. Thanki

PREFACE

In modern era, twenty-first-century world is running ahead. Life is getting busier day by day. Every second there is something is happening around the corner. There is so much today that sitting a day at home or being away from your daily tasks for a day seems to be like missing on a monthly task and at the end of it you feel like the one who out of the heard.

In fact, the wise and successful suggest that if you want to reach the heights, achieve your goal and finally want what you have longed for then the very first step is to value your time.

Time is a very necessity of life and if you want to walk along with the world then you have to keep a hold on to your time. Time is such a resource that cannot store it or save it for latter and dare if you are careless about managing your time then no great power can stop time slipping off your hands. Always keep in mind that you get the same 24 hours of the day that others get and to make a difference you have to make a difference you have to make use of your 24 hours in a different and better way than others.

Prof. Benjamin Franklin has been quoted as saying, "If time be of all things most precious, wasting time must be the greatest prodigality, since lost time is never found again." This is such a true and insightful comment that rings as true today and it did during Franklin's life.

Time is the great equalizer. Now matter how important or rich or famous you are. Everyday 24 hours, 1440 minutes or 86,400 seconds. This is your daily time account and you decide how to make use of this valuable resource by retrieving minutes and seconds similar to a bank account. The big difference is that you cannot make savings because the next day will start with an opening balancing of exactly 86,400 seconds again. Time that has not been used properly is vain. This concept gives you an idea how important it is use our time in the right way since there are no savings nor overdrafts. You should keep this in mind when you set your goals and plan each day.

Time is something that you can never take back. What's done is done. Nothing in history can be changed. The most, we can do about anything that has already been done is to take counter measures to prevent the damage from spreading. However, there is one more effective way to stop damage and that is to prevent it. You must have heard it said that "prevention is better than cure". This quote is most often used in terms of illness, however, this can also be done for future mistakes. Time-management is a form of prevention. Why is time management so important? Time is the most important commodity. Time never comes back. It never rewinds like videotape. You can get more money, but you cannot get more time! Here are the most common reasons why time is so important.

1. Time cannot be Stored

Everyone no matter how rich or poor spends time the

same way, it does speed-up for the rich and slow down the poor. Time management is equal to wise usage of time. This may be the difference between fame and failure.

2. Time is Rare

Yes, everybody has the same number of hours, but haven't you noticed that people are complaining that they don't have enough of it? There is just "so little time and so much to do" that people go out of focus. Time management means giving importance to priorities and nearer deadline and these give you enough for the crucial activities in life.

3. Time is a Limited Resource

Remember that time is a limited source. There is a Chinese proverb that say's "No amount of gold will buy you time has passed". Knowing that time is a limited resource, you would naturally need to cherish it. After all, deadlines to work will continue to inch closer to you whether or not you have started or you are slow on it. Once time is lost, you can never make-up for it. Your work will have to be compromised given that you have not managed your time.

4. Small Steps Buiid into Big Goals

To achieve career success, one important thing is to set goals. And goals needs to be mapped on to a timeline. That timeline needs to be managed. Any goal that does not have a timeline is as good as a moving goal post. Career success does not come in a day. It takes time.

Understand the importance of time management as your career success depends on these small steps across time. If you not take care of the seconds, the minutes will waste, and so will the hours and days. All these will accumulate into poor results. The importance of time management is to understand that small steps across time build into a big goals. And a main part of achieving goals is about time management.

5. Efficiency of Your Work Relates to Time

Being efficient at work is about managing your time. Optimum use of your time means you accomplish more in the least possible time. Being able to manage your time well gives you a competitive advantage over your colleagues. You get more done and hence you get assigned to more important projects in the future.

When boss see you as an efficient worker, you become a competitive advantage to your unit. This translates to better performance score, more trust, and respect from colleagues and boss. The importance of time management in this aspect should be kept in mind if you want to climb higher in the corporater ladder.

6. Knowing Your Priority at Work

The importance of time management in your career success also comes in the form of allowing you to prioritize. Part of good time management skills involves knowing when to do when to do what is urgent and important. Being able to recognize work that needs focus at the right time is a skill that is important to achieving career success.

When you are able to crystallize what is important, you will attend to the actual task that needs focus. You become more effective. Becoming efficient and effective at your workplace will automatically contribute significantly to your career success.

Moreover time management not only makes your work

and life systematic. It also helps you to spare time of day for your own self, we all have heard of the saying which goes "A STICH IN TIME SAVE NINE", however, there are very less people who have realized the proper meaning of this saying. This means, that if do your work at the very moment when it is scheduled for, then you are saved for a hundred for, then you are saved for a hundred hurdles that you would have to face in case you would have deleted it!!!

With good time management skills you are in control of your time and your life, of your stress and energy levels. You make progress at work. You are able to maintain balance between your work, personal, and family tasks.

Time is running everywhere. . . clocks and watches remind us how time files. Time management skills help to organize and prioritize your activities. It is one of the skills that is much needed in day-to-day life. Are you not being able to finish your work on time? Is the pending work increasing everyday? Are you unable to manage work and studies? Nowadays almost everyone multi-tasks, Is that good or bad? It depends upon time management, hard work and a right chance are the most important factors for success, but doing things on time adds extra percentage in the probability of successful in any profession.

We keep hearing the word "busy" a lot. There are two kinds of busy, chaotic, disorganized busy and calm effective busy. It goes without saying that being the latter helps to pack in more productivity in your work. Improving our "effective quotient" calls for mastery of basic time management skill. We constantly hear the retrain that we do not know where the time goes. Whether you are an executive, a student or a home maker, you need to achieve more in every minute of day and to enjoy each task that you take up. We will be well on our way to top if we know how squeeze the most out of even a minute. The first thing in mind is to question whether you have a personal sense of time or a time log. This helps you to keep track of how you spend each hour. There is a way to do this, divide each day for a period of two weeks into one hour intervals and jot down what you do in them. You can divide the activities under such heading as meetings—writing making phone calls, reading, time-spent with the family, etc. At the end of the week examine your time log.

Good time management simply means deciding what you want to get out of life and efficiently pursuing these goals. Time management does not mean being busy all the time it means using your time the way you want to use it, which can include large dose of day dreaming and doing nothing. "Good time management brings with it increased relaxation, less stress, more satisfaction and greater accomplishment."

Time management is a vehicle that can carry you from wherever you are to wherever, you want to go. Know and use your prime time, that time during the day when you are most likely to be alert, enthusiustic and creative. If you don't know where you are going and road will take you there. Conversely, if you do know your destination, you can quickly determine which route is best for you.

Are you willing to pay the price to get the prize? If so, you are ready to exchange your old time wasting habits for good time management behaviour. In a society enamoured with efficiency and productivity, it is a vital that we manage our time and our lives so that, we as individuals and as communities of men and women live healthier, happier more peace-filled lives.

Setting aside as little as 10 minutes per day for yourself adds up to more than 60 hours per year. Make it 15 minutes per day, and you will have enjoyed 90 hours of "reward time"!

CONTENTS

1

EVOLUTION OF TIME MANAGEMENT IN WORLD

"It is those who make the worst use of their time who most complain of it's shorteness."

— Jean De La Bruyere

"Time is the most valuable thing a man can spend."

— Laertius Diogness

"Lost time is never, found again."

— Benjamin Franklin

"Time is the wisest counsellor of all."

— Pericles

Content of this Chapter

Introduction; Time Management Quotes; Importance of Time Management in our Daily Life; Evolution of Time Management in the World; Concept and Structure of Time Management; Evolution of Time Management in India; Conclusion

1.1 INTRODUCTION

Time is the most precious resource in business and capital society. Unlike other resources like peopl϶ and capital, time is often considered fixed. However, the way people subjectively experience and utilize time varies substantially between people. Human development provides the basis for breakthrough improvement in time management. In particular, in higher, states of consciousness it may be possible to transcend the limitations of time so that time ceases to be a factor limiting our accomplishments in life. In order to realize in practice a transformation to improved time management. First of all, here we will discuss about the help with your time management, enjoy the following time management quotes.

1.2. TIME MANAGEMENT QUOTES / IMPORTANCE OF TIME MANAGEMENT IN OUR DAILY LIFE

1. I wasted time and now time doth waste me.

   —William Shakespeare

2. Time is really the only capital that any human being has, and the only thing he can't afford to lose.

   —Thomas Edison

3. Time is the most valuable thing a man can spend.

   —Laertius Diogenes

4. Money; I can only gain or lose. But time I can only lose. So, I must spend it carefully.

   —Author Unknown

5. Dost thou love life? Then do not squander time, for that is the stuff life is made of.

   —Benjamin Franklin

6. A man who dares to waste one hour of life has not discovered the value of life.

   —Charles Darwin

7. Being rich is having money: being wealthy is having time. —Margaret Bonnano

8. Lost time is never found again.

   —Banjamin Franklin

9. Time passes you say, But no !
   Alas, time is staying and we pass by.

   —Dobson A.

10. It is only in appearance that time is a river. It is a vast landscape and it is the eye of the beholder that moves.

    —Thornton Wilder

11. People who cannot find time for recreation are obliged sooner or later to find time for illness.

    —John Wanamaker

12. The trouble with our times is that the future is not what it used to be.

    —Paul Valery

13. Half our life is spent trying to find something to do with the time we have rushed through life trying to save.

    —Will Rogers Jr.

14. Better three Hours too soon, than one minute too late.

    —William Shakespeare

15. The moment has no time.

    —Leonardo Da Vinci

16. Time is the measurable unit of concerning a before and an after.

    —Aristotle

17. Try as they may to saver the taste of eternity their thoughts still twist and turn upon the ebb and flow of things in past and future time. But if only their

minds could be seized and held steady, they would be still for a while and for that short moment, they would glimpse the splendour of eternity, which is forever still.

—St. Augustine

18. Time and tide wait for no man.

—Geoffrey Chaucer

19. What we love to do we find time to do.

—John L. Spalding

20. There is time for everything.

—Thomas Edison

21. It is only possible to live happily-ever-after on a day-to-day basis.

—Margaret Bonnano

22. Time stays long enough for those who use it.

—Leonardo Da Vinci

23. The . . . silent, never resting thing called time, rolling, rushing on, swift, silent, like an all-embracing ocean tide . . . this is forever very literally a miracle; a thing to strike us dumb."

—Thomas Carlyle

24. Time is the moving image of unmoving eternity.

—Plato

25. We must use time wisely and forever realize that the time is always ripe to do right.

—Nelson Mandela

26. We must use time as a tool, not as a couch.

-John F. Kennedy

27. This time like all times is a very good one if we but know what to do with it.

—Ralph Waldo Emerson

28. Killing time is like committing slow suicide.

—Anonymous

29. You cannot kill time without injuring eternity.

—Herry David Thoreau

30. One thing you can't recycle is wasted time.

—Anonymous

31. One makes a time of time.

—Breton

32. Not time is the measure of movement but: . . . each constant periodic appearance of ideas.

—Locke

33. What then is time? If no one asks me, I know what it is, If I wish to explain it to him who asks, I do not know.

—St. Augustine

34. Time is the Supreme Law of nature.

—Arthur Stanley Eddington

35. To know the secret of time one must first fathom the mystry of the timeless moment, and this is accomplished through transcendental meditation.

—Charles F. Lutes

36. Life is endless, not punctuated by nights, days, months and years for all are one in the eternal stream.

—Sathya Sai Baba

37. The calendar is intolerable to all wisdom, the horror of all astronomy, and a laughing stock from a mathematician's point of view.

—Roger Bacon

38. But at my back I always hear times's winged chariot hurrying near.

—Andrew Marvell

39. While we are postponing, life speeds by.

—Seneces

40. The time for action is now. It's never too late to do something.

—Carl Sandburg

41. . . . Every moment is the right moment.

—Sathya Sai Baba

42. To me every hour of the light and dark is a miracle, Every cubic inch of space is a miracle.

—Walt Whitman

43. Time is the wiset counsellor of all.

—Pericles

44. Time is patient . . . it devours man one second at a time.

—Maheshvarnath

45. Time is the school in which we learn, time is the fire in which we burn.

—Delmore Schwartz

46. Time is a fire that consumes me, But I am the fire.

—Borges

47. Do not Dwell in the past, Do not dream of

the future, concentrate the mind on the present moment.

—Buddha

48. Don't let yesterday use up too much of today.

—Will Rogers

49. If God calls me tomorrow I will go without a moment's turning back."

—Paramhans Yogananda

50. Everthing happens to everybody sooner or later if there is time enough.

—George Bernard Shaw

51. Live as if you were to die tomorrow. Learn as if you were to live forever.

—Mahatma Gandhi

52. Live as if there is no forever, die as if forever is.

—Maheshvarnath

53. Live your spiritual life as if you were to die tomorrow. Live your material life as if you were to live for 100 years.

—Guy Banner

54. You cannot do a kindness too soon, for you never know-how soon it will be to late.

—Ralph Waldo Emerson

55. You may delay, but time will not.

—Benjamin Franklin

56. For he lives twice who can at once employ, The present well, and even the past enjoy.

—Alexander Pope

57. The happiest people spend much time in a state of

flow—the state in which people are so involved in an activity that nothing else seems to matter, the experience itself is so enjoyable that people will do it even at great cost, for the sheer sake of doing it.

—Mihaly Csikszentimihalyi

58. Time is what we want most, but what we use worst. —William Penn

59. Years of love have been forgot,
In the hatred of a minute.

—Edgar Allan Pol

60. Life is not so short but that there is always time enough for courtesy.

—Ralph Waldo Emerson

61. Too slow for those who wait,
Too swift for those who fear,
Too Long for those who grieve,
Too short for those who rejoice,
But for those who Love
Time is not.

—Herry Van Dyke

62. Time as be grows old teaches many lessons.

—Aeschylzes

63. Histories make men wise poets, witty: the mathematics, subtile, natural philosophy, deep, moral, grave, logic and rhetoric, able to contend.

—Francis Bacon

64. Whoever controls the past controls the future who even controls the present controls the past.

—

65. Pick my left pocket of its silver dime, but spare the right it holds my golden time.

—Oliver Wendell Holmes

66. The common man is not concerned about the passage of time, the man of time talent is drives by it.

—Shoppenhauer

67. Can anybody remember when the times were not hard and money not scarce?

—Ralph Waldo Emerson

68. Time is the coin of your life,
It is the only coin you have,
and only you can determine how it will be spent.
Be careful lest you let other people spend it for you.

—Carl Sandburg

69. Time has been transformed, and we have changed,
it has advanced and set us in motion,
it has unveiled its face,
inspiring us with bewilderment and exhilaration.

—Khalil Jibran

70. Time is the greatest innovator.

—Francis Bacon

71. See, if you can, eternity in the hour that passes.

—Arabian proverb

72. To see the the world in a grain of sand,
and to see heaven in a wild flower.
hold infinity in the palm of your hands,
and eternity in an hour.

—William Blake

73. Time is the meaning of life.

—Claudel

74. This is the beginning of a new day.
God has given me this day to use as I will.
I can waste it or use it for good.
What I do today is important, because
I am exchanging a day of my life for it.
When tomorrow comes.
this day will gone forever
leaving in its place something
that I have traded for it.
I want it to be gain not loss,
good not evil, success not failure
in order then I shall not regret
the price I paid for it.

—Anonymens

75. The factor of time is very vital in life. Those who have accomplished great things in the world have been those who valued in their life. The time of life is limited and a great amount of evolution has to be accomplished for fulfilment of life. Therefore, the factor of time must be valued above everything.

—Maharishi Mahesh Yogi

76. Awareness is crucial for successful time management. Everybody has heard the expression that time is money. One of my favourite writers, essayist Michael ventura, once wrote that time is life, meaning that how we use our time defines our life. And if we are unconscious about how we spend our time, then our life is [. . .].

—Anonymous

77. Time is the enemy of the poor business and the friend of the great business.

—Warren Buffett

78. Most people spend more time and energy into around problems there in trying to solve them.

—Henry Ford

79. We must use time creatively and forever realize that the time is always hope to do great things.

—Martin Luther

80. The ability to concentrate and to use time well is everything.

—Lee Iacocca

81. Time is the scarcest resource of the manager: if it is not managed, nothing else can be managed.

—Peter F. Drucker

82. Time management refers to the development of processes and tools that increase efficiency and productivity.

—

1.3 EVOLUTION OF TIME MANAGEMENT IN THE WORLD

For a couple weeks I have been thinking about history and the present with respect to utilizing time, as it time were something that could be braided, woven, folded or unravelled like colourful fabric. I am still lingering on time's malleable qualities because I have always thought of time as something too complex and vast to be affected by anything other than starts. If a key element in societal evolution is the dissemination of the perfect idea at its appropriate time and management.

Time investments can take two forms: creating foundations for future directed decisions and the actions necessary to implement future directed decisions. The actions may involve "design" thinking and operacy the thinking involved in doing. Thinking is the action in knowledge work.

Foundations for future directed decisions include the exploration of "places" our brains have never been in either our previous experiences or in time. Mentally placing oneself in 1950, 1970, 1980 or another different time in various life situations—geographical locations with their political climates and pursuits for making a living—reveals the limitations of traditional assumptions and the benefits of the "right" time investments. These mental foundations are our protection against taking the "wrong major rouds" in life. Incidentally the human brain—even when trying hard—wants to see the road behind rather than the road ahead. If the world's capable people keep thinking and doing what they are doing yesterday how can there be any progress or development? Are we leaving progress to the incapable?

In the unfashionable Kierkegaard, Peter Drucker wrote about the two poles of human existence life in society (life in time) and life in the spirit.

A man features of life in time is "change".

Society's tomorrows are always built on the foundations of yesterdays unfortunately the progression and changes aren't linear. The reality of (society) today isn't just a more up-to-date version of the worlds of 1650, 1850, 1950 or 1990. This non-linearity is a major source of challenge and difficulty.

A Society of Organizations

In the last hundred years or so society has become a society of organizations. We work in and with organizations plus the goods and servies we consume are the product of organizations. Our challenges are shaped in part by the organizations in which our lives are embedded. One of the key features of this environment is that the rules are subject to change with little or no prior notice. Another key feature is that "forward motion" is necessary to prevent obsolescence or being flattened by a competitor.

Organizational Evolution

For organizations to develop (to become something beyond their startup phase or their affairs in 1950, 1970, 1980. . .). Somebody has to do something to get beyond the yesterday that created today. Somebody has to create new and better for tomorrow. Somebody has to identify the work areas that are the core of development and these work areas have to make sense to the outside world.

The non-linear nature of knowledge advancement and therefore technology-coupled with competitive pressures almost guarantee organization performance crisis or worse. The organization may continue to operate, but it is not financially viable doesn't have a healthy financial structure for getting into the future.

In the waited states we predominately have product/ service-oriented organizations and functional activities with one time dimension. The adequacy of this approach can be judged by customer satisfaction and long-term financial performance.

Career Realities

Since careers (and jobs) are intertwined with organization futures it is vital to clarify and test assumptions. Employment in organizations that are exposed to competition may require vision, passion, hard work, keeping the boss happy, experience, high intelligence, transferable skills, educational and training credentials a GTD system, project management and high knowledge but these are not sufficient in the longer term.

The correlation between education attainment and income levels is based on a historical supply and demand situation rather than a functional mastery of the universe. Credentials can best be thought of as a passport to certain kinds of work rather than a guarantee of real world competitive competence, achievement or success.

One test of the adequacy of our work life aresenal is the ease of making a transition to an attractive, different organization. This point of transition tests the credibility of a career title. When the necessity arises is its not just an old job that is being left behind but a part of one's life. A work approach that is adequate to the challenges ahead is appropriate. This includes a foundation for future directed decisions it shapes our expectations. It also includes a search that makes sense to the individual and the outside world. The purpose of foregoing thoughts on career realities is to dispell the fantasy that someone else is going to look our for out best interests or that our careers will naturally evolve.

Career Evolution

We are responsible for our own development in an unfolding world. The "right" time investments in all major life areas major life areas: By definition, a changing world implies being outside one's comfort zone otherwise it wouldn't be real change.

Our changing world is not limited to external realities. Being prepared for and being prepared to move effectively forward requires. Time investments only way to get to tomorrow. We can only work with what's on our active *radar* and our *mental patterns.* Both of these are time dependent-moving targets. The "right" time investments are the secret to happiness, wealth, reputation, respect and shaping one's destiny.

Why we Need Time Investments: So, what's wrong with living our lives on a day-to-day basis, assuming that what's in our heads is all we need and ignoring the roads ahead? A highly condensed view can be obtained by picking *several earlier* points in history, superimposing the day-to-day approach and testing its adequacy examples are in the news everyday. Another view of time investments can be acquired by exploring the knowledge system view which includes the content and structure of the economy. The best time to work on this is when there is no apparent need when we are successful. Looking back on the primitive origins of human, where could we have acquired the capacity to deal with the challenges ahead?

Time management focuses on five dimensions of reality that form a foundation for future directed decisions.

1. *Organization Evolution:* Main change vehicle in a society of organizations moving in time,
2. *Work Life or Career Evolution:* (Main change initiator in a highly competitive global knowledge-based economy)

3. *Life-design:* Main change beneficiary.
4. *Financial Investing:* A Golden goose, and
5. *Life Navigation System:* The action sequencer.

The expanding world of the Internet is a radar blip? Because you are reading this on the Internet, through links and search ideas to everything that is reachable through the Internet-sites, words, pictures, etc. This type of interconnectivity is revolutionary and its full impact has not yet been reached not even close. This interconnectivity is a "sub-set" of the five dimensions above.

Good intensions are not sufficient. Tips from the time management field are not likely to produce the desired result because the experts in this field don't seem to know much of anything about time or management. A basic ideas is to identify and calendarize high impact work areas that fit our future interests.

Operational elements and steps potential work areas can be identified by exploring the site and creating a structured strategic interest profile your life *radar* consisting of any of the following:

I. The five dimensions listed above (seen separately and as a constellation moving in time).
II. navigations concepts (destinations in time and life: paths, and actions).
III. Conceptual resources (introduction directory list and concepts to daily action).
IV. Processes and tools (interest profile development and calendarization).

When we have a work approach blueprint we can test it against the news to see if it is adequate to our challenges ahead. Although, it is not possible for me to be more specific about the above because I can't occupy your mental space in tim—remember this is a prototype that users may adapt to fit them. Initially all of this may just be a foundation for future directed decisions.

The previous paragraphs concern time life navigations. The time element involves a society of organizations moving in non-linear time. The life dimension is both embedded in the non-personal time element and shaped by the personal challenges ahead. The life dimension may traverse several different time dimensions. The negative part involves determining where are want to go, how do we get there, where do we want to go from we thought we wanted to go and where we think, we want to go next. Implied in navigation is the mystifying our destinations, thinking through the obstacles we might encounter or the false pursuits and making adequete allowances. The navigation element involves a work approach blueprint for creating our futures. The navigation past requires lifetime investments. Time investments are different from just spending time or just reading.

Word Challenges

One of the challenges in working in this difficult area involves the multiple meanings of common (buzz) words—management, leadership, marketing, innovation, entrepreneurship, organization, teams, quality, value proposition, trust, profit, profitability, productivity, business model, growth, customers, markets, industry, best in class, customer service, perception, global, technology, outsourcing, brands, careers, human resources, human capital, knowledge, information, dates, oppurtunities (aim high), passions, strengths, weaknesses, objectives, transparency, strategic initiative, goals, performance metrics, getting things done, doing the right thing getting the right the done (effectiveness), time management, etc.

In one sense these words are used in an everyday operational sense in the media to explain some event and then these same words appear is "conceptual resources" created by capable people that deal with how the world works in time.

Imagine the words being used in the world of a hundred years ago, would the perceived meaning lead to the world of today, the worlds that intervened between then and now plus the worlds of tommorows?

Living Carefully

God has gives each of us a limited time on this earth. Here Paul exhorts us to use this precious commodity of time wisely, not wasting it in sin, but redeeming it by doing good works that will bring honour and glory to our heavenly father.

"Be very careful" or "see accurately". That means we must be governed by our minds, not our emotions. God has gives us the mind of Christ and we are to use it. Our eyes were blinded by Satan, but now the holy spirit of God has opened them so that we can see accurately. Now we can make decisions not as unwise but as wise, making the most of every opportunity, because the day are evil. "Therefore, do not be foolish, but understand what the Lord's will is." We are to exercise our minds, continuously thinking and learning, so that we can accurately perceive spiritual reality.

Why is it so important that we see clearly? Because, the world is under the control of the evil are and though we are human being, we still have sin dwelling in us. We are not yet perfect, thus we still sin, we do not have to, but we are quite capable of it. We are surrounded by traps and stumbling blocks and ditches. We are tempted daily, and there are times we succumb to these temptations. So, we are exhorted to walk carefully, and to look carefully before we walk. We must think (holistic), not according to the philosophies of this world. We must have carefully investigated everything from the beginning. It indicates doing careful research and understanding not mental laziness. We must have a correct perception of reality. So, we are to understand a situation before we make a dicision. We are not to be led by our emotions but by our sanctified reason. Look before you leap! In many countries today there are people who have lost limbs after stepping on landmines. Just so, there are spiritual landmines everywhere and if we walk carelessly, we will sutter great loss. So, watch out! Be careful how you live in the world."

The word "see" is translated watch out. Watch out for those dogs, those men who do evil, those mutilators of the flesh. Beware of them. Know what they are teaching and compare it with the gospel, the touchstone of truth, rather than being gullible and naivll. Don't be like blotting paper, absorbing all kinds of wrong ideas. The holy person takes always decisions to intelligently apprehend the doctrines of the gospel, so they would not be deceived by heretics teaching against salvations by grace through faith alone. We are not to believe everything, we must disc riminate. We must compare everything with the gospel and then reject what is not harmony with it. We must watch out for heretics, deceivers, emotionalists and antinomians, and reject non-human being philosophy of every turn. We must be intelligent God, guided by the gospel in our daily decisions.

"Let no one deceive you with empty words." Who are deceived? Those who refuse to exercise their minds to understand the gospel. The world's words are lies, void of reality. Blessed is the man who does not walk in the counsel of the wicked or stand in the way of sinners or sit in the seat of mockers we must exercise our minds so that we can resist the hollow philosophies of the world.

We are to do all things for the glory of God alone. Just as Lord Ram, Lord Krishna and our great saints, we must be follow in his footsteps. For we are his workmanship unto good works which God has foreordained that we should walk in them. It has nothing to do with what makes us happy, although the truth is, obedience to God will always make us happy in the long run. The chief end of man is to glosify God and enjoy him forever. Thus, we are to walk worthy of our calling, walk in love, and walk in wisdom.

God because of the ignorance that is in them due to the hardening of their hearts. Having lost of sensitivity, they have given themselves over to sensuality so as to indulge in every kind of impurity, with coutinuous lust for more. The fool has said in his heart, "There is no God, and that philosophy governs his every action. Who is a fool? A fool is cultivated by this world. He does not understand that this world is passing away. He is completely engrossed in eating, drinking, buying, selling, planting, harvesting, marrying and giving in marriage and has no interest in the world to come. He spends all his time and energy running after money, power, fame and pleasure, and then throws a party to show people that he has arrived. What a fool!

Once in a time. The ground of a certain rich man produced a good crop. He thought to himself, "What shall I do? I have no place to store my crops." Then he said, "This is what I will do. I will tear down my barns and build bigger ones, and there I will store all my grain and my goods. And I'll say to myself you have plenty of good things laid-up for many years. Take life easy, eat, drink and be merry. But God said to him, you fool!

This very night your life will be demanded from you. Then who will get what you have prepared for yourself? This is how it will be with anyone who stores up things for himself but is not rich toward God you fool! You live for your body. You don't think about immortal soul. But you have no control of your life.

Managing Time for Eternity

We are to "redeem" the time because the days are evil. "Bewise in the way you act toward outsiders, make the most of every opportunity." The idea is that we are to go to the marketplace and buy up time. But, how can we buy time? One way is to stop wasting time in various sectors and start doing the will of God. Though evil and moral darkness are everywhere, we are to shine as lights and resist every temptation.

The word used for time is kairors, not chronos. Chronos means the flow of time, hour after hour, day after day, year after year. One is born at a certain time, one and are dies at a certain time. That is chronos, from which we get chronology and chronometer. But kairos is different. Chronos is a straight-line, kairos speaks about certain points is that line—certain significant, opportune moments within the chronology of one's life. "My kairos has come", "My time has come." He did not mean that it was twelve o'clock. He meant "My time to die, for which God sent me, has come, and I am going to do that." So "redeem the time" can be thanslated "redeem the many opportunities we have in our lives". You see, you go to temple, that is kairos. God can do wonderful things when you are listening to the word of God. It is kairos, not merely chronos.

A time to born and a time to die, a time to plant and a time to uproot and so on. This is the kairors—certain significant, opportune moments in your life. There are certain things we must undrestand about time if we are to redeem it.

1. *Our time is limited:* Our chronology is limited, therefore our kairos also is limited. Our certain opportunities are ours within our life span, additionally, our time is short "Teaches to number our days right." It is referring to chronology, but within that chronology there are certain opportunities for us are may gain heart of wisdom.
2. *Our times are in his hands:* We must recognize that we have no control of our time. Sometimes, we think that "we will do it at a kairos at another convenient time" it will never happen. If you say you will do something tomorrow, you must realize that tomorrow may never come. Time and tide wait for no man. Opportune moments are passing

by, our kairos is slipping away. It is like split milk. We cannot recapture it. *"Use it or lose it!"* But use it for God and selfless services and make it eternally significant.

3. *There is a time for everything:* There is time to study, a time to pray, a time to repeat and trust in God, a time to marry, a time to train our children in the temple. There is a time work hard, a time to good works, a time to be generous, a time to help others. There is a time to make a call, to write a letter, to visit somebody and encourage that person. There is a time to be with the family and a time to be with God's people. There is a time to resist temptation and the youthful lusts. There is a time to say no and a time to say yes.
4. *Time is precious:* Time is precious because it is limited and we have certain things to do in this life. It is appointed for man once to die and then comes the judgement. The rich man went to hell, and there was no way for him to be saved. When you die, that is the end of it.
5. *Time has a purpose:* Whether it is chronology or the opportunities wihtin that chronology, there is a specific purpose for all time. God performed his redemptive work in time, and he applies that redemption to his people in time. That is the message of God. So, the purpose of our time on earth is not make money or to become famous, but to know the soul of ourselves.
6. *We cannot be certain of tomorrow:* This moment is all that we can be certain of it alone is ours. "Now

is the accepted time, now is the day of salvation." "Today, if you hear his voice, harden not your heart." To think, oh well, I can God tomorrow is utter foolishness. How dare you think that you have control of your life.

7. *Redeeming the time:* How, then, are we to redeem the time? "For you have spent enough time in the past doing what pagans choose to do." Don't waste your time doing the same old wicked things, do the will of God! We are God's workmanship, created in God for what purpose? To do good works. Good works are those we do for God's glory alone, not merry for our pleasure. Our pleasure should not be the determinate of our work.

Let me assure you, when you get up early in the morning to pray and read the *Geeta*, you are doing good works. When you are get up and go to work, you are doing the will of God, because the *Geeta* says you have to take care of your family. When you go to school and study hard. You are doing the will of God. When you go to workmanship, you clean the house, when you discipline your children, you are working for God and redeeming the time. When you bear children, when you submit to your husband, when you obey your parents, when you help the need, when you dress modestly, when you save your money, when you clean your car, when you study God's word, when you resist temptation, when you fast and pray all these things are good works, because they are the will of God. This, then is, what it means to redeem the time.

What motivates us to good works? *Geeta* says, "so, we

make it our goal to please him, whether we are at home in the body or away from it. For we must all appear before the judgement seat of Guru, that each one may receive what is due him for the things done while in the body, whether good or bad." Whatsoever you have done to the least of my brothers, you have done it to me. Come blessed of the Guru or saint. Let us not become weary in doing good, for at the proper time we will reap a harvest if we do not give up. Therefore, as we have opportunity—the word is kairos—"let us do good to all people, especially to those who belong to the family of believers."

Now is the accepted time, now is the day of salvation. Saint says that energized by the Holy Spirit of God, labouring for God, and redeeming the time. Seek opportunities to serve God and others in his name. Avoid laziness and self-indulgence. Get rid of all selfish activities and inerease in activities of eternal significance. Avoid sin like a plague, because it is a waste of precious time, make use of all opportunities in your life. "Never to lose one moment of time, but to improve it in the most profitable way I possibly can."

Time is precious. Time is limited. Time is purposeful. Time is under God's control and we can do mighty things in time. Time can be of external significance. Expect great things from God, and attempt great things for God today. Lay up for yourselves treasure in heaven.

Evolution of Time Management

With the growth of knowledge and widening of the dimensions of our intellect, it has become much more acclaimed that the work of time management is done, brings more output. Greater input of time bring more rewards and accomplishments. From the very early man's age, the value of time was scrutinized in all the respects. It was accepted that working as a farmer had more stability and longevity attached to it rather than working as a hunter with unprecedented lifestyle.

Benedictine monks had given the earlier reference to time managemant as to how to make a proper timetable? How to schedule the work load? How to organize the daily chores. This happened in the very sixth century. With more of urban development and industrialization, the necessity to be with time has crept in. In many countries, there was an account of how to spend the time and what time management was but there was no reference as how to increase the time limits and maximize the outputs. Since there is no accurate way of measuring time, the changes in the day. For example, morning, afternoon, dusk and night meant the changes in time. We already know that till the beginning of fifteenth century, there was no discovery of clocks and only after the end of seventeenth century a need was felt to innovate devices that could help in time keeping.

Adam Smith, during the development of theories based on inquiry of nature and causes of the wealth of nations, revealed that the amount of output done by the labourers is determined by the time taken in the activity. This theory gained mass acceptance also because at that time, revolutions had already cropped up and the factory owners were beginning to bring more of discipline and seriousness ino the working with imposition in terms of fine for the workers who came late. Smith fought for the division of labour so that the efficiency increased.

Benjamin Franklin, who is considered as the father of

the time-management had to suffer a great deal in order to understand how much importance our attitude is in terms of respecting the time. He had been twice bankrupt and thus he taught himself to keep a daily planner so that he can keep an account of all his activities and not ignore them. This made him less lethargic and more focused in his approach. His performance increased manifolds. Later he coined the quotation that "time is money". Something which has become the essence of the rat race we breathe in. He also revealed the fact that the greatest luxury in life is to have enough time for oneself so that one could plan more about the future prospects and live accordingly.

Eli Whitney is the American inventor who has been famous for his invention of "cotton gin", but what he taught about time holds true even after ages. . . After being rebuked in the business he worked for making markets during US's with France. He applied the division of lablour theory and worked with machines rather than employing man. The impossible task of producing 10,000 markets was done by him, which later led to ideas of mass production which bought a through evolution all around the world. Henry Ford also held the view that most of the people get ahead of other people when the other grumbled about the scarcity of time. The ones, who have to get things done, try every hard nut, crack it and finally devour the results. Slowly and slowly the demand of time manage grew and the first book regarding this subject was published in the 1960s.

But in the beginning time management was related to making notes and having reminders. Later on usage of calendars and planning out the routine also came in picture.

Today, time management has emerged to be more of discipline, goal setting and controlling.

Time is the only source that we have that confers different results with different finite juridiction and management. In the initial phases of our life, we are directed to do things and we really don't have to ponder over. The effective steps that we should adopt are that the outout of the allocated time increases our need. But as we evolve and get more into demand, our need to have a dominating control over our time increases because it affects a lot of people under us. From here the concept of time management emerges in full swing. Time manaement is not a concept that can be trained or imitated rather its process that has to be you from the very day one. The skill of time management is natural and it is very necessary for a good manager take into action. The basic flow with us is that we unknowingly sit all day through and doing wrong things at the right time, eventually causing us to complain by the end that there was scarcity of the endowed time. So the need to adopt an attitude that triggers to getting the goals executed within a limited time frame with efficiency and productivity is what time management stands for.

There have been stories that have guided people to get more efficient just by managing the time well. Some of them are.

The UK super market ASDA felt the emergent need to improve staff retention and reduce absenteesim.

So in 1995 the decision was taken to employ thousands of works. It introduced a number of innovations to go through. There were child care leave in which parents can drop off from the hectic schedule to spend time with their children without deduction in payment, swift swapping that catered to allowing the staff to be absent during domestic problems, school starter scheme that allows the parents to just take leave from the office for a half day for the admission of the child and his first day at school, paternity leave, it was regardless of the time, maternity leave that included the time period even after delivery. The others were adoption, study and emergency leave. There was also reorganization of the high women workforce taking into account that they also have a family to attend. There were more of innovations so that the productivity gets customized and the clients needs, can be met before the deadlines.

1.4 CONCEPT AND STRUCTURE OF TIME MANAGEMENT

Time is defined as the part of the life cycle elapsed between facts. It is considered a functional measurement of actions. Choronological time is a conventional factual measure of life cycles. The same choronological time has different meanings according to the length of the lifecycle of the participants of an event.

Time management is the human capacity to organize actions fulfilling external objective needs (external time) and respecting the universal time implicit in a specific scenario within the limits of the internal time of an individual.

Adapted individuals are those who are able to manage their internal time requirments to produce the external actions on time.

Structure of the concept of Time Management:

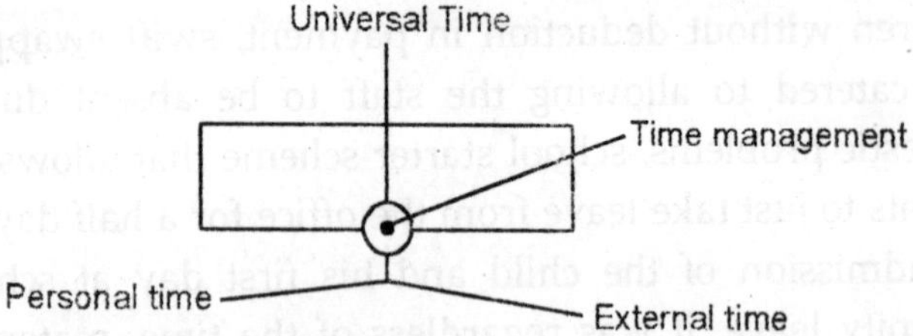

1. Universal Time

It is the time driven by the evolution of a certain environment, its entropy and irreversibility. Understanding the universal time of an environment defines the external limits of time management. Universal time has to be respected and it defines the general taxonomy of actions.

2. External Time

It is the time that defines when "things" have to be functional and working. External timing is the human capacity to influence reality when it is needed to make things happen.

In an activity or working context the external time prevails over the internal time within the limits of the universal time. "Work" has to be done where and when it is needed.

3. Personal Time

It is the time needed by an individual to get ready to make external timing work. Internal time depends on the capactiy of individuals. It includes the time necessary to use the reactive and active intelligence to make decisions within the limits of their into intelligence frustration's elaboration speed is the main inhibitor of internal time management.

4. Time Management Structure

Human speed requires an extreme learning process in order to be changed. That is why it is necessary to organize based on the internal time of individuals when defining responsibilities because they are a limit of the human capacity. There are two extreme segments with different velocities: the action driven segments and the energy conservation segments. The action driven segments are based on the external needs of the environment and the energy conservation segments are focused on their internal need of time. The action driven segments are based on the introjection of reality while the energy conservation segments are based on projection.

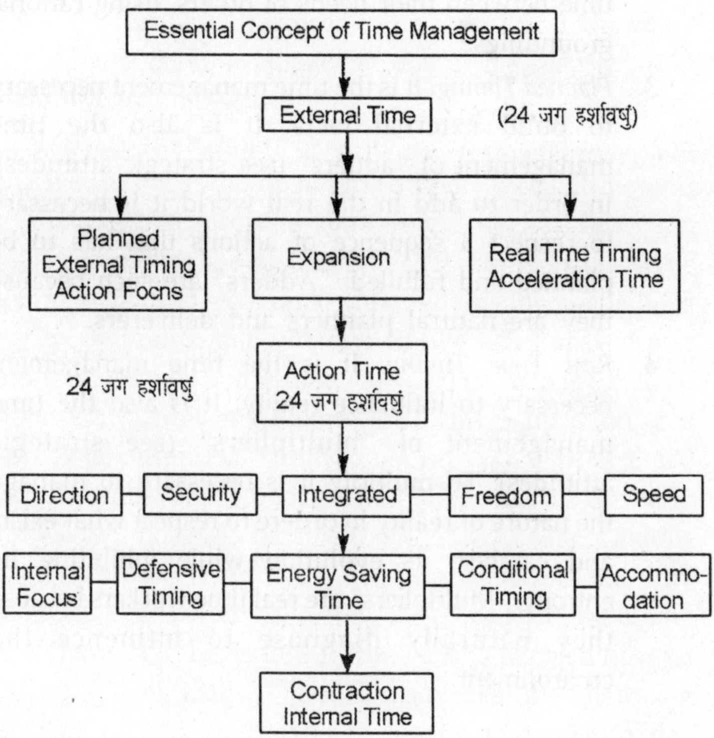

Time management Segments

1. *Conditional Timing:* It is the time management necessary to face external threatening conditions. It is also the time management of "difference makers" (see strategic attitudes). "Difference makers' are such because they naturally manage time in a reactive way.
2. *Defensive Timing:* It is the time management necessary to deal with reflection on complex problems. It is also the time management of "dividers" (see strategic attitudes) who provoke the division between the internal and external needs. Dividers are such because they separate time between their needs of others, using rational groundings.
3. *Planned Timing:* It is the time management necessary to build external facts. It is also the time management of "adders" (see strategic attitudes). In order to add in the real world it is necessary to respect a sequence of actions that has to be planned and fulfilled. "Adders" are such because they are natural planners and deliverers.
4. *Real Time Timing:* It is the time management necessary to influence reality. It is also the time management of "multipliers" (see strategic attitudes). To multiply it is necessary to manage the nature of reality in ordere to respect what exists and catalyse its evolution while inhibiting its entropy. "Multipliers" are real time workers because they naturally diagnose to influence the environment.

Maximal and Minimum Strategy in Time Management

The maximal and minimum strategies can be defined as follows:

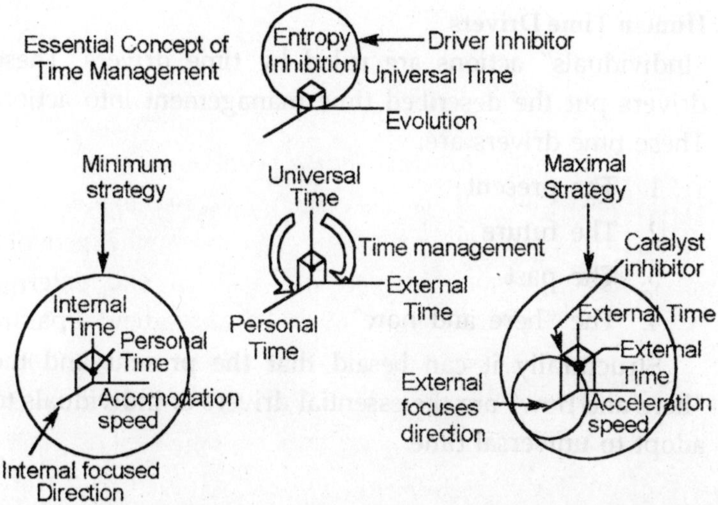

It has to be considered that the driver of time management is to avoid the entropy implicit in universal time. Time management has to provoke the facts that ensure that evolution prevails over entropy.

The maximal strategy is possible when the individual adapts to the needs of the external time. To do so the individual needs to have the necessary acceleration speed and direction to meet the needs of the external reality and to make things happen.

The minimum strategy is given by the internal time of individuals in order to accomodate to the external environment focusing on their internal needs to do so.

When individuals at work begin their time management

by focusing on their internal time needs they are in evolution, because personal necessities prevail over external needs.

Human Time Drivers

"Individuals" actions are ruled by time drivers. These drivers put the described time management into action. These time drivers are:

1. The present
2. The future
3. The past
4. The "here and now".

Structurally it can besaid that the present and the "here and now" are the essential drivers of individuals to adopt to universal time.

Structure of the Concept Human Time Drivers

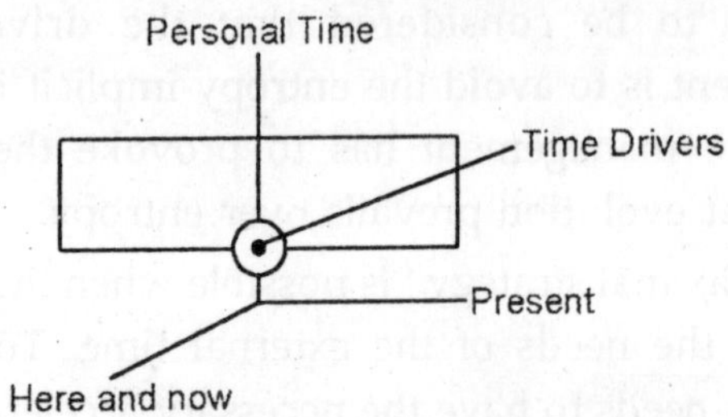

But the research on time management demonstrated that there are two major segments: individuals with a proactive action and individuals with a reactive action on the environment.

It ·/as also seen that individuals with a reactive action on the environment systematically struggle avoiding evolution while individuals with a proactive action fall in that situation when they do not include a minimal strategy to deal with the "here and now."

Essential Concept of Human Times Drivers

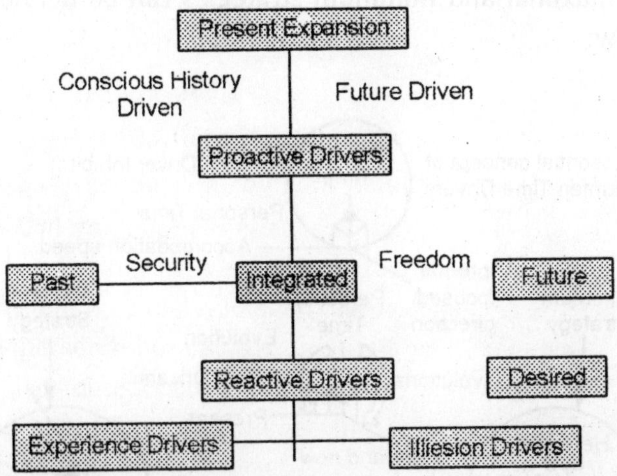

The segments discovered are:

1. *Illusion driven individuals:* They are those whose goal behind action is the fulfilment of an illusion. This time management attitude gives them a sense of freedom and power.
2. *Experience driven individuals:* They are those who use their experience in order to define their today's actions. This time management attitude provides them an extreem sense security and invulneribility.
3. *History driven individuals:* They are those who use a conscious experiential analysis to define today's actions. They find what has to be done in the structure of history.

4. *Future driven individuals:* They are those who forecast the future to define today's actions. They find in innovation and forecast the basis for their decisions.

Maximal and Minimum Strategies Using Time Drivers

The maximal and minimum strategies can be defined as follow:

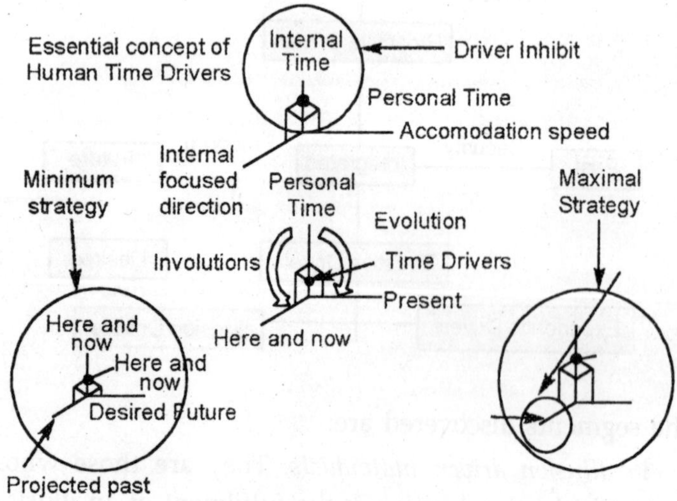

Personal time is the driver of "human time drivers". The maximal strategy is defined by managing present actions considering the possible future and based on the conscious past experience. It fosters human responsibility for what happens in the future. This can only happen in the limits of human possibilities. The minimum strategy avoids human responsibility on the environment. Involution is the consequence of individuals beginning their capacity to deal with external time by focusing on the "here and now" actions. The minimum strategy in this field ensures an energy saving environment to compensate the high risk implicit in the definition of possible future scenarios.

1.5. EVOLUTION OF TIME MANAGEMENT IN INDIA

Nowadays almost everyone multitasks, Is that good or bad? Well, it depends . . . juggling with time for example most of us fumble for this one thing in life . . . Time . . . Ever wondered why!

(*i*) **Time Management How to Start:** Hard work and a right chance are the most important factors for success, but doing things on time adds extra percentage in the probability of getting successful in any profession. If you are a student pursuing some degree, a professional working on some project (may be a software project or some other king of project), a teacher, a businessman, etc., then you must learns to utilize every bit of time that you have been allotted with.

(*ii*) **Value of Time:** Success does not depend on hard you try, it depends on when you choose to go for your goal at first chance! Everything is tied to TIME and to WIN everyone needs to take care of it.

(*iii*) **How to Understand the Mystries of Time:** Time is something you don't really pay much attention to, yet it guides, rules and dominates your life in a way nothing else does, therefore, you need to have a better understanding of time, if you are to make the most of time. It demands a good RO!

(*iv*) **Balancing Work and Life:** While we are all looking for "balance of life", few know where to find it. The digital age has brought about significant changes in the way. We work and live, and it is as if our work and home lives have morphed into a never ending list of commitments from the board room to the soccer field. People have become so disorganized, those few who know where there is suppose to be and what they are suppose to be doing outperform the rest.

(*v*) **Self-care and Time Management (How to Keep your life in balance at all times):** Self-care is far different from self-centredness . . . learn to support . . . spiritual, pschological, physical and energetic aspects of your whole being . . . to manage your time and balance your life.

Every success starts with a decision. The biggest of time, the biggest waste of life, for most people is the decision they need to make but haven't made because they can't make up their mind.

Time is a unique, unrenewable resource. It matches onward at a state of 60 minutes every hour. It shows no favouritism. No one immune to the relentless, unforgiving passage of time. Consider this: two days from now, tomorrow will be yesterday or how about this: two days ago, yesterday was tomorrow.

In today's competitive environment, workloads have become swollen by increasingly learner and meaner companies. There are fewer positions on company organizational charts, and the average workload of those wh́o remain has been growing. Sales people now have to spend more time in the office distracted from selling by fulfilling administrative obligations. You must appreciate that companies today pay for results, not the number of hours you work. Companies no longer reward busyness. In many cases, working long hours, a 60 or 70 hour week, is simply a smoke screen concealing inefficiencies and poor work habits. Nothing is easier than being busy and few things are more difficult than being more efficient. It requires discipline. Imagine having the time to get your work done, leaving the office at a resonable hour and spending the rest of your day with family or friends.

The One Universal Distribution of Equity is Time

Everybody on the planet has ownership of 24 hours per day. We all receive the same allotment, day in and day out. Each new day brings an automatic deposit of 24 hours into our "time account". I refer to it as time equity. Although each day brings a new deposit, each day the entire amount must be withdrawn, with no balance carried over to tomorrow use it or lose it. The challenge we face is how and where to invest our time equity. These decisions determine success, career path, productivity and family status. The truth is that where we are in life is a direct reflection of how well we have managed our time portfolio how and where we "spent our time". We often hear people refer to personal activities in terms of time equity: "How did you spend your weekend?" Time equity is the essence of a full and complete life. We often take it for granted and succumb to its harsh, unforgiving consequences we have to take responsibility for ourselves and consciously appreciate the positive impact time management can have on our lives.

Time cannot think for you, but it can certainly work for you. Like any other investment, time produces returns if invested wisely and treated with respect. Sales professionals constantly explore investment opportunities for their time and maximizing their ROT.

Principle 1: Maximize your ROT

Spending your time wisely starts with paying attention to how you spend it. Only when you decide to take control of your time will have the power to stop squandering it. The best starting point to better ROT is to conduct your time-efficiency study. Evaluate your current use of time by breaking down a typical day into hourly increments. Be objective. Include everything throughout your entire day, even the time you sleep. You may need to truck a full week or two to get a clear picture of your time usage.

The next step is to review your time log and classify the activities as time wasters, obligations or priorities. Time-wasters are just that, activities that distract you and contribute nothing toward your goals. Eliminate them. The danger is that time-wasters are activities performed out of habit. Usually, they create a false sense of productivity but actually product few or no results. The cure comes in the form of personal organization, the process of incorporating structure into your day.

Obligations are the dutiful responsibilities of your job. They are necessary yet important activities, usually performed throughout the day. They contribute indirectly to your goals. They are the administrative aspects of your job such as call reports, expense reports, quartery forecasts, and various other required duties. Despite the challenges of limited time coupled with increased responsibilities, you can be productive by evaluating your current usage of 24 hours and maximizing ROT, obligations cannot be overlooked but be cognizant of the negative impact they have on daily productivity. As you become better organized you can streamline your activities, minimizing the time spent fulfilling obligations. You may be in a position to delegate of your administrative duties to support within your office.

As you evaluate your current use of time, the time-wasters will become clear, allowing you to rethink your activities. Make the shift from a long dáy filled with unproductive busyness to a shorter day focusing as priorities. As a sales entrepreneur, challenge yourself to be more productive by prioritizing your tasks. Take control of the activities that prey on your efficiency, comprising your ROT. Once you complete your time efficiency study. You will be shocked to see the time wasted reacting to other people's demands and requests. Most of us habitually spend our days reacting instead of being productive, unware of the costly consequence, suggest that up to 75 per cent of our day is reactive.

Principle 2: Know What Time It Is

If you are like most sales people, you have too much to do and not enough time to get it all done. To get ahead in today's fast-paced world, you have got to be aware of what time it is. I am not talking about telling time, you learned that years ago. What I am talking about is: it's not enough that you are doing a particular job right, you have got to be sure that you are doing right activity at the right time. Common sense tells us that we should spend the majority of our time working on high priority A and B accounts. Most of us don't. We waste a lot of time is the adult day care reacting to the demands of C accounts or even performing C activities. The first step is to take control of your entire day by knowing what time it is.

Principle 3: Manage Your Time

Time management is a personal process. It takes a strong commitment to change long established habits. According to the 80/20 rule, we get 80 per cent of our results from 20 per cent of the things we do. This statistic supports the observation that we spend a lot of time on time wasters and obligations. You just (imagine) image the impact on our time efficiency if we increased the 20 per cent to 30 per cent.

What takes us from a starved day of routine, frustration and stress to a productive day filled with accomplishments? Change, one definition of time management is doing fewer things in less time. Wouldn't that be great?

Recent research suggests that effective time management straties can free up a minimum of two hours per day. For example, time management studies show that we spend up 70 minutes a day just looking for stuff. How many times have you said, "just a minute, I know it's here somewhere". We misplace files, reports, memos, and letters, and our desks look like the movie twister was filmed in our office clutter can be a huge time waster, not to mention the embarrassment of lost of unanswered requests. Your goals isn't to have a nice neat desk, but to get organized so that you can convert wasted time into productive time. However, with a clean, orderly desk, you will improve your time working on priorities that will make you money. Your quality of work will also improve.

The underlying objective of time management is to utilize all available resources to increase face-time, the time spent talking face-to-face with existing customers or potential customers. If you are an inside sales person, increase talk-time. Take some time to determine how much time you actually spend with customers. Take a stop-watch and clock total face-time in one entire week. On average, it's only two to four hours shocking! This statistic serves as additional proof of the inordinate amount of time consumed by time wasters and obligations.

I recognize that with learner companies sales person/ sales people are often saddled with more of the administrative aspects of the job. Unfortunately they become high-priced administrators. How many times a day should you ask yourself if you are making the best use of your time? If you answered "several" you are right. Only you can answer that question honestly. As the president of ME Inc., don't comprise your ROT by blindly filling your day with busyness. Restructure your day to eliminate the time-wasters and minimize the time spent fulfilling obligations. Sometimes working in the office on a project or on a presentation could very well be the best use of your time. I doubt that you can never eliminate time spent in the adult day care centre, but you certainly need to minimize it. Use janitoria time to fulfil your obligations.

As part of your time efficiency study, you should

determine the time of day that you are most efficient and productive. Know your peak time, the time of day you are at high energy. Not everyone has the same peak time. Some of us are morning people and others are afternoons or everning people. Pay attention to your moods and high energy time of day to determine when you are most productive morning people can accomplish more simply by getting-up an hour earlier each day, and night owls can carve out time for administrative activities in the evenings.

Once you have identified your peak time, do your worst jobs then. They won't go away so you might as well get them done when you are feeling energized. Some authors suggest doing them first thing in the morning when you are feeling fresh. This approach works well if you are a morning person but could be disastrous if you are an afternoon person. Imagine doing your worst job at your worst time of day. Two "worsts" don't make a right.

Another suggestion in the interest of maximizing your ROT is learn how to say no. Many of us are our own worst enemies. You will never have enough time to finish your own tasks if you are always taking on more than time permits. Don't be afraid to politely refuse a request or task if your plate is already full. This includes saying no to your sales manager. When given a tasks, simply ask you manager, "Would you like me to do this now or would you prefer I spend the time selling?" Your manager may decide to delegate the task elsewhere.

Principle 4: Use the Right Tool

A professional (sales enterpreneur included) is anyone paid to perform a task or a job at an acceptable level of proficiency while utilizing the tools of the trade to enhance efficiency and effectiveness. I am amazed at how often I see sales people conducting business with inappropriate tools. It's as though they use exempt from the requirement to be a prefessional. Imagine your doctor or dentist using anything but the best instruments. Your customers expect no less of you. As a sales entrepreneur, you have an obligations to invest in the best. You may have heard it before, "A carpenter is only as good as his tools."

The solution begins with a personal planner a time managemment system that offers the conveniences of portability while organizing your activities, mapping your week and, most importantly, planning your day. A good planner includes twelve months at a galance, 365 individiual day pages, a daily to-do list section, and an oppointments section. Some planners come with a rigid set of instructions, so pick a planner that offers simplicity and the flexibility to meet your personal preferences. A planner used effectively not only buys you time; it helps you stay in balance throughout your week, including weekends. Poor time management skills result in overspending your time, running out of day before you get everything done. Without the oppropriate tool to track your time related activities, you quickly find yourself out of balance, over-drawn on your time account.

Principle 5: Be Proactive, not Reactive

I would suggest that up to 75 per cent of our day is spent reacting to the needs and requests of other people such us customers, managers, internal customers, family and friends. We are constantly bombarded with demands on our limited time, leaving us unable to accomplish our own goals and objectives. No wonder we feel the frustration of, "So much to do, so little time."

We often succumb to the demands and requests of others because we think it is socially in appropriate to say no. We become victimized by others who may have a strong interest in controlling our activities or behaviour such as a spouse or a manager. Unfortunately many people, including sales people, are content to be regulated and manipulated rather than committing to SMART goals and living life guided by their agenda, not someone else's. No one ever accomplished a personal goal by being subservient to others. Successful sales entrepreneur refuse to be swayed by the whims of others and are quitely effective at managing their own agendas. Employers and managers sometimes do more to demotivate rather than to motivate. Demotivation can take the form of intimidation or high performance expectations constrained by rigid management policies and limited resources to perform the job.

A productive strategy means developing the discipline to stay focus on your agenda, your goals and your objectives. Part of this discipline comes in the form of qualifying the severity of a problem prior to reacting to it. For example, next time a customer informs you of a problem or a concern, resist the temptation to immediately jump into react mode, drop what you are doing and race over to console your customer. It may not be necessary. The next time you get an irate customer (or internal customer) demanding to see you right away, follow these two steps:

(*i*) **Acknowledge the problem:** Allow the customer to vent by explaining the situation and then clearify your understanding of it by paraphrasing. Be sure to take notes of your discussion for future reference. By acknowledging the concern and showing empathy, the customer will begin to feel better about it and may become somewhat flexible as to how and when you resolve the concern. A sympathetic attitude to a real or imginary product or service failure cannot be overemphasized. A 10 minute Phone call to determine the facts and the seriousness of the problem may be a valuable investment, possibly saving you hours of unnecessary running around. Work smart, not hard.

(ii) **Suggest another time**: Tell the customer that your day is full with appointments and commitments and ask if first thing tomorrow morning would be okay to get together. Your business and time are just as important and legitimate as that of your customer. You are equals. In the majority of cases, your customer will appreciate your schedule and agree to meet with the next day. Too often, we assume that we must respond immediately, but by following these steps you will save yourself valuable time.

Another good tactic is to start building flexibility into your day. By this I mean schedule your day to allow for "poop happens". Allow time (management) between appointments or activities to deal with interruptions that are sure to occur. Interruptions and problems are a natural component of everbody's day so don't ignore the fact that they happen and plan accordingly. Don't try to puck too much into one day by scheduling consecutive appointments and meetings.

Plan what you can reasonably expect to get accomplished that day and allow time to deal with inevitable interruptions. I suggest that you let the 60/40 rule be your guide, don't place more than 60per cent of your day. The remaining 40 per cent is reserved to deal with unforeseen yet inevitable interruptions. It also helps prevent the list-lay over syndrome where we put unfinished to do items onto tomorrows schedule. If your workday is ten hours, don't plan for than six hours. Once again, if you pack too much into a day, you will surely have to make rigorous cuts, deal with unfinished tasks and wrestle with unneccessary stress. Remember, one of the aspects of a SMART goal is "attainable". Make your daily activities attainable.

1.6. CONCLUSION

Here we discussed about the importance of time management, evolution of time management in world and evolution of time management in India. Above this detail discussion of time management we can say that, if we want to achieve our target, we want to make our career. We should do proper time management of day-to-day and week-to-week and month-to-month otherwise we can't achieve our targets or our ambitions.

Because, time is the most precious resource in commerce, trade business and also in society. Unlike other resources like people and capital, time is often considered fixed. However, the way people substantially between people. Human development provides the basis for break through improvements in time management. In particular, in higher states of conscious it may be possible to transcend the limitations of time so that ceases to be a factor limiting our accomplishments in life. In order to realize in practice a transformation to improved time management. We will succeed in our life.

SELF-ASSESSMENT

1. What is the importance of time management in human life?
2. Explain the evolution of time management in world?
3. Discuss the evolution of time management in India?

REFERENCES

1. Time management for the creative person.

   By *Lee silber* — amazon.com
2. The Time Trap: The classic book on time management.

   By *Alec Mackenzie*

   WWW. Vikas publishing.com
3. The complete Idiot's to Managing your Time.

   By *Jeff Duvidson*
4. Time Tactics of very Successful people.

   By *B. Eugene Griessman*
5. How to Get Control of your Time and your Life.

   By *Alan Lakein*
6. Time Management for Dummies

   By *Jeffrey J. Mayor*
7. Time Management for Busy People.

   By *Roberts Roesch*
8. You can't Manage Time: But you can Manage Many Priorities

   By *Susan de la Vergene*

2

PRINCIPLES OF TIME MANAGEMENT

"Time management is one of the important factors that can make one's life full and well lived. But, how well we manage our time can be understand only when wre analyse or make an effort to study our life patterns. Today the whole world is moving fast and in today's fast paced lifestyle, if you want to make out most from your personal as well as official life, then time management is very important in your life."

—Dr. Jan Yager & Mask Forster

Content of the Chapter

Introduction, Basic Principles of Time Management, Pareto's Principles of Time Management, Principles of Time Management in India, Conclusion

2.1 INTRODUCTION

Time is one of our most prescious resources. In today's hectic world, time is more become difficult to find out the time to complete all of our tasks or reach our goals. Being unfamilier with the basic principles of prioritization good time management. It is not possible to make everyone happy all of the time. Some people all of the time. If we are not focused on our goals it can be tempting to activities. Understanding what our goals are and making a focused effort to every aspect of good time management.

Poor time management skills are a major contributor to stress. However, this stress good news is that it can be easily prevented, if we understand apply and stick time management. In the previous chapter, we discussed about the importance of time management evolution of time management in world and also in India. In this chapter we shall discuss about the basic principles of time management, Pareto's principles of time management and principles of time management in India first of all, we shall discuss the basic principles of time management.

2.2 BASIC PRINCIPLES OF TIME MANAGEMENT

As a new graduate, one of the biggest challenges you may face in your first position is organizing and using your time efficiently a process known as time management. As a student, the number of patients assigned to your care was typically fewer than those you are assigned as a regular employee. In addition, you have not had time to become efficient in many of the technical procedures required in your job. Because, time is finite—there are just 60 minutes in each hour and 24 hours in each day—time management skills become essential. Like many other areas you have already mastered, time management can be learned.

As you work at learening to manage time more effectively, the following general principles will be of assistance to you. They can be applied in every setting and will facilitate your work in any role.

(*i*) **Understand yourself:** Learning to manage your time begins as many other behaviour related concerns, with a through assessment of yourself. This includes giving attention to your basic physcian needs and identifying things that restore and enhance your level of energy, as well as examining individual patterns of behaviour. Adequate nutrition, sufficient rest, appropriate exercise and relaxation are all part of appearing in the work environment in the best possible condition to perform. Analyse your body rhythms and determine when your energy is at it highest peak. You will want to plan activities requiring the greatest energy output and concerntration to coincide with these peaks whenever possible. Are there things that boost your energy, such as a cup of tea a break or a power bar? Gerenally, it is considered unwise to skip breaks or lunch to capture moe time. Your efficiency and perhaps your disposition, will suffer. What things create the greatest stress for you? How can they be mitigated or avoided? What activities help you best deal with stress?

(*ii*) **Take control of your own time:** Responding to the requests of others results in one of the greatest expenditures of time. These requests may be for assistance or simply directed toward socialization. In either case, they can rob you of needed minutes and hours.

We recognize that it is difficult to say "no", especially when a colleague is asking for assistance. However, there are some clear-cut situations in which it is easier. The first of these occurs when you are asked to assist with something for which you lack the necessary skill. You need to honestly recognize these instances and decline involvement when they occur. For example, if a seasoned nurse on the unit asks you, as a new graduate, to watch for effective time management.

Many of us realize that we are not able to manage the time efficiently to do or devote to the things which matter most for us. It is common to hear somebody saying "I don't have time" to do this or that. Generally, principles of time management will help you not only to deliver or achieve more in less time but also helps you to do the tasks in more systemized way.

No Procrastination

This is one of the main reasons of many people who are able to achieve their goals in their lives. Procrastinating a work to do it latter will lead to less or no interesting in doing it and in the process you will put it off altogether. Try as much as possible not to procrastinate a task nd complete it as soon as possible. Be a Go-Getter. You will learn how to avoid this is effective principles discussed below.

> *"There is an old saying which I have learnt in my school days, by a famous saint: whatever you want to do tomorrow, do it today and whatever you want to do today, do it now, you never know if you can do it latter."*

Assign Priority

Do the tasks based an priority. This will help you to divide your time between least important and most important tasks.

Assign priority to each task or activity, either by making a mental note or putting it on a paper. I recommend you list down all the tasks or activities to be done on a day in a planner and then assign priority to each one like numbers one, two, three, etc., or in the sequence of priority with most important on the top of the list and least important task at the bottom of the list. This way you can decide which task you should first work and there-by achieving your potential. Most of the successful people to do the things according to priority and in order to become. Successful, it is always advisable to follow the successful people.

Task Log

Most of time we wonder where our entire time has gone or how have we achieved very less with so much time spending whole day working. This can be avoided by maintaining a task or activity log and recording the time spent on each one for at least a week or month. Many times, we do not consider the time we have spent on a task like reading a newspaper, calling a client or customer on an issue, taking a coffee break, talking to a friend on phone or in a coffee, etc. At the end of this period, i.e., week or month check that list and then you will find where you have spent more time and where less time. Spend less time on unimportant or less important tasks and more time on the important or high priority tasks.

Planner

Plan all tasks and activities in advance and enter them in a planner. There are wide varieties of planners available in the market. Pick one and start using them. This will help you to do your tasks systematically and without any confusion of which task should be done first and which one last or fear of missing one altogether. Always carry that planner before and note down the tasks, activities, appointments, meetings, call reminders, etc., in that planner. Check that planner commiting to some task to see if you have time for it on that day or in that week. Politely convey the same to others and schedule it when you are free.

Use this principle in combination of above principle of assigning priority to each task.

Discipline

This is very important to make use of your time efficiently. All the successful people have discipline in doing things and thus achieve tremendous success make this a habit and you will cerainly see the difference. Try following the above principles religiously for a month or so and you will see how efficient you have become in doing things and managing your time. Once you are on this track, it would not be difficult to continue as it becomes a habit for you and thus achieve tremendous success. Just remember, time is money. If you waste time, you are effectively loosing the money and your future.

Time management involves making the best use of time and getting more done in the time available. It means not wasting time on irrelevant things, instead focusing on important parts of the job. Ultimately this means working calmly and effectively, avoiding the panic and anxiety of the last minute rush.

In the Western world, time is treated as a valuable resource which people spend. Most of managers claim that they do not have enough time often this is blamed on the organization and colleagues for making too many demands. However, we all have at least some control over we spend our time. We can and do make choices. Recognizing this is the first step on the path to effective time management.

Time management means taking more control over how we spend our time and making sensible decisions about the way we use it. If good time management is about taking control, it involves finding those areas where you do have control, and also finding those where you think you don't, but really you do. For example, you may have far too many things to do and this makes you feel happiness, but may be you have the option of renegotiating some parts of your work, or even delegating some activities. There may still some areas where you don't have control, for example, if a key part of the job is to be available at a certain time to provide advice to others, you cannot just decide to be absent or you may have a coursework assignment to submit some deadlines are not renegotiable. In this areas it is more sensible not to waste time ralling against these commitments, instead concentrate on finding those areas you do have the power to change, and make the changes that will help you to become more effective.

Exercises 2.1 and 2.2 should start to help you identify those problem areas and areas where you would like to make changes.

Preparation for Change

Before reading in this chapter it is helpful for you to have an idea of how effective you are as a time manager.

Reflecting on your own time bandits and traps will make this chapter more useful and relevant to you.

Being by brainstorming three barriers that you think prevent from being effective at work, or at study, as indicated in Exersice 2.1. Now go on to Exercise 2.2 and rate your effectiveness using the list provided. This list has been developed by distilling some of the common problems that have been identified by several hundred staff and students in workshops held over the last five year at imperial college.

Exercise 2.1: Barriers to Being Effective

What are the three barriers you have that prevent you bring effective?

Exercise 2.2: Diagnosing Your Time Management Problems

Go through the list of time management problems below and rate each one with relation to its frequency as a problem for you and also its severity using the following ratings:

0 = this problem does not relate to me

1 = this problem partly relates to me, relates some of the time

2 = this is a regular problem for me

3 = this is a major problem for me, it severely hampers my effectiveness.

Note: Assess your behaviour us it is not as you would like it to be.

(A) Prioritization and Scheduling	
1. I am not sure what tasks I have to do each day, I don't make a to-do list.	0-1-2-3
2. When I have finished one job I just go on to the next without checking on my priority	0-1-2-3
3. I don't work out which tasks have the biggest gain for me	0-1-2-3
4. I have difficulty in setting priorities	0-1-2-3
5. I have difficulty in keeping to priorities or a schedule I have set	0-1-2-3
6. I am a perfectionist and even if I have several tasks to do I allow myself to spend ages on one task to get it right, which can cause problems in completing my work	0-1-2-3
7. I often do trivial tasks at my high-energy time of day	0-1-2-3
8. I don't stop to think when my best time of day is for working	0-1-2-3

(B) Persistence, Procrastination and Focus	
9. I fit from task to task, starting a lot of things but not always finishing them	0-1-2-3
10. I feel very intimidated by large important tasks, and don't break them down into smaller ones	0-1-2-3
11. I put off difficult taks until the last possible moment	0-1-2-3

12. I put thing off until the last minute and then I have to work in a rush and panic	0-1-2-3
13. I procrastinate, prevaricate and can't decide what to do, nor make decisions	0-1-2-3
14. I allow myself to be interrupted from my work, for example by the phone, talking to others, distractions, new e-mails coming in	0-1-2-3
15. I spend ages on the telephone, surfing the net, or answering e-mails	0-1-2-3
16. Once I get started, I cannot stop a task, even if it is taking far too much time and there are other pressing things to do	0-1-2-3
17. I don't have protected time in the day when I can get on with my priorities	0-1-2-3
(C) ***Role Definition***	
18. I am not sure what my key objectives are	0-1-2-3
19. I am unclear of my role definitions and line of responsibility	0-1-2-3
20. I am not sure how long certain tasks take so find it hard to allocate the appropriate time to them	0-1-2-3
21. I try and do everything myself, and do not consider whether it would be better to delegate tasks, or ask for more help and support	0-1-2-3

(D) *Work Environment and Organization*	
22. My workspace is a mess, I can never find anything at work, and papers pile-up around me without being field	0-1-2-3
23. I don't know what to do with paper-I just leave it hanging around	0-1-2-3
24. I don't have anywhere where I can work uninterrupted	0-1-2-3
25. My work environment is noisy and distracting and I don't find ways to deal with this	0-1-2-3
26. If I find myself free time in the day, for example, when commuting, waiting for an appointment, I don't have things with me to do.	0-1-2-3

(E) *Study Skills*	
27. I take ages to read anything and find it hard to remember what I have read	0-1-2-3
28. I am not sure how to go about academic or work related reading	0-1-2-3

(F) *Assertiveness*	
29. I find it very hard to say "no" to other people	0-1-2-3
30. I feeel guilty if I am getting on with my own agenda and not focusing on helping others	0-1-2-3
31. I spend most of my time doing things for other people, and hardly any time getting on with my agenda	0-1-2-3

(G) *Anxiety, Stress and Emotion*	
32. I worry a lot and regulary suffer from work related anxiety and stress	0-1-2-3
33. I don't feel very confident so I often worry that I am not doing well or going about my work in the right way	0-1-2-3
34. I never have fun at work, I don't enjoy my work	0-1-2-3
35. I get very bored at work and this slows me down or allows me to get sidetracked	0-1-2-3
36. I find it hard to concentrate	0-1-2-3

(H) *Life Balance*	
37. I don't have time for exercise, health, leisure, family, I just work all the time	0-1-2-3
38. I get very tired and exhausted at work	0-1-2-3

Scoring

(1) 0-38 averaging 0s and 1s

You are an excellent time manager.

(2) 39-76 Averaging 1s and 2s

You have some areas to work on but over all you are an effective time manager.

(3) 77-114 averaging 2s and 3s

You have a big problem with time management and need to take action now to get yourself more in control of your time (but don't worry—that is what this chapter aims to do).

Where Does All My Time Go ?

The Time Bandits And Traps :

A time bandit is a work practice, attitude or behaviour that leads to ineffective working practices or your time getting stolen or expropriated away from your care priorities and frittered on less important activities.

Epicurus and the Pleasure Principle

Think about your own time management bandit and traps, do you see any patterns? One common pattern is to put the fun, exciting, interesting, easy things first and put off doing the boring, dull, difficult tasks until later. It is a king of pleasure principle going for the short-term gains, surrounding to wants and desires as they arise immediately. Epicurus, the philosopher who is attributed with setting up the foundations for a pleasure principle, believed in following desires. However, he is often mistake thought to have been a slave to advance and pleasure, indulging himself in whatever desire arose at a given moment. This is not actually true. Epicurus followed a simple life, one of healthy food, friendship and good company, freedom and thought, not an undisciplined response to every whim and fancy. In relation to your own work or study, following the Epicurian principle will lead you to doing things you enjoy instead of focusing on your principles.

It is a mistake to think that taking the easy route will improve things in the long run. In reality, giving into the pleasure principle in the short-term results in a mess lateraon, because over time what happens is the accumulation of a whole mountain of tasks that have been ignored. This can lead to misery, anxiety and depression.

A lot of thought and planning went into Epicurus way of life and creating time for a balanced, enjoyable life takes planning and self-discipline.

The Last Minute Rush and Adrenaline Junky

Some people like to live fast, and so working in a calm systematic way can seem very boring. Waiting for a burst of energy, or the adrenaline rush that comes with the fear of deadline looming can become a way of life, but does usually mean that when the job actually gets done, it is done in a haphazard panicky way, leaving the person exhausted after late-night working and long hours in order to finish it on time. In the long run health can be affected, as the fight or flight impulse that triggers adrenaline is intended for moments of danger, not a lifetime of stress.

Hamlet: The Procrastinator

"To be or not to be", some people say that they don't know! It isn't noble to play Hamlet unless you are Lawrence Olivier! If it can't be faced now, it might be worse later! What is more, as well as getting nothing done, the agony is repeated over and over again, and usually by tomorrow there is no change except the increased anxiety of another day gone by without completing the task. There are different reasons for procrastations and prevarication: not having the energy (which is represented by the aderaline junky above) not having a starting point or the right information (but will you have the information tomorrow?), or being indecisive over what exactly to get on and do. All that happens is that work piles up.

It's All Too Much

However, for some people, being busy is a way of life. They may ask themselves.

–Where does all my time go?

–Why are there not enough house in the day?

Typically these people then fool themselves with the thought. Well, this is just a busy period, once I've got this assignment or deadline over then life will be easier and I can relax. This is fine if true, but often one deadline out of the way can just open someone up to a new deadline, as they rush from one hectic task to the next. Sometimes this is self-generated they can't help but take on more and more.

Another way they fool themselves is to say "I am a no-limit person. I can keep on taking on more and more and more". No one is superman or superwoman, there are only1,440 minutes in a day, 1,000 when we deduct sleeping, washing, dressing, eating, etc. In our lives we probably spend six months waiting things, 24 years asleep . . . There is only so much time left and time is not infinitely elastic, we do have limits. After all, no one ever said on their deathbed. I wish I had spent more time at the office.

The Headless Chicken: Action Wihtout Thought

There may be other reasons for taking on too much work, being too busy on feeling driven. Some people may be working hard but without having clear priorities, and without planning. Spending much too much time on things that are not at all important. Giving the illusion of working hard but not working productively.

The Butterfly: Flitting from Task to Task

Helen arrives at work, puts her out on the door peg, sit down and turns on the computer. She intends to spend the morning writing the proposal for the new performance appraisal system—a very important part of her job. But first she listens to her telephone messages and realises Gerald wants her to produce some figures for a meeting the following week she accesses her computer to pull-out the figures, and notices she has (21) e-mails and begins trawling through these. The first few she just looks at and leaves open to come back to later, the sixth one asks her to give some dates for a meeting and she opens her diary to look at dates, and sees that for one of the dates she has a presentation to give on that day. Oh she must remember to take the files home for preparing the presentation so she can do it at the weekend. She gets up and opens her cabinet to retrieve them . . . Oh dear, she is feeling giddy . . . She hasn't got anything done and she has been at work an hour already . . . She feels so confused, she thinks . . . I'd better go and get a coffee.

One result of not planning or sticking to priorities can be butterly. This is someone who flits from task to task in downward spiral of panic and anxiety, getting in a mess, never getting the boost and closure of completion. Many managers have to be butterflies, for example, Mintzberg (1973) and Kotter (1982) showed that managers spend nine minutes or less on 50 per cent of their activities are subject to constant interruptions and that management is a very fragmented activity. Good time management brings order to this fragmentation, rather than exacerbates it.

Interruptions, Interruptions

There are two types of interruptions: interruptions from others that distract us from our work, and self-interruptions, ways in which we distract ourselves from our intended activities.

What is your working environment like quite and easy to concentrate in, or noisy and busy? Some people work in open plan office environments where they cannot help but get drawn into conversation with others. Think how you manage your interruptions, what happens if you are concentrating on something really important and somebody starts casually chatting to you as they pass your desk or door?

The proliferation of communication technologies has meant there are myriad of way in which we can be interrupted at any time of day The ding of a near e-mail arriving in the computer, the ringing telephone, the mobile phone, just ensure you are available 24 hours a day 7 days a week. Take the telephone this is designed for people to contact you when it is convenient for them, not necessarily for you. Some people spend a long time on the phone, not getting to the point, getting side tracked into talk. How long are your phone calls, could they be shorter? E-mail is also a tempter. In some roles people are receiving 50-100 e-mails a day and if every time one arrives on the computer they stopped what they were doing to look at it, it would never be possible to concentrate.

The Escapologist: It and Other Escapes

However, it isn't just the requirements of others that interrupt us we also interrupt ourselves, For example, may be not being able to resist surfing the net for another couple of hours, just having a look at a couple more search paths for a holiday or outing.

Some are self-interrupters, may be finding it difficult to concentrate they just have to go off for another coffee or go and chat to someone else, because they can't quite get down to it. This can be even worse at home—when you spot the washing or ironing or vacuuming out of the comer of your eye. It is amazing how you can suddenly feel the urge to do a bit of gardening or even jobs you normally hate like cleaning the cooker suddenly seem compelling when you are trying to get down work on a challenging report.

The Doormat: Yes, Yes, Yes

One problem can be unassertiveness or unwillngness to say 'no': This may be because of low internal self-esteem, wanting to 'please others' in order to feel good, or even being too scared to say no. Ironically always saying 'yes' may just mean a person is taken for granted, not necessarily respected and liked. In the end, they can cause more problems for other people, because they become ill or are too busy to do evening to which they have commited which can be very imitating for others.

Presenteeism

Sam was always first into the office everyday and last to leave in the evening. Everyone commented on how committed he was, what a hard working member of staff. One day Sarah wondered what Sam was actually working on all day at the computer screen, she wondered up to his desk and looked over his shoulder, and found he was playing solltaires.

Being at a desk doesn't mean the same as working—it is passing time instead of spending time. Sometimes the most effective people are those you don't see, may be they find somewhere quite to work where they don't get interrupted. Effective people don't necessarily need to impress on others how hard they work—their output is more important than the appearance of work. Some office environments, however, encourage presenteesim-focusing performance evaluation on time spent at the desk, clock watching, rather than on the quality of work.

Wasted Spaces

It has been calculated that people lose up 20 per cent of their time waiting. All that time spent sitting on the train into work, or waiting for the printer to finish or a lecture or meeting to start are wasted periods that could have been used to complete a small task, or even begin a bigger one. Do you sit and stare realizing you don't have any work at hand for such type of work occasions or does it even occur to you in the first place to fill these spaces?

Habit: Two Clear Priorities

Identify your priorities and distinguish tasks that are urgent from tasks which are important, urgent tasks have an immediate impact. Important tasks have a significant impact. Do tasks in this order.

– Urgent and important
– Urgent (but do them quickly)
– Important.

Try to prioritize important tasks. Don't be tempted to fill in old moments with low-rated tasks. Try and at least start a more important tasks. If you don't watch out you will find at the end of the day that you haven't any of the important tasks but have merely cleared away some of the less important tasks but have merely cleared away some of the less important ones.

Be clear what the critical 20 per cent of your tasks are Pareto's Law suggests that 20 per cent of the work produces 80 per cent of the results. Be clear what the critical 20 per cent of your tasks are and prioritize them.

Look at Table 2.1 below. In which box do you spend most of your time? Too much time in box one means being irresponsible and over dependent, as well as in effective you don't get down to anything important or urgent. Too much time in Box 2 leads to short-termism and crisis management you are ruled by urgency but don't do anything that is important. Working in Box 3 on a regular rather than occasional basis leads to stress and burn out as everything you do seems very important and urgent you are constantly under pressure (see Example 2.2).

Table 2.1 Time spent on urgent and important tasks

4	3
Not urgent Quadrant of opportunity • development • innovation • planning	Urgent/Important Quadrant of pressure • Crises • pressing problems • deadline driven projects
1	2
Not urgent/Not important Quadrant of waste • escapes • routines • office politics	Urgent/Important Quadrant of busyness • mail and e-mail • telephone • interruptions

Source

Ideally you should be looking to be spending a significant proportion of your time in Box 4 where your work can be more meaningful, effective, balanced and disciplined as well as more in your control.

Example 2.2: Too Much Pressure

Sally the Social Worker

Sally is a social worker. For the past two years she had worked in a tough inner city borough with a very challenging environment and above average levels of poverty, crime and drug use and mental illness. She had a very case load of mentally ill clients.

Example 2.2

Some of whom could have been a danger to themselves or others, and she needed to monitor their position. She felt responsible for their well-being, knowing that one mistake from her, and someone could be seriously injured on die. Even worse, there were five vacancies in her department and the council didn't seem able to recruit anyone to fill them. Her managers didn't listen to her view that her job was too much, and certainly didn't give her the support she needed to do a good job. Instead, as a result of the vacancies they louded her up with more clients to cover the shortfall. She became exhausted, keeping their reports up to date, attending case work meetings, making decisions about their future. She went to see her doctor, as she was not sleeping, worrying about her job, her clients and her persistent headaches, as well as experiencing palpitations. The doctor refused to give her more sleeping pills, and stronger painkillers, instead pointing out that she was heading for a nervous breakdown if she carried on working in that fashion. When she returned home from the doctor she thought through some of the things he had said and concluded "I don't have to live like that". That evening she prepared her CV and applied for as similar role in another brough where she knew the pressures weren't as great, and where there were more staff, greater support, and lower case loads. Two months later she is enjoying her new job and wonders 'why didn't I move before?'.

Perfectionist

The perfectionist pays attention to detail, agonizes over every decision, every word in report. They must get it right. But what is the point if it is too late, or they have ignored several other things—is it all really necessary? Not all tasks have to done to the same high standard: Writing a routine e-mail for example, does it really matter if the grammar is correct?

Paper Mountains

Some people allow a mountain of paper to pile-up on their desk, around their floor—a trail of paper that doesn't allow them to be able to find anything they need. They can waste lots of time trying to find things, and the paper mountains doesn't make for good office sculpture, it festers and exudes stress and incompetence.

I Am in a Meeting

Consider the costs of 10 people in a one hour meeting £ 50 per hour each plus all the overheads and opportunity costs, the time spend travelling, preparation—is it worth it? Worse still are those meetings where people are unprepared, there is no agenda, the chair allows the discussions on trivial items to go on for ages without coming to any decisions.

"Heather was chairing student union General Purposes Committee meeting. The meeting discussed for an hour the subject of what colour the new minibus should be. The labour society rep suggested red, the Conservative Group rep blue, the liberal democrat member orange, and the chap from the Greens said they shouldn't have a minibus at all! Eventually the meeting ran out of time and the main item on the agenda – what to do about the student debt situation never got discussed." Poorly run meetings are only a waste of time, but also very demoralizing.

D-I-Y Enthusiast

The D-I-Y enthusiast thinks they can do everything themselves, never giving, a thought to delegation or sharing the work with others. Moreover, when they get into trouble, they don't go and task for help, they soldier or miserably, not getting anywhere except lost and desperate. If you have too much to do, or are stuck, do you look to see how the work can be allocated differently, do you call in for help or the support of others?

Why oh why do D-I-Y? Refusing to ask for help may be due to lack assertiveness, but it may also be arrogance the belief that no one can do it as well, so it is better done single handed. Other people will never learn the skills if they are not given a chance to start. Delegation is not just a downward action, it can also move upwards, for example, where something really isn't a person's job may be they need to refer it back.

The Good Habits of Time Management

Habit 1 The 'to do' list

Make a 'to do' list. This could be either on a palm or computer, or in a filofax or diary, through ideally this should be portable, as you will want to add to the list whenever you think of a new task and this may not occur when you are at your desk. This will prevent you going off task every time you remember another thing to do. Simply add it to you list and return to the task in hand. This will stop the butterfly. Writing things down will help you remember them and is a better recorder than your memory. You need to devise a system to suit you, but many people have a general list, and then a specific daily or weekly list of tasks to be achieved within a certain time frame pulled out from the general list. A lot of people find it helpful to rank the items on their 'to-do' list in order of importance. Not everything is of equal importance.

More importantly, ticking jobs off a 'to-do' list can help you see and enjoy your achievements.

Habit 2: Clear Priorities

Note: Identify your priorities and distingush tasks that are urgent from tasks which are important, urgent tasks have an immediate impact. Important tasks have a significant impact. Do tasks in this order:

- Urgent and important
- Urgent (but do them quickly)
- Important

Habit 3: Saying no and Delegation

Not all tasks are relevant or appropriate for you to do. Ask yourself what will happen if you don't do a certain task? Does it matter? Some tasks can be deprioritized, or put on hold, or you can say 'no' if you decide not to do them all.

Alternatively some jobs are more appropriate to delegate. As you become more senior you may find you need to change your work role so you are doing less directly yourself, and spending more time delegating work to others. Delegating is not activity dumping you. You need to check that the task is suitable for the person, and you need to clarify with them what needs to be done and to what performance standard and check they have the ability to do it and that it is appropirate to their role or development. You may also need to provide them with some coaching and other support, and ensure they have the responsibility and authority required. Many managers are afraid of 'letting go' feeling that they either are the only ones that can do the job effectively, or alternatively it will look as if they are a shirker, continually passing work on to others. This is often not to the case, especially if they have considered carefully which tasks to delegate. It is worth examining your job and working out which tasks are most suitable for you to do and which tasks would more appropriately be done by a sub ordinate, celleague or even someone higher up the organization.

Habit 4: The Best Use

Try not to drift between tasks as you complete one task don't float onto another. Stand back and ask yourself.

What is the best use of my time now?

Be honest—it is very unlikely to be something trivial. It is more likely to be getting started on 'the big one'.

Habit 5: Achieving the Big One – Break it Down

Nuclear power stations get built, rockets are launched into space, large, difficult projects happen. How? They are broken down into smaller and smaller chunks until each piece of the project, each stage of the schedule is do-able. The same principle is at work for us on our big, difficult tasks. We often avoid tackling large, important projects because they overwhelm us with their size and importance. If something appears to be too difficult, them the first thing you need to do is break it down into smaller, achievable tasks. These tasks, which you can put on your to-do list, can then be given a schedule, and priority, as in Example 2.3

Example 2.3: Achieving The Big One by Breaking IT Down

Steve had a presentation to do that he was dreading, it seemed so daunting 200 people would be there, including some very important people, and it would be the culumation of months of work on a project. He decided to brainstorm a 'to-do' list of all the tasks involved in doing the presentation: identify the message, the audience and their needs. Key ideas and points for the content, having an introduction, a middle and an end, work out what IT support and other aids he would use, decide on the extra reading and research needed. He then decided to fit all these into a logical order. Instead of panicking, he decided his first hour should be spent that evening at home where he wouldn't be interrupted, with some classical music on the CD, planning it, writing down his key message, followed by producing an outline structure. For the following day at work he scheduled a couple of hours in the afternoon for reading and research, getting the materials together to build-up his evidence and information. In a third session he decided to design some slides and pay more attention to making the presentation stimulating for the audience, introduce some one codes and illustrations, may be even having a practice run through in his head. In a fourth session he decided, he would rope in a friend, Tony get him round for a drink and get him to listen to him practising the presentation. Tony was an experienced presenter, he would be bound to have some tips and he owed him one for fixing his computer. In the last session few days before the presentation he would allow time to redesign his slides, change around the format of the session and may be write a short hand out to accompany it. That would allow for any slippage should anything go wrong.

Listing out tasks and then making a schedule is an important place to start, because you can get into a mess by omitting to create something tangible and concrete. Having a schedule gives you a feeling of control, and also means that in each session your mind can concentrate on the task in hand, rather than the project in its entirely, facing one do able task at a time, thus avoiding the feeling of overload.

Habit 6: Do it Now Get Started

Of course, finding a task too difficult is not the only reason for delay. Procrastration is a great time bandit, and the irony is that all it does is increase feeling of anxiety. Anticipatory anxiety is 9 times out of 10 worse than actually getting on and doing something. Work out where your block is and gently lift it out of the way.

Think of a child who is scared of the dark, may be she

sees shadows dancing on her bedroom wall, and she starts fearing that a robber is going to come through her window. However, when she returns the light on, she finds the shadows were nothing more than the trees waving outside, and there is nothing thereafter all. Metaphonically we need to 'turn the light on': getting started means working out what needs to be done and starting, rather than freezing in the headlights of your own fear.

Sometimes it is not anxiety that makes you defer, but indecisiveness. In 95 per cent (at least) of cases you won't have better information later so you might as well begin immediately and clear the task.

A common fear is putting pen to paper, particurlarly for the perfectionist, yet it is amazing how once you get started, you can even find enjoyment in that difficult job you have been dreading. In any case, a written draft is rarely very polished, so it may be a good idea to lower your expectations and tell yourself it is more important to finish a draft, however poor, in order to create something to work on and polish, than not begin at all and miss an important deadline. Beware of disappearing into a lot of unimportant, not urgent activities to give yourself the illusion of action.

The adrenaline junky mentioned above need to go one step further and find a way of putting pressure on that bit earlier. One way of doing this is to set an earlier deadline and externalize it. See for example James in Example 2.4.

Example 2.4: Create an Early Deadline

James is a research scientist who has paper to do for a conference that takes place 1 May. It is now 1 April. Normally he would spend days avoiding the task, and then a couple of days befor the conference stay up all night working on it, arriving at the conference tired and exhausted. Instead James could contact his group manager and suggest that he get a first draft of the paper to him by 14 April, or alternatively suggest he circulate a draft to his research group for comments on that date. By creating an earlier deadline, and then externalizing it, he can give himself the feeling of pressure he needs to work, but without having to go through the process of turning into a nervous wreck.

Habit 7: Re-engineer Your Day best Time for Best Tasks

Some people are tasks they get up early in the morning bright to runing to go, yet by mid-afternoon they are flugging. Others are owls, they drag themselves out of bed, sit sleeply at their desk in the morning, but then by evening they are ready to work, full of energy, burning the midnight oil. Different people have different 'best times' —what is your best time of day for working? Ideally you should aim to re-engineer your day so that you undertake your critical 20 per cent and your top priorities when you are at your best. Likewise you could save your routine work for when you are tired and your energy is low.

Example 2.5: David Hockney and the Tea Bags

On a visit to the Tate Modern I looked at a piece of art by David Hockney. If consisted of a packet of tea-bags. What made him paint tea bags I wondered? I listened through the earphones to hear the commentary to this painting. Apparently Hockney liked to get-up early in the morning to do his painting then, but at that time the cafe wasn't open so he had to bring his own tea bags into his workplace. By mid-afternoon he was often really tired, so regularly he would down tools, pack up and go and watch a film, may be coming back latter refreshed. How much more effective do you think you could be if you resigned your working day to fit with your own natural rhythm. This may be a daily rhythm, or even one over longer periods of time. Certainly some people like to work in quick bursts, other work more steadily.

Example 2.6: A Lion or a Dung Beetle?

At a talk at Imperial College given by the top biographer Victoria Glendining someone asked how she worked. Victoria gave the analogy of the lion and dung beetle. The lion sits there lazily for hour upon hour, and then suddenly sees her prey and is full of energy. Violently chasing and capturing it. A hurricane of energy and vitality. When the activity is finished, the lion returns, lazily to sitting and basking in the sun or shade, until her appetite prompts her back into action. On the other hand, the dung beetle finds a small lamp of dung and laboriously pushes it and pushes it until eventually it rolls over the blade of grass, and it carries on laboriously pushing and pushing and pushing, on and on and on. Victoria said she would really like to be a lion in the way she worked, working with short bursts of high energy. Regrettably she said, she was more like a dung beetle, plodding away day after day.

Habit 8: Cut Yourself Off: Find a Hideway

Re-engineering your day also may mean training others to respect your concentration time. This may not always be possible in noisy office environments. You may need to find somewhere quiet where you can work effectively. It may even mean taking work home, or working in a library, or at least away from the office and distractions of colleagues. For this to be effective, you need to make sure your performance is being judged by outcomes and not process.

Example 2.7: Xerox and Re-engineering the Day
Lotte Bailyn, a professor at MIT helped staff at xerox to re-engineer their working lives. As well as changing their work shedule, it meant that staff had to learn that others may gave times when they weren't available. For this to be successful it also meant that staff needed to provide times. When they were available, and advertise these so that they could be contacted.

The principle is that if you remove something, such as your constant availability all times of the day, you need to provide something to replace it, such as office hours when you can guarantee to be available and give others your attention. For example, you may decide your best work times are 10-12 a.m. and you may hide yourself away at these times, removing yourself from the office or putting up a 1.00-3.00 p.m. for inquiries. Alternatively, work at home one day communication technologies mean you can be reached if absolutely necessary, and you can connect to your workplace by computer.

Habit 9: Wait Productively
Now is the to start using up those odd 5-10 minutes slot which everyone has in their days and which we tend to think can't be used productively. They can't if you have trouble getting started on tasks you dislike, use one of the

small slots to face up to it. Often knowing that you will only have to spend a few minutes on it is enough to get you to face up to it. Once you have started it you can usually continue it. Alternatively reading is good space-filler, and you may find you get to like habit, looking forward to your computer journey, and uninterrupted time for reading those books or reports, you just need to make sure you bring the documents with you, but beware, don't cruise with documents, don't become laden down with work to do as you go too and from work. Only take with you what you will need otherwise the work will become like a milstone you carry around with you.

Habit 10: Killing Two Birds with One Stone

Type A personalities are people who are driving, ambitious, competitive, restless, always liking to be on the go, unlike type B people who are more laid back, clam and take life a bit more easily. These different types are discussed more fully in next chapter. Type As like this habit doing two tasks at once. This works particularly well then you have lots of trivial tasks to do, for example, you could be signing letters as viewing e-mails when on the telephone to that manager who does tend to go on rather.

Example 2.8: Killing Two Birds with One Stone

Stephanie had a research student, Richard, who wanted her to provide him with some reading on a topic. Stephanie had been asked to do a book review for a journal on the same topic by mid-January, and it was now the middle of December and at first glance the book seemed to be on up to date review of the literature in this area. Stephanie really didn't have the time to get started on the book review, not spend time getting more references for Richard. She had on idea, she proposed to Richard that he borrow the book over Christmas to read and they do the book review jointly, with him making notes on the book over the vacation. Richard was delighted, he had also wanted to ask Stephanie to help him start publishing material and doing a joint book review seemed a good place to start practising his skills.

Although in Stephanie's case the action meant she had less to do, in some cases it can make you busier. If you are a type A person, don't over do it: type A's are also more prone to heart attacks! Likewise if you are a butterfly don't use this as an excuse to get in a mess, and remember difficult tasks will require your whole attention.

Another related techniques is to take a number of trivial tasks or related tasks and bunch them together. Often you can build up greater speed if you are clearing up several tasks, such as form-filling, at once. Order tasks so you cut down on travelling, for example, pick-up the office stationery next time you are down in the basement photocopying in the room along the corridor, rather than making an extra visit—it also means you don't just stand at the photocopier staring into space.

Habit 11: Once is Enough

There are four things you can do with a piece of paper: 1. bin it, 2. act on it, 3. pass it on, or 4. file use another time. Picking up a note, putting it down again picking it up later shuffling it round your desk until the next piece of paper comes into busy it underneath—is not doing one of those four things. Handle each piece of paper once. This is not easy, but it is rewarding why do people let paper hover round their workspace? Often because they are indecisive, they don't know what to do with it. Stop defering decisions. Don't hoard items to read later you won't you never have so far, so it is unlikely you are about to start. The bin is a business information neutralizer that should be used more often, and the 'delete' button on the computer under utilized tool—use it, rather than letting clutter build-up and paralyse you with a pile of 'indecisions'.

Of course, there is some material that doesn't need immediate attention, and you may be about to get started on something important and don't want to allow bits of paper to divert you from that important task. In that case mark the material you need to return to later with the relevant date and put a note in your diary 'to-do' list to remind you. Or set up a reminder system and use recall notes. Sometimes people use computer packages such as Microsoft office and calender to input dates so that the computer reminds them when to turn attention to task or activity.

Habit 12: Tidy Up

You need to have a place for everything and everything in its place. If you have allowed your workspace to become untidy and cluttered tacking it can seem intimidating. It is made more daunting by the likelihood that it is full of those papers you don't know what to do with, are too indecisive to deal with, find too difficult to tackle, so that you don't know where to begin. So how do you start? Habit 11 will have set up the first method dealing with new material using the four alternatives idea. As for the rest, you need to schedule a time in your dairy, in low energy time of day, may be after lunch or at the end of the day to catch up with filing.

Begin by obtaining whatever equipment you need to climb this paper mountain: filling cabinets, files and folders, and try and make them appealing to look at. Then start the climb up the paper moutain by tackling the paper on your desk. Once you have a clear desk you will feel more relaxed at work. Try and move all paper extraneous to whatever you are working on out of sight it will be less likely to distract you then. Next, move to the other surfaces and then the floor. Horizontal filling (that is, in filling cabinets) is time more effective than vertical filing (piles on the floor). A note on the geology of paper mountains: they form very easily, stroking encourages their formation dust makes them fester.

If you are still feeling it is all too much to tackle, just imgaine what you will feel like walking into a tidy office. Picture how your office could look when you arrive in the morning isn't that a much more pleasurable start to the day? If you find it very difficult to throw away material, take the zero based rule. Imagine there had been a fire in your office, and all the paper was burnt which files, pieces of paper or data would you really miss? Or imagine this was your first day at work which bits of paper would you find essential to be able to do your job? This is the information you need and for electronic data make sure you have a copy backed up in a separate place on the computer. Some paper is difficult to throw away because it is represents our history. Other bits of paper may useful at some point in the future. If you are really not certain, box the material up, label it and put it in a loft or somewhere out of way, and then see whether you need to get it down over the next year. If you haven't you could then throw it away.

Habit 13: The Electronic Battlefield

It is not just paper that can clutter our work space there is now the electronic battlefield also, and the never-ending stream of e-mails and SPAM that arrives on our computers. Just because it is in electronic form doesn't mean it's not rubbish. Delete and file as you go rather than letting old messages hang around and clog-up your system.

Begin by limiting the times of day you are going to look at your e-mails and stick to them. For many people it won't be more than three times: first thing in the morning, after lunch and when you finish work, when look at your e-mails skim through them to check if anything is urgent or very important. If it is not, decide a time of day when you can deal with non-important/ urgent messages as a group and make sure it is not your best time!

You could also go one step further and set-up electronic folders for your filing to mirror any filing system you have. You could even divert your e-mails into these folders automatically, for example, anything personal into a separate folder to look at later. Do not let other people's agendas rule your day immediate responses are not often required.

If you are feeling like taking this even further you could arrange to get yourself training in all the functions of your office software, such as the diary and calender, many of which are designed to help with time management. Alternatively when you have a free half-hour, explore the functions on your office software or read the manual, or an introductory basic guide, you may be amazed at what you could do. However, the computer is just as often a hindrance as a help, and there may be times when you need to unplug yourself in order to concentrate and not get distracted from the important task in hand.

Habit 14: Active Reading

Students have particular time management difficulties related to reading. It is quite easy for someone to spend hours, even days, reading a book, only to discover a couple of weeks later they can't remember anything they read, their time has effectively been wasted. The situation is made even more difficult with internet search engines and electonic access to journals, making more books and articles available than ever before.

Effectively, the number of publications on any topic is infinite; it is certainly not possible to read everything on a given subject. Reading can become like painting the Forth Bridge, a never-ending activity, unless you prioritise. Therefore you have to be selective and engine in active reading.

The first step in active reading is to skim abstracts to see how relevant materials is. Go for quality rather than quantity, don't download everything. Is it relevant, is it widely cited, does it appear in a top journal?

Once you have narrowed down the focus for your reading you can then concentrate on how you read, skim through first of all to check how useful it is really going to be. Then you start reading in detail make sure you are actively engaging with the material by asking the following:

– How would I sum up the message in this article in a few sentences?

- What are the key points?
- In what way will I use this article does it provide me with material for an argument in an essay, an example mehtodology to use, or what? How can I use this material?
- How would I critique this article, what are its strengths and weaknesses, do I agree with it, how would I classify it in the literature, are there holes in its argument and approach?
- Are there any quotes I need to take down exactly?
- What information do I need about the reference itself?

The third step is to consider, note taking. Are you going to use a highlighter pen and jot down some notes in the margin and keep a photocopy on electronic copy of the article? You may decide to keep all your references in endnote or reference manager or some proprietary software for referencing. There is nothing more time wasting than to find you need a full reference and haven't got it, so need to go and track down the source, or the page numbers or authors.

Habit 15: Look After Goose

Steven Covey (1969), in his book *The 7 Habits of Effective People* provides the example of the goose that lays the golden egg. If you exhaust yourself, work yourself into the ground, how can you expect to be able to continue to produce the golden eggs? Everyone knows organic, free-range produced eggs are better than battery farmed ones. Why allow yourself to become a battery farmed animal? Take care of yourself, value yourself enough to give yourself time to relax, time off, not life as one hard slog. So work productively rather than to burn out.

This applies especially over exams: working longer and longer without break can lead to exhaustion and in-effectiveness. You deserve a break and need to keep replenishing your batteries. It is not just long working hours that you need to avoid, but also destructive 'self-talk'. Examine the self-talk that stops you from doing things immediately. "I can't do this", "I am no good" , and put in place more constructive self-talk, and find others to reinforce it. You can do it.

Example 2.9: Albert Kushlick: A Truly Fallible Human Being

Some people went to the memorial service for a good personal friend. Albert Kushlick was one of the most incredible therapists. I have come across. Albert, South African who had come to England to escape the Apartheid regime and imprisonment for his work alongside Mandela, had become an eminent rational emotive therapist. No one who knew Albert was not affected by him even chose to spend the night before my own Ph.D. viva at his house, because I knew that if anyone could calm me down and help me feel confident. It was Albert. He made a significant impact on many people's lives and it was not surprising to see many come to his memorial service to pay their respects. On the booklet for the service there was a picture of Albert, and instead of the expected list of all the amazing deeds he had done in his life, there was the simple statement: "Albert Kushlick, a truly fallible human being". That had made me laugh, and remember a story Albert had once told me about how he had travelled across America to arrive at 10 o'clock at night on the doorstep of the therapist he saw as a master of the profession. He was late, but he had travelled for over a day, and when the man opened the door he had grumpily said 'Get lost, you are too late, I am going to bed.'

We are all fallible human beings, even experts at the top of their profession. Generally, we try to do the best that we can. No one has foresight. So you can do is make the best decisions you can in the circumstances and move on, even if events later prove you to have been wrong. So stop beating yourself up and do the best you can. Put mistakes down to experience and move on constructively.

Habit 16: Adopt a Habit

Time management is a habit. You are trying to change deeply entrenched habits. This takes time. Adopt one knew habit at a time. Move from theory to practise. . . practise. . . practise, dipping your toe in the water and having a go will show you that you can do it. . . But before you move on to fill in the personal contract it is worth just having a quick practice at these new skill by using the scenarios below!

Time Management Scenarios

Take 15 minutes to read the following scenario and to write down what you would do next in each case. You may like to also consider whether what you would really do differs significantly from what you think you ought to do, looking at the habits listed above.

Exercise 2.3: The Scenarios

Scenario-2

8.00 a.m. Monday morning, uggh! you had a fantastic

week away at a conference, and didn't get back until 2.00 a.m. last night, having stopped off a friend's house to break-up the drive home, but wish you hadn't. You have got a whole afternoon of meetings, a team presentation to organize for tomorrow to give another department on the work your team does, and report to get in by the end of the week. You make your way downstairs to make a cup of tea, and oooh, there are about 10 letters waiting for you on the doormat. You ideally turn your computer as you wait for the kettle to boil, and your curiosity is aroused by 17 e-mails waiting for you, and one looks as if it is about a possible project idea that you have been pursuing, which might lead to a lucrative new contract. You get out your briefcase, and notice two documents that should be back at your work library in two hours, and it will take you 50 minutes on the table to get into work. As you open the fridge to get out the milk, oh no, it's stale, and there is nothing else in the fridge,you forgot to shop, and yes, the calender next to the fridge reminds you that you offered to have your team round for dinner tonight. As you start getting dressed, your heart starts to pump and you can feel that knot of anxiety beginning to clench in your stomach. Oh no not another of those days where you run round like a headless chicken, panicked out and getting now here.

How Do You Spend Your First Hour?

Scenario 2

11.00 a.m. Monday morning and you are sat at your desk at work trying to get on with your report.

How did the conference go? I am dying to hear all the

news, and I have got some ideas on that plan you were presenting, It's Mike, a member of your team, come for a quiet chat you would so love him the rundown on how it all went, but say: I am so busy.

'Oh I know, tell me about it, it's so hectic around here, you will never believe what has been going on. I have got a really juicy bit of news to tell you. And he makes to sit down and start launching into his history.

What do you do and say?

Scenario 3

You are just getting back to your report when you realize that you have left some of the most important statistics that you had down loaded from the internet, at home. As you search in vain through the pile of papers on your desk, you find a visa card statement that you need to pay off today, and the bank is only five minutes away. You also find the birthday card you meant to send of your sister, for which you still need to get a stamp. You also feel it would have helped to e-mail your boss to clarify some details about this report, such as how long it should be, and should you focus more on providing one solution to the problem or alternatively provide several options. You are now beginning to feel confused. Oh you need a coffee to clear your head, it is spinning and haven't put pen to paper yet.

What do you do?

Debriefing

Actually, it is not easy as you think. It is likely you are

between what you know you would be likely to do, that may include bad habits, and what you think you should do having read through the suggested list of good habits. It is likely take you a bit more effort to move from the should to the 'do' but that is what the personal contract is intended to do below. Taking scenario I, given the predicament, a good place to start would be writing a long list of things to do, and then prioritizing them in a grid identifying urgent and important(see habits 1 and 2). For example, in the urgent and important box you could put the presentation and your afternoon meetings, in the important but not urgent box the report, in the urgent but not important box scanning e-mails and messages, getting the documents back to the library, buying milk, the shopping and the dinner party. In the not urgent and not important box are the letters and many e-mails. Looking at an effective path through this, you could consider beginning by scanning e-mails, then going into work to get going on your report, stopping at the library on the way in. You have a killing two birds with one stone possibility of e-mailing your group before you leave to suggest that you all discuss the presentation over dinner, and renegotiation opportunity to save time is that you may suggest dinner will be moved to your local pizzeria. The trap is to get caught answering e-mails, but you could print off the project opportunity to read on your computer journey into work.

Scenario 2 is a common way in which we get interrupted. The sensible approach would be short and sweet and to the point: "I am too busy now, but I'd love to talk later, how about we meet for launch?" Don't get drawn into talking about your busyness that could mean you just get lost in a moan. Keep it brief and use your body language to confirm your statement. Other techniques people employ to avoid length interruptions are:

- to set a time limit. I have five minutes only
- Set the stage in advance – I am leaving in five minutes
- remain standing – it is harder to get into a long relaxed conservation that way.
- meet others away from your office and workspace – preferably in their office, because if makes our get away easier and is more difficult to get trapped.
- avoid small talk, be ruthless but polite get them to the point.
- don't get dragged into long excuses that open the way to more conversation.
- don't get roll roaded.

Scenario 3

Again places potential interruptions your way – paying your visa and buying a stump for a birthday card. These are also killing two birds opportunities (on your way somewhere for example) and can also be clustered with other small jobs after you have go on with something more important. Plan when you are going to do these and don't just go off into 'the pleasure principle' of easy fun things like writing and sending a card. Making a note of when you will do things can ease. 'Your anxiety and stop it buzzing round in your head. Move the pile of papers off your desk to stop them distracting you, make a note of the papers you want to get hold of download later' and get back to preparing your report. Don't let the lack of certain information stop your getting started. You can always slot in later, and getting going may help you identify more clearly exactly what additional information you need, and what you may not actually require after all.

Ultimately, the best way of dealing with 'busyness' anxiety is to build-up your self-esteem, respect yourself enough to enable you to do one job at a time, not run around frantically, protect the other jobs by putting them in your schedule, and focus on the one job you have decided to begin.

Aristotic and the Habit of the Good Life

It is quite likely that in identifying your own time bandits, you already had an idea what they were. You may even have a good idea of what you should be doing differently. This chapter is not about knowing what to do, it is about putting thought into action and this requires behavioural change which is a bit trickier to effect.

Artistotle talked about the habit of the good life. The good life is not an abstract idea, it is a habit that is nurtured and acted upon over a period of time. Time management is a habit. It is likely you are accustomed to your habits, may even be comfortable with the way you do things, and they won't be easy to change, because that requires effort and persistence. Therefore, it won't be enough if this chapter merely identifies for you what you should be doing differently. You have to break a habit, create a habit and preserve to maintain it.

Below are some good habits, but for them to work and guarantee you more time, you will need to put them into practice. When, we start something new, it is easier to take one step at a time, building up competence and new habits gradually.

Glance at this contract now, and you will see it requires you to identify three changes you intend to make, and to put the first step into practice in the following. As you read through the good habits think which one would be most relevant for you to start with, which will give you the biggest gain, and which relates most closely to the problems you identified in Exercies 2.1 and 2.2.

Example 2.1: Examples of Time Management Problem Work Related

I work on a project to implement IT in my organization, but I report to two bosses, the head of IT Department, and the Project Leader their demands of me are diverse and sometimes conflicting and very confusing as a result I get in a mess.

I work in an open plan office. I constantly get distracted by people talking on the phone, chatting across desks, stopping to talk to me. I cannot concentrate on my work, and I end-up frittering my time on superficial tasks whilst at work, and then well into the night at home to catch up with the tougher parts of my work.

I am a design engineer and each part of the work I do seems to take at least three time longer than we estimate it will take, meaning that I spend a lot of time explaining why the work is late and reorganizing schedules and activites. This impacts negatively on people further down the development process. "I set myself priorities but because I also work as a support service for other people in the organization. I get in undated by e-mails and requests from others. I spend all my time meeting other people's demands and my priorities go out of the window!"

Last year, I spent ages developing a balanced scorecard system for the organization to performance manage the managerial team, then a new director was appointed and he passed the plug on months of work and asked me to set up a totally different scheme. It seems like much of my work is a waste of time? Now, we shall discuss about the Pareto's Principles of time management.

Principles of Time Management

According to Prof. Pareto, "when we look at time management and its 'prodcut' from calendars to training sessions, he believed that Although, Today there is a fundamental problem. The underlying assumption that if you can get more things done in less time, you will have more free time is flawed. Because as any truly effective and efficient person can tell you, that is complete nonesense! They always have more things to do than they can ever finish in a given day, week or month. No matter how much they complete, there will always be more.

So prepare yourself for a shock: If you really want to be more productive and have the free time to do other things besides work, then time management is not the answer.

It can be helpful, but to really make a difference, you will need to take a different approach. Before I share this with you, let me ask you this: What would you do with you" time if you had more of it? What would you like to be doing with your time that you aren't already doing?

(*i*) Spending more time with friends and family?

(*ii*) Taking more breaks, mini vacations and full on vacations?

(*iii*) Being able to be more creative and not worry about your business so much ?

(*iv*) Taking a month off to travel the world?

(*v*) Taking three-day weekends?

(*vi*) Working 25 hourwork weeks?

Why Some People Work Best Under Pressure

Are you somwone that works best under pressure? Do you need the rush of a deadline that's almost impossible to reach in order to churn out your very best? There are three reasons for this:

First, when you have a deadline and a project is due 'tomorrow', you give yourself permission to do crappy work. You don't have a lot of time, you are working really fast, so if this isn't amazing, you have a perfect excuse. Your inner critic can go to sleep and you can get to work.

Second, when you are under pressure, you have to come up with something. Instead of worrying and thinking. "I don't know what to write" or "I don't know how to do this", because of the pressure of the deadline, you just "make yourself" come up with something. Good or bad, right or wrong, you get to work.

Finally, when you are under pressure, you get a surge of adrenaline, this gives you great levels of energy and your brain is fried up in the moment giving you more creativity and more power to accomplish what you are working on.

Someone has rightly said that the 'dark side' of the pressure cooker: of course, the reasons why people work, better under pressure are part of the reason why you might find yourself in this situation so often yet even though 'in the moment', when you are working on a project with a deadline, you might feel great, it comes with a high price tag. Because when you are done with a project like this, there's usually a crash that comes right after it. Sometimes a big one, sometimes a small one. Some people have a history of getting ill the first day of their holidays. This constant up and down is quite exhausting, especially when there are so many projects to work on. The best work is actually done from a state of peace and calm, but because people have an 'inner critc' that is expecting simply all of their ideas to be great ones and all of their work to be perfect, sometimes it's not until the pressure is on that you can put the critic to sleep. However, if you could put the critic to sleep for ever, you wouldn't need the threat of a deadline to make it OK to go for it. When you are working, "in the flow" at a peaceful and relaxed place, the energy isn't coming from adrenaline, it's coming from a purer place.

There is also another reason why this way of working is problematic: every project team has people who just can't motivate themselves to keep a deadline in the early stages of the project, when nothing much will happen yet and this starts a very unflattering track record.

The Price of Being "Hurried, Worried, Rushed and Stressed"

Many people I know who are working around the clock are missing out on a lot. But it's usually not very clear what they are missing. It is not just that the miss-out on doing fun stuff that they might rather be doing. They miss-out on a high quality of life, because after all, how you spend your time? Is how you spend your life?

When you are stressed out by things you need to do to grow your business and feel hurried and worried, it can be very hard to stay present even when you are able technically free to enjoy yourself after work. Why? Because, there's a part of your mind that is still thinking about all the things you need to do, and worrying that something might fall through the cracks.

This impacts your health, your relationships. Your attractiveness (to clients and co-workers) as well as your general feeling of aliveness. On top of it all, when you are feeling this way and working this way, your work can actually suffer by producing less than desirable results. A typical example; people who have their nose buried too deep in their computer tend to miss out an apportunities to go unnoticed but you probably don't want your life to pass you by.

Many people know that numerous clinical studies show that people who are under lots of stress are at greater risk for health issues such as heart attacks and cancer. Just like they also know that stress weakens our immune system, increasing our chances of getting sick (especially, again, with cancer). But they do precious little with knowledge.

Become "Time Abundant"

I have been coaching busy managers and busy owners for the last eight years. And among the top three reasons they hire me are variations of "to have more free time". But, for the last eight years. I have not been teaching time management strategies. What does that mean? Do I not provide something my clients clearly want? The answer is that I do deliver what my clients want, just not through the means they might be expecting. There is no 'programme' that I teach my clients that's not how I work. Although I do use a few time management strategies that work for me (more about them in a moment), I never felt good advising my clients to use them.

So, I don't know about you, but I could never get myself to fit my life-style into the structured "time-management boxes" that most expert profess. I just couldn't imagine my solution was in a new type of dairy or not-taking. . . and since I have always been quite disciplined, I knew the solution wasn't there either. The following is what worked for me because I am the one person I really know most about.

Today, I realize whenever I hear, a client say "I don't have enough time to get everything done", that, I have more time abundance than most people I know. Somehow, I have managed to achieve something that has eluded so many, How? Why have I so much time abundance in my life, in spite of the fact that I have a growing coaching business, and handle all my clients, from e-mail to the actual coaching, myself.

When, I started my career, I had a lot to do, but somehow it was always possible to finish what I had on my agenda for any given week. It might mean putting a couple of extra hours in here and there, but by and large, it worked. As a consultant, some evenings got longer and longer, but I still hardly ever worked over the weekend. Of course, that changed entirely when I had my own company with millions of things to do myself and a handful of co-workers that needed to be trained and overseen. The handful then became 15 people, and then 25 and more work than I could handle. And I what I now know many people do, I panicked and took care of more urgent stuff than important stuff. In my case, 'creating systems' (which constiuted an important part of my job role) was per se not an urgent task. But, my mistake was that I become cluttered and unclear in my oriorities, trying to make as many things a priority as possible. The result was six and a half day workweeks. Our cleaning people always came after 8 p.m. and I knew all of them and was sometimes still working when they had left. I was so overworked and at the same time noticed that other people in the office didn't fully realize what exactly I was so busy with, because they didn't see much of the output.

It was only when I started my coaching training than I started turning the situation around. I had to into this workload, I suddenly needed to make time for two and half days every six weeks (one was a Saturday), but since I worked Saturdays anyway, it did feel like, I was losing two and a half one and a half days. One of the question that this raised was "what are the things I cannot compromise on?", and I realized there weren't that many. I also realized I could delegate who chunk of work to others people in my support team, if I changed my attitude towards their competence and created systems that would allow them to do more which they loved, by the way! That was the beginning.

Of Course, I wouldn't have it like that back them, but what I was really on my way to doing was implementing the first five principles that I had just read in a book from Michalson. The more I applied the following principles, the better I felt and the more resourceful and resilient I became.

(*i*) Principle 1 = Free your mind of time scarcity
(*ii*) Principle 2 = Love what you do
(*iii*) Principle 3 = Develop patient timelines
(*iv*) Principle 4 = Simplify your life (de-clutter)
(*v*) Principle 5 = Upgrade your energy sources
(*vi*) Principle 6 = Follow your changing needs.

Principle 1: Free Your Mind of Time Scarcity (Rid yourself of constantly thinking "lack of time")

When the worst comes to the worst, spend a few minutes finding our what will happen if you can't make the deadline, chances are you discover that others have built a little leeway into their time lines, so that you may end-up having an extra two-to-three days, or even a whole week. They you are take a deep breath and be ready to start working in your priorities. This won't work every single time but I know lots of people who are stressed and overworked that they can't produce anything for hours and end-up browsing the internet only to find themselves working (that way) until the week hours of the morning. If you are really can't work don't (see principle 6)

Principle 2: Love What You Do

"My friends sometimes say "... but you work quite hard too", as if working was somehting bad! If you love your work, why wouldn't you want to work! But if you really don't enjoy your work and, for some reason, still want to stay in that line of business, I strongly advise you to look for at least some chuncks of activities that you can enjoy!

Principle 3: Develop Patient Timelines

I think we can all benefit from some principles of project management here. Many activities within a project can happen in various moments during that project. Others are absolutely critically determined by their position in a sequence, and obviously these will then be your priorities in that moment. But often the pressure we create is entirely of our own making and this applies especially to the self employed and entrepreneurs. Be actively patient with yourself and overcome the fear of not offering the tightest schedule and losing the bid. It is often your choice!

Principle 4: Simplify Your Life

There is a flourishing trade in books, tapes and CDs, all based around that one principles of de-cluttering. Throw out what doesn't serve you anymore. Whether these are jsut objects or demands you make on yourself. When you can hardly remember what you need something for, you probably won't need it at all. If you are a careful type, don't throw it away just yet, but box it and put it in the basement figuratively speaking.

Principle 5: Upgrade Your Energy Sources

Whether it's yoga or salsa, meditaiton or track-and-field there is something that gives you energy, and you know what it is! Don't give up such activities, but devote some time to them on a regular basis. And if sometimes doesn't work out, just make a new appointment with yourself.

Principle 6: Follow Your Changing Needs

If you can't work do something else take a walk, if necessary do a breathing exercise or use the "cheapest anti-depressant know to man gratitude", as Ben Furman a famous finish colleague says, Monitor how you are and take care of what you really need. Do you really that bar of chocolate, or is it just that you are tired but don't allow yourself to take a break? Try to get the real message. Whatever you do, don't 'self-reproach'!

Imagine if you applied these principles, and as a result–

(*i*) You felt more relaxed.

(*ii*) You were in the "flow of life"

(*iii*) Your work would just "happen" (no more forcing things now the ideas just come to you find more come throught you)

(*iv*) You had more time of play and fun and for the people that really matter in your life.

(*v*) The work you did was for more effective.

Now we shall discuss about the Pareto's principle of time management.

2.3 PARETO'S PRINCIPLES OF TIME MANAGEMENT

In 1906, Italian economist Vi!fredo Pareto created a mathematical formula to describe the unequal distribution of wealth in his country, observing that 20 per cent of the people owned 80 per cent of the wealth. In the late 1940s, Dr. Joseph M. Juran in accurately attributed the 80/20 Rule to pareto, calling it pareto's principle. While, it may be misnamed, Pareto's principle or Pareto's Law as it is sometimes called, can be a very effective tool to help you manage effectively.

Where it Came From

After Pareto made his observation and created his formula,

many others observed similar phenomena in their own areas of expertise. Quality Managements Pioneer, Dr. Joseph Juran, working in the US in the 1930s and 1940s recognized a universal principle he called the "vital few and trivial many" and reduced it to writing.

In an early work, a lack of precision on Juran's part made it appear that he was applying Pareto's observations about economics to a broader body of work. The name Pareto's Principle stuck, probably because it sounded better than Juran's principle.

As a result, Dr. Juran's observation of the "Vital few and trivial many", the principle that 20 per cent of the something always are responsible for 80 per cent of the results, became known as Pareto's Principle or the 80/20 Rule.

What It Means

The 80/20 Rule means that in anything a few 20 per cent are vital and many (80 per cent) are trivial. In Pareto's case it meant 20 per cent of the people owned 80 per cent of the wealth. In Juran's initial work be identified 20 per cent of the defects causing 80 per cent of the problems.

Project manager know that 20 per cent of the work (the first 10 per cent and the last 10 per cent) consume 80 per cent of your time and resources. You can apply the rule 80/20 Rule to almost anything from the science management to the physical world.

You know 20 per cent of you stock takes up 80 per cent of your warehouse space and that 80 per cent of your stock comes from 20 per cent of your suppliers. Also 80 per cent of your sales will come from 20 per cent of your sales staff, 20 per cent of your staff will cause 80 per cent of your problems, but another 20 per cent of your staff will provide 80 per cent of your production. It works both ways.

How It Can Help You

The value of the Pareto Principle for a manager is that it reminds you to focus on the 20 per cent that matters of the things you do during your day, only 20 per cent really matter. Those 20 per cent product 80 per cent of your results. Identify and focus on those things. When the fire drill of the day begin to sap your time, remind yourself of the 20 per cent you need to focus on. If something in the schedule has to slip, if something isn't going to get done, make sure it's not part of that 20 per cent.

There is a management theory floating around at the moment that proposes to interpret Pareto's principle in such a way as to produce what is called superstar management. The theory's supporter's claim that since 20 per cent of your people produce 80 per cent of your results you should focus your limited time on managing only that 20 per cent, the superstars. The theory is flawed, as we are discussing here because it overlooks the fact that 80 per cent of your time should be spent doing what is really important. Helping the good become better is a better use of your time than helping the great become terrific. Apply the Pareto principle to all you do, but use it wisely.

Manage This Issue

Pareto's principle, the 80/20 rule, should serve as a daily reminder to focus 80 per cent ot your time and energy on the 20 per cent of you work that is really important. Don't just "work smart", work smark on the right things.

This may come as a surprise, but despite all the talk about life balance, you can benefit tremendously from introducing a little imbalance into your day. I am referring to the 80/20 rule of time-management, which is rooted in what is known as the Pareto principle.

Vilfredo Pareto, an Italian Economist, "discoverd" this principle in 1897 when he observed that 80 per cent of the land in England (and every country he subsequently studied) was owred by 20 per cent of the populution. Pareto's of predictable imblalance has since been applied to almost every aspect of modern life. Given a chance, it can make a difference in yours.

Recognizing your 20 per cent

Simply put the 80/20 rule states taht the relationship between input and output is rarely, if ever, balanced. When applied to work, it means that approximately 20 per cent of your efforts, produce 80 per cent of teh results. Learning to recognize and then focus on that 20 per cent is the key to making the most effective use of your time. Here are two quick tips to develop 80/20 thinking.

Take a Good Look at the People Around You

Twenty per cent of your collegues, staff and patients probably give you 80 per cent of the support and satisfaction you need. They are your true advocates. Take good care of them. Likewise, you can probably name several friends and family members who would be there for you under any circumstances. In other words, we can say that 20 per cent of your efforts produce 80 per cent of the results.

Examine Your Work

Ask yourself, "What do I really want to do with my life and my time? What 20 per cent of my work should I be focusing on?"

Implementing the 80/20 Rule

Even if you are skeptical, follow the 80/20 principle for a few days just to see what happens. You can start by implementing these "20 per cent" tasks right now.

Read less: Identify the 20 per cent of the journals you get that are most valuable. Read them and trash the rest.

Keep Current: Make yourself aware of new technological innovations. At the very least, you may be to challege established routine that could be shifting your focus away from your 20 per cent.

80 per cent or 20 per cent

Here are some signs that will help you to recognize whether you are spending your time as you should: you are in your 80 per cent if the following statements ring true:

1. You are working on tasks other people want you, to but you have no investment in them.
2. You are frequently working on tasks labelled 'urgent'.
3. You are spending time on tasks you are not usually good at doing.
4. Activities are taking a lot longer than you expected.
5. You find yourself complaining all the time.
6. You are smiling.

If you would like more information on this time

management principle, I would suggest the 80/20 pricnciple 'The secret of Achieving More with Less" by Richard Koch (New York Bantam University, Delhi publishing, 1998). Gain more control over your time and your work by taking one small step right now. This is increase awarness of what's vital to your life and your life's work may be all you really need to start using your time more effectively.

Koch has also used his concepts to make a fortune from several private equity investments made personally. He also emphasizes that 80/20 principle should not only be seen as method for making decisions or selections, but it should be combined with W. Brian Arthur's concepts of positive feedback and increasing returns.

In business, the 80/20 rule can be applied in many areas. For example:

1. *Supplies*– 80 per cent of your supplies comes from 20 per cent of your vendors.
2. *Inventory*–80 per cent of your product comes from 20 per cent of your vendors intventory.
3. *Sales productivity*–80 per cent of your suppliers sales comes from 20 per cent of your sales force.
4. *Employees*–80 per cent of the work will be done by 20 per cent of the employees.
5. *Customers*–80 per cent of sales will come from 20 per cent of your customers.
6. *Complaints*–80 per cent of complaints come from 20 per cent of your customers.
7. *Advertising*–80 per cent of business from advertising will come from 20 per cent of the advertising.

It's important to keep in mind that the 80/20 rule is ratio. This means, if the total selection is less, then the total sales will also be less. Pareto's principle, the 80/20 rule, should serve as a daily reminder to focus 80 per cent of your time and energy on the 20 per cent of those activities that are really important. It's not enough to just 'smart', you also need to work smart on the right things.

Time Management Tips: The 80/20 Rule or the Pareto Principle

The 80/20 rule is one of the most helpful of all concepts of time and life management. It is also called the Pareto principle after its founder, the Italian economist Vilfred Pareto, who first wrote about it in 1895. Pareto noticed that people in his society seemed to divide naturally into what he called the 'vital few' the top 2 per cent in terms of money and influence and the 'trivial many', the bottom 80 per cent.

This means that if you have a list of 10 items to do, two of those items will turn out to be worth as much or more than the other eight items put together. Here is an interesting discovery. Each of these tasks may take the same amount of time accomplish. But one or two of those tasks will contribute five or 10 times the values as any of the others. Often, one item on a list of 10 things that you have to do can be worth more than all the other nine items put together. This tasks is invariably the one that you should do first.

The most valuable tasks you can do each day are often the hardest and most complex. But the pay off and rewards for completing these tasks efficiently can be tremendous. For this reason, you must adamantly refuse to work on tasks in the bottom 80 per cent while you still have tasks in the top 20 per cent left to be done. Before you begin work, always ask yourslef, "Is this task in the top per cent of my activities or in the bottom 80 per cent?"

The hardest part of any important task is getting started on it in the place. Once you actually begin work on a valuable task, you seem to be naturally motivated to continue. There is a part of your mind that loves to busy working on significant tasks that can really make a difference. Your job is to feed this part of your mind continually.

Time management is really life management, personal management. It is really taking control over the sequence of events. Time management is control over what you do next/ And you are always free to choose the task that you will do next? your ability to choose between the important and unimportant is the key determinant of your success in life and work.

Effective, productive people discipline themselves to start on the most important task. That is before them make a list of all the key goals, activities, projects and responsibilities in your life today. Which of them are or could be in the top 10 per cent or 20 per cent of tasks that represent or could represent, 80 per cent or 90 per cent of your results?

Resolve today that you are going to spend more and more of your time working in those few areas that can really make a difference in your life and career and less and less time on lower value activities.

Pareto Chart

In QI a Pareto chart provides facts needed for settings

priorities. It organizes and displays information to show the relative importance of various problems or causes of problems. It is essentially a special form of a vertical bar chart that puts items in order (from the highest to the lowest) relative to some measurable effect to interest: frequency, cost, time. The chart is based on the Pareto principle which states that when several factor affect a situation a few factors will account for most of the impact. The Pareto principle describes a phenomenon mere 20 per cent of the causes of that variation. (Chart 2.1, Pureto Chart).

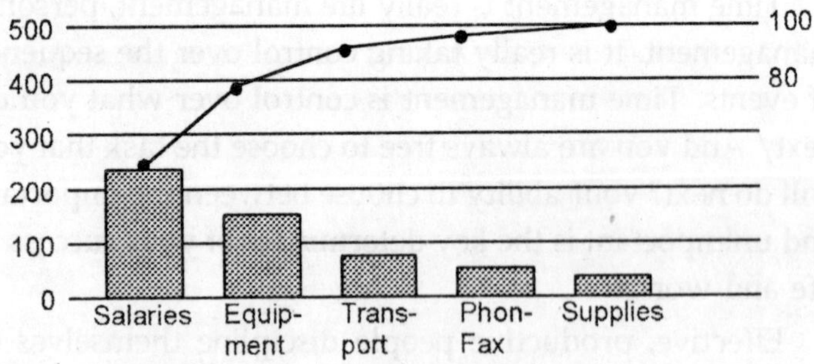

Fig. 2.1

We can see chart. 2.1 that the placing the items in descending order of frequency makes it easy to discern those problems that are of great importance of those causes that appear to account for most of the variation. Thus, a Pareto chart helps teams to focus their efforts where they can have the greatest potential impact.

When to Use It

Pareto charts help teams focus on the number of really important problems or causes of problems. Pareto charts are useful in establishing priorities by showing which are the most critical problems to be tackled or causes to be addressed. Comparing Pareto charts of a given situation over time can also determine whether an implemented solutions reduced the relative frequency or cost of that problem or cause.

How to Use It

Step 1: Develop a list of problems, items or causes to be compared.

Step 2: Develop a standard measure for comparing the items.

- How often it occurs: frequency (e.g., utilization, complications, errors)
- How long it takes: time
- How many resources it uses: cost

Step 3 : Choose a time frame for collecting the data.

Step 4 : Tally, for each item, how often it occurred (or cost or total time it took). Then add these amounts to detemine the grand total for all items. Find the per cent of each item in the grand total by taking the sum of the item, dividing it by the grand total and multiplying by 100.

Table 2.1: Tallying Items in a compilation table

Cause for Late Arrival	Number of occasions	Percentage
Family problems	8	11
Work up late	20	27
Had to take the bus	4	6

Traffic tie up	32	44
Sick	6	8
Bad weather	3	4
Total	**73**	**100**

Step-5 : List the items being compared in decreasing order of the measure of comparison. For example, the most frequent to the least frequent. The cumulative per cent for an item is the sum of that item's per cent of the total and that of all the other items that come before it in the ordering by rank.

Table 2.2

Return to Resources causes of late (Return to Top) Arrival Decreasing order	Number of occasions	Percentage	Cumulative per centage
Traffic tie-up	32	44	44
Wake up late	20	28	71
Family problems	8	10	82
Slick	6	8	90
Had to take the Bus	4	6	96
Bad weather	3	4	100

Step 6: List the items on the horizontal axis of a graph from highest to lowest. Label the left vertical axis with the number (frequency, time or cost) then label the right vertical axis with the cumulative per centages the (cumulative total should equal 100 per cent) draw in the bars for each item.

Step 7: Draw a line graph of the cumulative per centages,

The first point on the line graph should line up with the top of the first bar.

2.4 PRINCIPLES OF TIME MANAGEMENT IN INDIA

(*i*) **Accomplished Time Manager**: Prof. Peter Drucker is a most accomplished time manager. He works as a professor consultant and author. His time budget for consulting and speaking is 100 days in a year. Probably another 100 days, he spends on his teaching work and for the list of the year he works in his study. He goes on producing illuminating books year after year. He works without any staff. He keeps down demands on his time by use of pointed mail-back cards saying, for instance, Drucker regrets that he cannot accept any speaking assignment for the time being. In his eminently read a book *The Effective Exclusive* he explains the principles of time management in his time table style.

(*ii*) **Super Time Manager:** At the outset Drucker refers to the president of a bank with whom he had to work as consultant for several months. To Drucker's surprise the president was even a more accomplished time manager.

Every meeting would be exactly of 90 minutes. There would always be only one item on the agenda. After 80 minutes Drucker had to summarize the discussion and to outline the topic for the next session and within ten minutes the president would be shaking hand with him. There were no visitors or telephone calls to interrupt the meeting. The secretary never stuck her head in the door announcing some important visitor. Only the president of the U.S.A or the bank president's wife could telephone while the meeting was in progress. The wife knew better and never rang up. The president rang up only in a national crisis, which was very rare.

This is an ideal way of conducting a meeting. It illustrates a number of principles of effective time management.

(*iii*) **Span of Attention:** The duration of this meeting was always 90 minutes. The president of the bank had found that he could not concentrate on the subject after 90 minutes. That was his attention span. On the other hand, no useful discussion could take place in shorter time say half an hour. It is difficult to get the roots of the matter and to concentrate on the subject in a short time. This leads to the next principle of time management time being made available in sufficiently large chunks.

(*iv*) **Large Chunks of Time:** Suppose you want to prepare a report for which you estimate that you would require in all 48 per cent hours. Then you decide to work 112 hours a day for four days and finish the work. You find that you cannot working so long on a single day and it is better to devote half an hour a day and do the job perfectly. But you soon find that in an hour no work gets done and the time is simply wasted. If some important work is to be done, you must have sufficiently large chunks of time available in a strech. Executives often fritter away their time trying to use it in small driblets. No real work gets done in this manner.

(*v*) **Allocation of Time:** From the point of view of intellectual efficiently all clock hours are not identical. The hour during which your mind is fresh and you can think lucidity is worth several hours when you feel fatigued and dejected. The effective excutive reserves the hours when he is fresh and vigorous for the most important work. Another principle is to judge the relative importance of various items. A good executive knows what is trivial and what is important. His allocation of time is based on the relative importance of various matters. This appears to be a very simple matter but very often many executives occupy themselves with the trivial and neglect the fundamental.

(*vi*) **Time the Most Precious Resource:** Of all the resources of production, time is the most precious resource. It is also the most essential resource as all work is done in time. It is irreplaceble. Time lost is lost forever. The most loving care of his time therefore marks the effective executive. He plans his work carefully. His priorities are well fixed. He knows how to deal with time wasters. He also ensures that he does not waste the time of his assistant by keeping them waiting unnecessarily.

(*vii*) **The Golden Principles:** Management is not, and cannot be an exact science. There are exactly any laws in management, which are universally valid, like the law of gravitation. But, there are two golden principles; which are true at all times. The first concerns the proper use of one's time. To be effective in management is to be efficient in the use of one's time in the first place. And this one can practice and teach oneself. It does not require any capital investment. It is a matter of self-discipline. The other principle is that of integrity for which there is no substitute in management .

(1) Life is what you make it. No matter what profession you choose there should always be time to enjoy personal solitude and moments to spend with friends and family. Those who do not have time for fun are the ones that simply do not make time for it.

(2) Time management is your friend. How do I know? I used to seriously mismanage time by taking work home and borrowing time from other tasks. The mismanagement of time left me with a serious work life imbalance. As a result I was often stressed out and did not know the meaning of recreational time. Thankfully. I found resources like *Seven Habits of Hightly Effective People* by Steven Coven and *5 Leadership Essentials for Women* by Linda Clark. From them I knew the are of time management and principles for having a fun and full of life.

(3) Purpose, priorities and balance 90 hand in hand. When you know your purpose you can set priorities and balance every aspect of your life. Many of us fall short in one of these areas.

To make improvements that will keep everything in perspectives, identify your roles. Are you a spouse, a parent, a sidbling, or a business owner? Once you have defined your roles. You can set priorities and identify what you need to do in order to have the life you want to live. These principles will keep you from burning out.

Now use them and carve out some play time in your life today.

2.6. CONCLUSION

This chapter has identified ways in which you could improve your time management. At time management is about taking control and developing good habits, it has invited you to practise some time management skills. Through changing your behaviour step-by-step, you can become much more effective at setting and achieving priorities and objectives. Enjoy your achievements and learn to work in calmer more effective way.

In identifying the changes, make sure that these are written positively, things you will do and not things you won't do. For example, I will tidy-up my desk not I won't have a messy desk. You may like to consider the SMART methodology in setting your objectivities. Check that each objective is

S = specific (make it a clear specific aim such as "I will find somewhere to work where I can concentrate for a few hour-periods in the week rather than something vague and over general like I will re-arrange my working practices")

M = Measurable (How will you know you have achieved it?)

A = Achievable

R = Realistic

T = Time bound

You are likely to need some support in putting this into action and so you may be could design or discuss your personal contact and objectives in construction with work colleague, a personal tutor, or even a mentor at work and include this part of your (pc).

SELF ASSESSMENT

1. Discuss the basic principles of time management.
2. Examine practical examples of time management.
3. Describe the Pareto's principles of time management.
4. Discuss the principles of time management in India.

REFERENCES

Bailyin, L.(1993), *Breaking the Mold: Women, Men and Time in the New Corporate World.* New York Macmillan.

Clegge, C.K. Legge and S. Walsh, (1999), *The Experience of Managing: A Skills Guide,* Hunts: Macmillan chapte 31, D. Griffiths, Time management, 285-92.

Kotter, J.P. (1982), *The General Managers,* New York: Macmillan.

Maitland, I. (2001), *Managing Your Time,* London: CIPD.

Neenan, M. and W. Dryden (2002), *Life Coaching: A Cognitive-Behavioural Approach,* Hove Brunner-Routledge.

3

STRATEGY OF TIME MANAGEMENT

"That will cure every workaholic in the world. It will motivate any procrastination and encourage the utmost pessimist." *—Vivien Richardson*

"When you ask people what they would like to change most about the things they have done in the past, a lot of them will tell you something that is related to time." *— Peter Drucker*

Content of this Chapter

Introduction, Strategy of Time Management in World, Strategy of Time Management in India, Conclusion

3.1. INTRODUCTION

Have you ever wished to have more than 24 hours in a day, have you ever felt your head is about to explode as you are trying to assign at least a few check marks to your To Do List? Have tried every trick in a practical life on how to manage but still can't quite time this best? Despair no more the help is on its way, the real solutions from real life time management *gurus* who will anviel their secrets to one of the most challenging problems that most of us struggle with. These time management strategies will cure every workaholic in the world, will motivate any procrastinator and encourage the atmost pessimist to get things done in time and still have time left to enjoy life. Now learn from each other how to better manage your time, how to organize your day in a more efficient way, link to each other and become friends with, so elusive, but wise. His majesty time. In this chapter, we will discuss about the strategy of time management in world and in India. First of all, we will try to understand the strategy of time management in world.

3.2. STRATEGY OF TIME MANAGEMENT IN WORLD

Time Management Strategies—Revitalize Enthusiasm and Productivity using the 3 Gratitudes Exercise

Time management tips that inspire you to renew and deepen your gratitude also energize you, every single time you open your heart. If you really want to experience new zest, learn how to genuinely appreciate and care for your life, starting right now.

Cultivating the gift of gratitude is a powerful way to ground yourself and prepare yourself for any challenge. Gratitude enhances healthy humility that is based in self-respect. It also helps you assess your strengths and redirect your energy the following reflections provide a fresh window of understanding to your inner powerhouse.

Finding Time for Gratitude: 5 Central Insight

Gratitude's 3 Gifts to you

Gratitude immediately enriches your life in 3 ways:

1. How you look at your world.
2. How you move through your days.

3. How you experience your moments.

It is a fundamental value, and the ultimate way to make full use of your time. In *Character Strength and Virtues* by Christopher Peterson and Martin E.P. Seligman, gratitude is defined as "an enduring thankfulness that is across situations and over time."

There are two types of gratitude, personal and transpersonal.

Personal gratitude is about thankfulness towards an individual, whereas transpersonal gratitude is a constant and fundamental appreciation of the world.

Gratitude is a Very Special Gift to Children

According to studies, gratitude develops between 7 to 10 years of age. However, I belive that if a child is raised in an environment of appreciation, both specific and general, and if it is spoken about often and consistently, gratitude will begin to develop an earlier age. At the very least, the child will be surrounded by positive energy.

Experience and Express appreciation to Others Specifically and Frequently

How many times a day-to-day you actively thank someone? And how often do you feel the energy of awe and wonder? Don't deprive yourself or others of this wonderful, free gift that strengthens relationship!

As an Informative Exercise, Jot Down Each Time you Feel Grateful for Anything

After 3 or 4 weeks, go over your documentation and identify patterns in your gratitude. Are there days when you are so absorbed in the activities of daily living that you "forget" life's gifts? What does this tell you? What happens to your energy? Do you habitually see the glass as the "half empty" or "half full"?

There is a simple and wonderful exercise I've practised for many years.

Enjoy the "3 Gratitudes" Exercise

Each night, right before sleep, list at least 3 gratitudes you are aware of for that day. These blessings can be anything you notice and appreciate. Now ask yourself: How can you generate still more gratitude today by finding more time?

Managing the Minutes and Seconds of Your Life

Many people, myself included, search endlessly through life for the 'magic elixir' of wisdom that might prove beneficial by providing growth to a new level of maturity of character.

Is it perhaps a real skill in life to know-how to wisely make best use of each portion of time, the minutes and even the seconds? I think so.

Think of the fragmenting that occurs on the hard disk of a personal computer over time. When we 'de-frag' the computer we see a graphical image of the disk's profile on the monitor before us, it's all the fragments of the disk that have been wedged in there though deleted files and file corruptions mainly. When we de-frag were simply compressing all that usable disk memory into a smaller space, to make more space available on the disk for future use, hence a more efficient computer.

Now, our time is not that different to that fragmented disk but the fragments are recorded and imprinted in real time, and we don't get to see it graphically. We do waste many fragments of time (minutes, hours and seconds) through our days. We could probably argue in different ways that in some seasons of life waste days, weeks and even years.

The fragments of time that we waste we never get over again. Once it's gone. The Bible talks about making 'redeeming the time' as if time could be bought with tokens. It implies that we would plan our lives so well and considerably, for each moment, that we would forsee wasted time and passionately ensure it was covered staying awake and not falling asleep to oppurtunities in life.

This doesn't mean we wouldn't have down time and time to play and rest. On the contrary, we would have the best and most rejuvenating rest and play time.

Gandhi once said, "Learn as if you would live forever, live as if you would die tomorrow." Perhaps that's the crux here. To commit to lifelong voraciousness of learning and to live so smartly to pretend today was our last, direct's a life, doesn't it?

Managing our minutes and seconds—the purpose of a disciplined, ordered, wise life—is a good way to extract what we were meant to extract from it. It's there for us all we need to do is taken it. One moment at a time.

Combating Lunch Hour Boredom

Do you find yourself on your lunch break and you just don't have anything to occupy your time? How long does it really take to eat you lunch anyway? Fifteen minutes of your lunch hour is spent actually eating and what to do with the other 45? Make the most of your break with these easy solutions for combating the boredom.

1. **Go out side for some fresh air:** Take a walk and stretch your legs. Studies show that exercise in the middle of the work day can give you the energy you need to make through. The fresh air will invigorate you, raising your heart rate and keeping you feeling energetic for the rest of the day.
2. Runnings quick errands on time off will save you time later on pay your bills, drop off your mail at the post office or to do some light shopping. The more that you can get done during the week, the more free time you will have on the weekend.
3. Take a relaxing approach and free your mind from reality by playing online games. There are tons of online games to choose from including speed games and puzzle games. You are sure to find a game that will give your brain a break before getting back to work.
4. You can also take natural, holistic approach to spending your free time, with yoga and meditation. Yoga is excellent for physical and mental health and many moves can be done right from your office chair. Meditation will help clear your mind of any negative energy and get you ready for the second half of your work day.

There are many productive and relaxing things that you can do on your lunch break. Don't count down the minutes until you get back to work. Do something that will help you relax, and give you the energy to make it through the day. You will more productive when you get back from your lunch break hour and may be your boss will give you that raise you know that you deserve!

Repetition the Father of Time Management

What do invention and repitition share? They are both born from necessity. Necessity may well be "the mother of invention" —but necessity is the "mother of repitition" also.

Please think about these two pharses carefully. Invention or originality could not be more different from repetition. In fact, they appear to be contradictory. Yet they are both certainly true! For sure in many ways, on many occasions, necessity has provided the spark that has prompted original thinkers to devise unique and creative solutions.

Less glamorous, and certainly more commonplace, is the fact necessity has given birth to repetition those things that must be done habitually.

But what has that go to do with time management? Well, I could also have said that necessity is the mother or father of time management.

You will also have heard of the expression "use it or lose it" used in connection with the ability to do something athletic, or skillful maintaining skills is easire when we continue to use those skills regularly.

The same applies to being well organized for which you must decide what works well and suits your needs and then to keep doing it. Mindless repetition is pointless so of course you need to be sure that systems you have in place continue to suit your needs. However in many cases these tasks are carried out more efficiently simply because they become so well known to us.

Like it or not, the simple truth is that for most people in most situations, their life is dominated by things that they do routinely and repititively. Even those who engage in creative employment find that the means to express their creativity involves much that is routine. Does that sound tedious, dull and boring? Well it can be! Expect nothing inspirational to come from repetition.

Furthermore, for most of us, we are simply stuck with it. Almost all of us, must complete some uninteresting monotonous tasks. For example, we make few changes to the way we get us, shower and dress for the day and much of what we do in order to run a family home is routine ask a parent if one laundry basket offers anything very different to any other.

In fact, much of what we do routinely actually contributes enormously to our identity as the person we are and how others see us. We need that routine and continuity so that we might be able to express ourselves in other ways and do those things that really interest us.

Consequently we can say that necessity is needed the father or mother of repetition.

What you should avoid, if possible, is delay in completing tasks because they are repetitive and you find them boring. Interrupting or even putting off routine tasks nearly always results in the need for more time to be spent on them at some later time. But, if we ask ourselves whether we can do those things more quickly, or make better use of the time spent doing the repetitive tasks-in other words think of what we do in terms of time management then we can begin to make a difference to the tasks and alleviate the boredom that comes from repetition.

It is really possible to approach routine chores whilst simultaneously looking beyond the immediate task. The key lies with the attitude you adopt. If you incorporate the task into wider circumstances, then you can shift to a more positive frame of mind. For example, you can keep in mind how the task contributes to a larger goals or is time so that other more interesting tasks are dealt with immediately befor and after. You might also try to think of ways in which routine tasks can be done together and not one after the other. You might set time limits for completion of tasks and then try and finish ahead of time, in other words challenge yourself in some way. That part of you that would otherwise be aware of the tedium will be diverted to meeting the challenge.

Be imaginative in incentivising yourself with the trivial and in setting different (rewards) for different tasks at different times. Everyone has some inducement that will provide motivation to conclude tedius tasks. You could grant to yourself some incentive for the conclusion of a chore but be sure to do so. You might time rest breaks to be taken when a task is completed rather than at set time. We must do the routine less attractive and more boring tasks and they will always be a part of our lives. So we must find ways in which we can reduce that boredom and incenstivize ourselves to complete them as efficiently as possible.

So we come full circuit. We have been reminded that necessity is the mother of invention, but learned how necessity is also the father of repetition. The key is to ensure that these two parents work in harmony and not in conflict in order to nurture their child time management. The child will flourish with a healthy balance between the routine and more interesting aspects of our life. In fact, this balance is a preaequisite for good time management.

The Benefits of Time Blocking

How many times have you ended the day and wondered what did I accomplish today? So many times we get caught-up in being "busy" during our day and before we know what hit us? The day is over. We spend time doing this for a few minute or two, thus we do something else for a few minutes, and then come back to what we started earlier in the day. This is not good time management. In this day of multitasking, come people take a sense of pride in being overwhelmed and "just too busy" to get anything done. Hours go by, days go by and yes, even years go by without ever accomplishing anything.

Here is the solutions. Time blocking can provide structure in your day and allow you to complete tasks or at least complete a large part of a task before moving on to something else. Here is how it works. Decide on the tasks you will do for a particular day. Instead of just having a "to do" list with everything listed in order of importance and working down the list, take a few items from the list that are top priority for accomplishing what you need to accomplish, and block-out whatever time you want to allocate to that task. This can be 15 minutes, 30 minutes, 1 hour or 2 hour. The point is to only allocate the allotted time to each task.

Here is an example. Today, I want to write an article, follow-up with 3 contacts, go to a networking event. I will allocate 1 hour to writing the article. This is focused effort on just writing the article. Whether I finish the article or not is irrelevant. I will only spend one hour on writing the article. I will do the same for the other two tasks will allocate 30 minutes to following up with contacts and allocate 2 hours to the networking event. By doing this you are sure to, at the very least, accomplish these tasks. You will not and your day wondering where the time went and what you accomplished.

Give this a chance and try it for 5 consecutive days and if you have improved productivity, less stress and more time to do the things that are important to your business and your life.

Here's Why Trying to Manage Time is Causing you Additional Stress

There's not enough time. Sounds familiar doesn't it? How many times have you said that there just aren't enough hours in the day to get everything done? Time is such a precious commodity in our life and yet we never seem to have enough of it in our day.

Prof. Franklin has been quoted as saying, "If time be of all things most precious, wasting time must be the greatest prodigality, since lost time is never found again". This is such a true and insightful comment that rings as true today and it did during Franklin's life.

Time is the great equalizer. No matter how imporatnt or rich or famous you are, you still get the same number of hours as everyone else. We each get 1,440 minutes per day, 10,080 minutes per week and 5,25,600 minutes per year! I am sorry to say that neither I nor anyone else can get more of this precious commodity for you.

It's now how much we get, since we all get the same amount, its what we do with our precious hours that matters. Time management is a misnomer. We cannot may time, the best we can do is develop the skill not to let it manage us. Trying to do so we just cause you more stress because the minutes and hours will continue to tick away regardless of whether you are doing things you should be doing or not.

The way to change this is to learn priority management. It is the priorities you set in your life that dictate what you will accomplish in your life. Your definition of success should guide how you use your time from a macro level. Your life vision will direct your priority management so you invest your priorities to work on accomplishing your goals.

When something is trying to take your time, ask yourself, "Does this help me move close to my goals and my vision?" If the answer is "yes," then you should invest yourself in to do it with passion and purpose. If the answer is "no", then you should not invest yourself it. It really is that simple.

Notice that I used the term "invest" instead of "spend" your time. It is important to recognize the difference between these. Normally, when we talk about this, we use the consumption term "spend" when we should be talking in terms of "investing" meaning. We are getting a payback when we do something. The payback may be as simple as making your family happy or improving your health. It may be improving your knowledge or increasing the profits of your business. Time must repay you by getting you closer to your ultimate dream of success. Otherwise, if you spend it, you will never get that time back and will find yourself getting no closer to what you want to be. It is completely up to you what priorities to invest in, but let me give you this advice. It's life and your goals. Don't let time manage you. Don't let others take control of you time either. Other will want to interrupt you or impose their priorities on you. Let how to avoid these situations or minimize their impact on you. Those who stayed focus and stick to the plan they have developed are the ones who accomplish the most. May sure you keep your plan in a place wherer you can review it oftern. Stay focused on how you choose to invest yourself for the best payoff. You must be brutal in how you ratio out your time because no one else will do it for you. Take control of your priority management, and you will be amazed at how much progress you will make toward fulfilling your life mission.

The Illusion of Time Management

Because, we live in hyper busy world, chock full important and not-so-important distractions, we are constantly looking for a way to keep our heads above the tsunami of stuff. Because so much of this busyness is driven by our work lives. The concept of time management is pretty ridiculous, when you stop think about it. Exactly, how are we supposed to "manage" time? This is the completed problem for everybody. In this context, one is important factor to help in time management.

Is the Procrastination Obstacle Tripping you up?

I am sure that you have heard the saying "procrastination" is the thief of time. It is partly true. I say partly because it is not really the procrastination itself thats robs us of our time. We do it to ourselves when we yield to the temptation of procrastinating.

There are two main things we need to do in order to overcome any obstacles, temptation or problem.

1. We need to face the situation for what it really is.
2. We need to accept the responsibility for the part we play in the situation.

There are three main reasons that we human tend to put off till tomorrow what we could do today. Have you ever fallen into one of these attitudes?

1. You are facing something that tasks effort to solve. How many times have you looked at a task set before you and said some like this: Well, I think, I will do this tomorrow. It is going to take a lot of effort and I don't feel like doing it today. If you don't get started on it today, chances are tomorrow may never come. So do it now. At least get started now and then make an appointment with yourself to complete the task in the morning or as early as possible tomorrow.
2. You just don't feel like completing the task at hand. How many times have you heard some say:
   - I am just too lazy to do that today.
   - I can't be bothered doing that today, tomorrow is another day.

   Of course, you have never said anything like that right? I didn't think so.

   These thoughts are definitely attitudes of procrastination buy tries to hit you is to make yourself start the task. Once you get started, many times you wil find yourself easily completing it right away. Other times, at least it will be easier to continue the next day. It is always easier to continue doing something that is started, than it is to get started on something new.

   So get started on that difficult or boring task now
3. I just don't have time.

In these days we live in with so many pressures all

around, this may be true. You may not have time. However, you can at least find 10-15 minutes to get started. You may need to make some drastic decisions like cutting out your favourite TV programme. But let's face it, is your favourite programme going to take you to the success you are seeking or will the work you could complete in that 30-60 minutes give you a better opportunity to reach your goals? Yes procrastination is a choice. You don't have to gives into it. It now, or at least get started now.

Pracrastination is just one of the obstacles we face on a daily basis. There are many practical things you can do to train your mind to be ready to meet and overcome all kinds of obstacles.

Procrastination Sounds Good

"To think too long about doing a thing often becomes its undoing". *Eva Young*

"I will do it tomorrow". Does this sound familiar? Getting something done is easy when it is something we enjoy unfortunately, we all have lots of tasks that we don't particularly enjoy. Even when a thing simply must be done, almost all of us are pretty good at coming up with excuses for putting them off.

- So I am getting a little over-weight! who isn't?
- I am just not in the mood right how.
- I will go for a run tomorrow, the weather isn't that good today.
- I will got plenty of time to get it done.
- What's the point, I will just have to do it all over again in two days.
- It's not like they can't do it without me.

- I will leave it until the day before. I work better under pressure.

Do any of the above points sound familiar? I will bet you can add a few to the list without too much trouble! I know it sounds funny when you look at the issue like this but the trouble is procrastination wreaks have in most of our lives.

Why do we procrastinate?

- Some reasons are easy to spot but others are not so obvious.
- Some things just aren't fun!
- We are uncomfortable about doing some things (e.g., preparing a speech).
- We don't feel up to the job.
- We have had a bad experience in the past.

What we can do to procrastinate less?

This is tough one to kick-start because the first inclination of most of us is to put it off. Like most habits, we tend not to notice them (our own at least) most of the time. One way to break the habit is to replace it with another one. A good habit to replace it with is to examine your reasons for putting things off when you were using to procrastinate just won't stand up under examination. If you have to make a list of the pros and cons of doing vs. not doing the thing you are procrastinating on. I had be willing to bet that a good percentage of the time you will just get on with the task.

There is trap here.

Try not to put yourself down when you are examining why you procrastinate. Negative reinforcement is depressing and leads to bad self-image. There is nothing to be gained by telling yourself you are lazy or you are stupid or you aren't capable of doing something. It is self-defeating. Instead, list the positive things about getting it done straight away. Look at how it will make you feel it you get the job done.

Examine how others will see you in a more positive light. Consider how much more you will enjoy your leisure time when you know your jobs done. Realize how much grief you will save yourself by being proactive. In short, focusing on the positive aspects will have a much more motivating impact on you.

How can we make things easier?

Don't expect yourself to be perfect.

Perfection is difficult to achieve at the best of times. Most often it is not only unnecessary, but counter- productive. The law of diminishing returns comes into play here. Do the job well and get the result. Don't shoot for perfect unless there is a reward equal to the effort.

Be clear about what is the most important thing to get done and do that first. Leave the less important stuff for last. It is far more motivating to know you have the hard or important things completed. Once you have the job broken down it is easy to prioritize.

Break the job down.

Tackle the job in bite-sized pieces. Don't take on more than you can get done in the time you allocate. This guarantees that you feel good at the end of the task because you have completed it.

Reward yourself.

Make sure that when you get a job done you give

yourself a pat on the back. Reward yourself in some way for accomplishing what you set out to do. It gives you something to look forward to. Let me generalize a bit. The thing is, we are all suit pretty much the same way. A carrot is better than a stick even though they can both accomplish the same thing. But, what is more motivating? What make you more likely to tackle the job at hand? If you like carrots and you associate the jobs at hand with getting at the end, you are less likely to procrastinate. "Procrastination is something best put off until tomorrow".

Top 10 Tips for Managing your Time Effectively

We all heard the old saying that we sound 'work smarter, not harder', but how many of us actually abide by this? It's easier said than done, isn't it? Experts actually say the key to working smart is to be more effective, not necessarily more efficient. Efficiency is doing the job right. Effectiveness, on the other hand, is doing the right job. Think about that! Here are my ten tips for managing your time more effectively.

(1) **Figure out when you are at your peak:** I know, I work better from 9 a.m. to noon, So that's when I try to do my most important tasks. Figure out when you are at your prime and plan carefully around this

(2) **Turn off your e-mail notifier:** Do you really need the pop-up or 'ding' every few minutes? Try turning off your e-mail notifier when you need to concentrate on an important project, then you really can focus.

(3) **Expect the unexpected:** Block out some planning time. Everyone needs some time for thinking, so

try to build in some flexibility into our daily routine.

(4) **Say no occasionally**: Sometimes we may have to be assertive and say 'no' if something is not urgent or a priority. Saying no courteously may be seen as a strength rather a weakness.

(5) **Set priorities:** Categorises tasks according to priority, for example:

1. The task is urgent and important.
2. It's important but not urgent.
3. It's urgent not important.
4. It's not urgent and not important.

(6) **Stay focused in meetings:** How many meetings have you attended where people go off at tangents? It helps to be clear about the agenda before meetings and make sure everyone's knows what the objectives are. This will help you stayed focused and keep the discussion leading in the right direction.

(7) **Clear out clutter:** I know I can't work effectively if my desk is a mess with lots of paper work everywhere. So once, in a while. I have a good clearing and sorting session, and I clear out the clutter on my desk, trays drawers and files. It's amazing how much better I always feel once the clutter is gone!

(8) **Remember to take a break:** We all tend to make more mistakes when we are tired or stressed, so learns to recognize the symptoms when you are flagging and take a break from your work. I hear you. . . this is something I am not so good at!

(9) **Don't procrastinate:** Tackle what's right now in the present and don't let procrastination get in the way. It's amazing how great it feels when you can tick off those items on your to do list!

(10) **Adopt a positive attitude:** Keep your mindset positive. See solutions instead of prob!ems. See positive instead of negatives. Do your tasks with a happy heart, and smile!

How to Be Productive

Being productive means being able to accomplish tasks in as little time as possible. How to Be Productive Do you find yourself struggling to accomplish some project? Does your work consume your whole day? There certain steps you can take to learn how to be productive.

Being with the End in Mind

You should never start a project without defining how it would look like upon completion. For example, if you want to increase profits of your company, you should always understand exactly what turn over you want your business to generate.

If you fail to define an exact end product, you will end up spending far too much time doing activities of little importance. Therefore the completed project will be of poor quality. The more clearly you see how the completed project should turn out, the more determined you will become to achieve the goal.

Giving Your Undivided Attention to Your Current Project

No matter what project you are working on, for it to be finished in a perfect manner you need to put look of your attention to it. Try to block yourself from any possible distractions and always be aware of where your attention is.

Most often people go about their lives on autopilot. When they work on one project, their thoughts are completely somewhere else. Such people never understand how to be productive and always get average results.

By not giving your full attention to one project, you waste your energy on unnecessary external objects. Some of the energy goes into the project, but the rest is wasted on distractions such as unrelated thoughts, observation of the environment, or even eating whilst working. Because of that the results you are get always mediocre.

To get excellent results you will need to entirely focus on the project. You need to complete. When you concentrate on one subject, you put so much energy into it that it must turn out perfect.

This is such an under estimated advice on how to be productive. When you look at world's most successful people, you can tell that they are the best in their field only because they mastered the art of concentration.

On one hand it is very empowering to know that all you have to do succeed is entirely focus on one task at a time. Yes it is the hardest labour for most because many people do not have any control over their thinking process. They let any kinds of thoughts dewll in their mind which distract them from the main tasks. This, of course, brings poor results together with increasing dis satisfaction, anger and hopelessness.

Find Your Most Productive Time for Important Tasks

For example, my most productive time is from 5 a.m. to

7 a.m. This is the time when I write most of the articles. I am not distracted by anyone which gives me complete control over my thinking. I do not need to labour mentally because early in the morning ideas just flow out nowhere to me and I have to rush to record all of them. When it gets late I have so many thoughts on my mind that they constantly intervene in everything I do. Therefore my productivity drops significantly.

Some people can be most productive whilst others are in deep sleep at 2-3 a.m. That was my working time in the past. However, once I decided to try a complete shift of my working hours and I am much more productive early in the morning. Therefore it is worth shifting your patterns and noticing how your productivity changes depending on certain times. By such experimenting you will be able to find your most productive time, put all your efforts in that time frame, and spend the rest of the time relaxing or enjoying low energy activities.

Give Yourself a Deadline for the Project Completion

Parkinson's law states that "work expands so as to fill the time available for its completion". That is completely true, because if you have plenty of time for one project, you are certain get involves in unnecessary details of the project only to fill the time.

This causes you to become disengaged from the main project objective. You may lose your focus and start wasting your energy on minor project aspects. Because of that the entire work will be only average and you will end-up feeling. To avoid this you should put a deadline as each task you are performing. The shorter the deadline you assign, the better way the less time you have on each task, the more focused you will be perform the task in the most efficient manner possible, focusing only on the important and eliminating the minor tasks. This will bring excellent results as the work will always be clean, concise and relevant.

Divide Largest Project into Smaller Pieces until it Seems Manageable

Some projects may seem too big for you to accomplish. However, if you divide the project into manageable tasks you will notice that it is not as hard as you thought.

By following the above steps you will surely learn how to be productive. This will certainly give you more from time, deeper, satisfaction and greater self-esteem because you will be proud of what you can achieve.

Time Management Techniques—The Serial Work Flow Method as to Managing Time

Time management techniques tend to focus on making us, well focus on doing one thing at a time. And that may approach at times. But there are alternatives...Read on to find-out about one that you thought you had (would) never hear about.

What if you start a project (project A) and then suddenly get inspired about another project (project B) and as you start working on that project, you suddenly feel absolutely compelled to work on that report you have been meaning to get (project C). And then once you have just started to make some headway, project A beckons all over again.

Sounds like a mess to most people, doesn't it? But some people work that way. And while they may or may not manage to complete their projects right then and there thare is a way to approach things that way but in a somewhat more purposeful fashion, and actually get a lot done and completing the projects eventually.

How So?

Here are four principles you have to keep in mind if you want to make this serial work flow mehtod work for you.

(1) **Stop beating yourself up over it:** Stop feeling guilty or ashamed about your supposed lack of organizational will power. Do you have any idea how much that alone would rob you of energy and your ability to get things done?

(2) **Stop losing work you have already done:** The biggest problem with the serial approach is that we often forget where we were last time we worked on what-ever it was. That is a big productivity killer. But, it doesn't have to be that way. Yes, it will take a bit of discipline, but you should find it relatively easy to come-up with it since the reward will be that you can then move on to the next project-guilt-free!

(3) **Benefit of your brain's weird wanderings:** I am not kidding. Our brain is designed in weird and wonderful ways. It doesn't its thing even and especially while we are doing somethinng else. So while you have put project. A side project for the time being, you may get a brilliant ideas for it rght when you are supposely doing something else. Write it down. Accept that your brain works that way. In fact, embrace it. And schedule may be three projects together that you can alternate

between until you are done. If you finish are of them, phase in another project in its slot.

(4) Keep things Interesting and fast paced: Arranging projects into this serial pattern can keep otherwise boring tasks quite interesting since you will be switching back and forth between them and won't have to do any of them for longer than you feel like it.

So instead of beating yourself up, harm's your brain's unique ability to do things a serial rather than an all-at-once way. Many projects are too big to be completed all at once anyway. So why not break them down, and alternate tasks. One task for project A, one for project B and one for project C, adn repeat. You may be amazed at how much you get done. It may not be the most conventional time management technique, but it may well work for you and help you get even the most tedious jobs done eventually.

Personal Success—High Performance with Balance

We all have full schedules, learning how to determine what is truly important can free us up to enjoy time together with loved ones. A close friend of mind (mine) is studying 6-sigma, which means by default I am studying 6-sigma. One of the items I have taken away is the "5 why". The basic principle is to ask why five times to find the real reason you are performing a certain task. When we ask ourselves why we really do something we can start to move into a direction of balance.

When something new comes across your desk ask why you must be the one to do it. If, it can be delegated then delegate it. I know this sounds simple and you have heard this a thousand times but I bet like people, I talk to everyday you do things just because you; "want them done right the first time", or "Done your way," or some other reason, you must be the one to do the task. It you are a sole proprietor then skip to next paragraph. If you run a business with employees then train one of them to be a surrogate you. You need someone you can rely on to handle the task so you can cast the vision and lead the team. If you are running a business and you are the only one who knows how it runs you will never be able to relax or take a vacation. If you have to be on 24/7 then you are not getting the rest your body needs and it will catch you some time.

If you are like me and have no one to delegate to then you need a list of things to-do. I use no day-timer or calender system, I just lay out on a spiral notebook all of the things. I need to accomplish that week. Each night, I list the thing to-do the next day in order from most important down. If, something new comes in, I put it on the list, and it may or may not get done that day depending on priority. I check and write e-mail for 30 minutes in the morning and evening. When you do this all the other things will come.

The Time Management Struggle

Managing your time effectively is the life blood of any business. Time is many as the saying does. This is especially true when you own the business. You must learn to utilize your time correctly in order to gain financially. Time wasted is money thrown out the window. Do not let this one common mistake affect you and your dreams of working from home. Start by developing an action plan.

Write down your tasks and post them where you will see it everyday. I keep mine next to the computer. Another good place is the refrigerator or a wall near your computer, so you can look at it everyday.

Here are some points to consider when developing your action plan:

(*i*) What goals would you like to accomplish today?

(*ii*) What tasks have the highest priority?

(*iii*) When will you have some down time?

(*iv*) How much time will it take to complete your daily tasks?

The key to a successful home business is proper utilization of time, attenable goal setting, and prioritizing. Remember to allow your some relaxations of time too. This is a very important part of owning a business because it will help to rejuvenate you, keep you motivated, and give you some new ideas to implement.

So, do not under-estimate the power of rest periods. Rest can be just as important as actively working because without it, you will become overwhelmed and stressed out which is counter productive to any business. So get out that paper and start writing down your daily action plan. Follow it each and everyday and soon you will find that your new but exponentially just by taking tiny steps each day. Your business will thrive and you more contended human being, knowing that you can accomplish anything.

Seven Time Management Secrets

Without exception when you implement these 7 (seven) tested time management secrets you will see a doubling or quadrupling of your personal productivity. Your ability to effectively manage your time is directly related to your ability to discipline yourself to follow your time management plan and take the required action to complete daily tasks.

1. **Multi-Tasking:** Numerous studies prove that multi-tasking negatively effects personal productivity. When interrupted it takes humans up to 20 minutes to return to the state of focus held prior to be interrupted. People erroneously think that they are switching from task to task and paying attention to everything arround them but the human brain can not operate that way. What really happens is that the brain is switching back and forth with astonishing speed.
2. **Blocks of Time:** Schedule your time in 50 to 100 minutes blocks with breaks of 10 to 20 minute between each block. Block out quiet blocks due to tasks that require concentration and focus. Be diligent in protecting that time. The proverbial open door is a real drag on executive productivity.
3. **Scheduling:** Arrange your schedule to complement your bio-rhythms. If you do your best analytical work early in the day be sure to schedule it early. Analyse you personal preferences and schedule appropriately.
4. **20/80 Rule:** Clearly understand the 20 per cent of things you do that generate 80 per cent of your results. The key point is that most things in life (effort, reward, output) are not distributed evenly some contribute than others. But, remember that it may be true that 80 per cent of the bridge got

build in 20 per cent of the time, but you still need the rest of the bridge in order for work. The Paréto principle is an observation, not a law of nature. Beware of the law of Diminishing Returns.

5. **Segment the Activity or Tasks:** Analyse what needs to be completed and break the segment for efficiently. Do not try to eat the elephant in one bite.
6. **Plan Ahead:** Busy people have a plan. They have to do list with tasks broken in the segments. They work the list, avoid procrastinating and understand that they must far their day. The confirm all out of office appointments, they prioritize acccordingly and real they delegate effectively.
7. **Control meetings:** Avoid all meetings if at all possible. If you have to attend keep the hour maximum and have exist strategy ready if the meeting will run over an hour. Also the meeting and stick to it. Shut-up the people that love to hear themselves talk.

The 10 Most Common Time Wasters and How to Avoid Them

Just as saving money is a wise thing to do these days saving time may be even more important. The one resource that is absolutely limited is time. You have only so much, not a second more. You can not afford to waste your most precious gift-time. Here are ten easy tips to save some of that precious time:

1. **Resist procrastination:** It is a big time waster. If you must do it, do it, get it done and stop putting it off.

2. **Answer e-mail in Bunches:** Answer e-mail in bunches, not as they pop-up on the computer. Doing all of your small chores in grouped bunches is more productive and saves time.
3. **Keep Telephone calls short and to the point:** Avoid needless chit-chat.
4. **Find your purpose in what you are doing:** Once you have clearly defined what you want to be and why you waste less time and get it accomplished.
5. **Get organized:** Organize people are more productive and use their time more wisely. Take a little time to get organized it pays off.
6. **Write down your goals and refer to them:** People with goals are more achievement oriented and waste less time. People with written goals are many times more productive.
7. **Carry reading materials and work with you:** Everywhere you go (except vacation). When you have to kill time waiting at a train crossing or in a traffic jam you can get a lot done.
8. **When you need help ask for it:** Don't waste time floundering about a problem when you can get help and move on.
9. **Focus on your priorities:** Focus on your priority first thing in the morning. Work on your most time demanding have the most energy.
10. **Keep a record of how you spend your time for a week:** Keep a record of how you spend your time for a week. Analyxe it you will be surprise clearly see what you spend too much time on

and what you spend too little on. Adjust 80/20 rule, most of time you gain 80 per cent of your gain from 20 per cent of your work. Use the wiser you use time, and more you avoid wasting time, the more time, you will have need to do and want to do. Time is your one limited resource, it is one thing you steal. Use it wisely.

Saving Time With Deliverable Services

The world is in almost constant chaos. Everyone is so busy trying to get things done, that they sometimes get nothing done. When your mind is not in order, your life will not be either. You have to stop and think before you take on the daily tasks of life, ways to better manage your time are:

1. Think about what has to be done today. Make a list with everything you hope to accomplish. Don't make the list too lengthy, otherwise you will feel too overwhelmed.
2. Sort through the list, and choose only the most important tasks. If washing the car is going to cause you go into a panic attack, skip it. It can be done another day.
3. Use your time wisely. When you are working, work. Try not to spend working time doing other things.
4. Delegate responsibilities whenever possible. If there is a way to have someone else do it, then utilize their services. If you can have someone come to you to give you a haircut take advantage of it. If you need a relaxaing message after a hard day, let the mass-use come to you.

5. Don't beat yourself up if you can not accomplish everything in one day. This will only make you frustrated and less apt to want to do it later.
6. Let others in the household help with chores and cooking. If your children are old enough, now is a good time to teach them valuable life skills, and give your self extra time to do other things.
7. Relax: Take some time-out everyday for you. Even if it is only a few minutes. Every little bit helps in the search for serenity.

In this crazy world, we often forget to take a deep breath and be satisfied with what we have. We spend too much time worrying about things that we cannot control. Learning to manage our time wisely can help us lead to more happy and fulfilled lives. Giving others the chance to bear some of our burdens can make for a less stressful life.

To make your life easier, and help to alleviate unnecessary stress, consider hiring online to come to your work or home (you can get just any). Above we discussed about strategy of time management in world. Now we shall discuss about the strategy of time management in India.

3.3 STRATEGY OF TIME MANAGEMENT IN INDIA

Having A Good Time Management Strategy Keeps you Ahead of Competition

To be successful in modern business you need to have a time management strategy. In every sector you will stiff (tough) competition and a lot of people who are willing to work very hard to get ahead. So, you need to use all of the tools at your disposal to stay ahead of the game. One of the best tools you can have is a good time management strategy.

The real secret of good time management is knowing, really knowing, how you want to spend your time. If you know what your goals are in both your personal and professional life then you can manage your days around these goals.

So, Before, drawing up a time management strategy you should become clear on how you want to spend your time. Now compare it how you spend your time at the moments, and you will begin to see the changes that need to be made. Now, you can really start working on your time management strategy. Some of the changes that will be big, even daunting while others will be small. You need to begin making these changes in a way that is comfortable for you. It is probably better to start with small changes. When you take on big changes do it step by step.

I encourage you to be methodical about this write down your immediate and long-term goals and keep track of which ones you are working on. Each day, keep a time plan and in corporate something that takes you towards your chosen goals. This could be something small like getting 30 minutes exercise, or a step towards. Something big, like looking at alternative employment opportunities. Here, we will discuss about how to get more done in less time, the top "7 time management truths are as below:

1. **Effective time management:** Do you ever end your days feeling like you just haven't achieved enough? Do you find your self-staying late at work to get everything finished? Do you feel like you are

missing out on the best things in life because you don't have enough time?

If you answered yes to any or all of the above questions you are probably not feeling too good right now. May be work is not going how you would like. Or you do not have time to spend with your children that you feel they deserve.

Do not fret, your worries could soon be over. These time worries are flexible, and it is not as difficult to your think. Simply by changing the way you approach the use of your time you can find the hours to do all the things you want to, and even have some time left over. Not only will this help you manage your time more effectively, it can help you to achieve the things you really want to in life.

2. **For effective time management, manage yourself:** We have only so much time in each-day. This is something that you have to accept because it will not change. While you may not be able to control this, you can manage yourself. Once you realize this you have taken the first step towards effective time management. You must train yourself to focus on the things that really matter to you and spend your time on this things only. Everything else should be eliminated from your life.

Making the changes necessary to manage your time effectively can be rewarding and fun, but some of these changes will take a leap of faith on your part. However, there is no need to rush, you can make the necessary changes at your own pace.

If you bite off more than you can chew at the beginning there is a chance you may fall.

3. **For effective time management, understand yourself:** To really manage your time effectively you must first learn to know yourself. In modern society there are so many distractions we can easily lose our focus on what we want in our lives. It is amazing that we can let this happen to us, but it happens all too easily.

   So, Before, you can really begin to look at your time management you need to figure out what you want out of life. This is where you find your vision. Cast yourself back to when you were an adolescent or a young adult, a time anything seemed possible. What were your dreams and aims when you were that age? What you wanted then may really be what you went now, it may just be that you have lost sight of your true vision. No doubt, some priorities will have changed, but many will have remained the same.

   Also ask yourself how you would like your personal and professional life to be. And think about what is possible for you? and what you can really achieve. We call this your vision.

4. **Where are you now:** By now, you should have a reasonable idea of what you would like your life to like. So here comes the tough part, you need to look at your life now and compare it to your vision, to how you would realy like your life to be like. If you are writing all of this down, the difference between the two probably will not make for very pleasant reading.

However, no matter how wide the gap is between your ideal reality and how you live your life now, it can be bridged. You may think of effective time management as a tool that will help you to get you to meetings on time. Not true. Effective time management can transform your life on a much more fundamental level.

Achieving your ideal reality will involve little changes and big changes in your life. A small change would be something like taking a walk every evening. A Big change might be starting up your own business. However, if you put your mind to it you could achieve either of these. You will have to take a close look at how your hours are spent and make the necessary adjustments so you can achieve what you want to achieve.

5. **The 4 Ds of time management**: Now you can move onto looking more closely at the things. You need to do each day and deciding how to handle them. This is where the 4 Ds of time management come in. They are: "*Do it*: This needs to be done immediately". Delegate it, it needs to be done, but someone else can take care of it. Dump it. This is not important, thrash it, defer it, something for the to do pile come back to it later.

   You should be able to file any task that arises in your average day under one of the four Ds.

6. **Time wasters:** Now let's look at time wasters. Time wasters can destroy any attempt at effective time management if they are not identified and eliminated. This is mainly because they can be very hard to spot and are often the most trivial things:

These are some time wasters to watch out for

(*i*) **Lack of poor planning:** File things properly, write down appointments, that kind of thing. Basically, you need to be organized to use your time effectively.

(*ii*) **Procrastination:** If you keep putting things off you will miss all the best opportunities in life.

(*iii*) **Not delegating:** You can't do it all yourself. Do the things that you are good at and enjoy. Someone else can do the rest.

(*iv*) **Interruptions:** Don't let clutter and noise out into your productive time. Make sure there are no interruptions when you want to work.

Try to identify the time wasters that are holding you back and eliminate them from your life.

These pointers should help you in your first step towards effective time management. Breaking old habits isn't easy to take the changes you need to make one step at a time. As you take it step by step, you will gradually move closer to your ideal life, a life where there is plenty of time for the things you want to do.

7. **Time Management for Working Mothers:** Do you stuggle to find time for all the things you want to do? Is overtime becoming the norm for you? Do you feel like you are missing out on the best things in life because you don't have enough time?

If you do it is okay as most of us feel like this on a regular basis. It could be that the pressures of your professional life are getting you down. Or you just do not have enough leisure time to pursue your hobbies and do the things you enjoy.

However, don't worry just yet. There is a solution to this problem and it is far easier than you might think. Simply by changing the way you approach the use of your time you can find the hours to do all the things. You want to, and even have some time left over. Not only will this help you manage your time more effectively, it can help you to achieve the things you really want to in life.

Manage Yourself

We have only so much in each. This is something that will not change and we can do nothing about it. Time cannot be changed, but the way you approach it can. This is the secret of effective time management. You must train yourself to focus on the things that really matter to you and spend your time on these things only. Everything else should be eliminated from your life.

It is important to point-out at this stage that making the changes necessary to manage your time effectively can mean making some fundamental changes in your lifestyle. For this reason it is important to take it at your own pace and make one chage at a time. If you bite off more than you can chew at the beginning there is a chance you may fail.

Know Yourself

To really manage your time effectively you must first learn to know yourself. With the pressures of modern life it is easy to lose sight of what we really want in our lives. For most people, this is an unfortunate fact to life.

So before, you can really begin to look at your time management you need to figure-out what you want out of life. You need to get in touch with yourself and discover your vision. Try to remember yourself as a child or a young adult when you felt you could achieve anything. How did your dream life look then, what did your really want in your heart? This could help you to get in touch with your vision. No doubt, the some priorities will have changed, but many will have remained the same. Also ask yourself how you would like your personal and professional life to be. And think about what is possible for you and what you can really achieve. This is your vision.

Where are You Now

If you followed the steps above you should be able picture your ideal life accurately. Now comes the scary part. You need to look at your life now and compare it to your vision, to how you would really like your life to be like. Be prepared for a shock here as there will most likely be a vast.

Don't worry if this is the case as bridging the gap between your ideal reality and your life now is much easier than you would expect. Many people think effective time management is all about calendars and diaries. This is not the case. Effective time management goes much deeper than and can make major changes to the way you live your life.

Achieving your ideal reality will involve little changes and big changes in your life. A small change would be something like taking a walk every evening. A big change might be starting up your own business. There is a big difference between the two, but both goals are attainable. You need to look at how you spend your days and plan your time with a view to achieving these goals.

Planning Your Day

You should start by picking two things you want to achieve, one big and one small. Now, you want to think of one small step you can take towards achieving these that you can incorporate into one day. If you can complete the one step towards achieving each goal then you have made an excellent start.

In truth, there is much more to it than this but this will show you that it is far from impossible can be very rewarding. Now you need to make sure that everything you do each day is taking you towards your goals, and that you plan in such a way that you complete all of the tasks you need to each day.

This is why you need a clear time plan for everyday. You need to have a very clear idea of what needs to be done, how long it will take, and when it is going to be done. At the beginning it can be difficult to know-how long each task will take so it may be a good idea to keep a time log for a week before starting to keep a time plan. In your time log you need to write down what you do everyday and how long it takes. Keeping a time log for a week should give you a clear picture of how long the various taks you need to do take. When you know this you can plan your days much more accurately and effectively.

The 4 Ds of Time Management

Now, as you make your time plan for each day you need

to decide how to handle the various tasks that need doing and how to deal with any new tasks that may rise.

These are just a few of the time wasters that could be effecting your effective time management. These pointers should help you in your first steps towards effective time management. If you take this process in small steps it will be much easier to incorporate the necessary changes into your life. Each of these small steps will bring you closer to your vision and leave you with time to do all of the things you want each day.

Time Management for Working Mothers: Suffering from Time Poverty?

Many people struggle to find the time to do the things they want to. There are only 24 hours in a day and that is never going to change. However, we can change how we look at time and how we use it to help us lead a fuller and more productive life.

If you have a to do list that is longer than your arm and only limited time available you are probably wondering how you can get it all done. Most likely you are feeling stressed out and helpless. However, with a little commitment and effort you can learn how to manage your time more effectively.

Write down what is important to you and compare it to how you plan to spend the coming days. There will most likely be many things that are not important to you and that are not essential to get done. First, remove these from your lists and you will find that your schedule now looks much more manageable.

There will, of course, remain some things on the list that are not important to you that simply have to be done.

At the beginning at least, this will be fact of life. However, effective time management can lead of some life-changing choices and help you achieve what you really want in your life.

The mis-matches between how you currently spend your time and how would like to spend your time can be very revealing as they help you identify where you need to make changes. Some of these changes may be very small while others may be life changing.

You can start on the small changes right away. These could include simple things like getting fit or learning a new hobby so all you will need to do is schedule a little time to devote to these each day.

Bigger chanages will require a lot more thought and commitment, but are achievable. Perhaps you want to move house or change profession. You cannot do things like this at the drop of a hut so you need to identify the steps you need to take to achieve them.

I encourage you to break these steps into small, manageable tasks that can be easily scheduled. Using the changing profession example, a first task might to be research courses available to train you in the skills you need for your chosen new-profession. This small task can easily be scheduled into one of your days. Once you begin to take action to move you in the right direction you will feel satisfied with your life.

Time Management for Working Mothers:

Stop and Re-evaluate

If things are getting on top of you and you feel like there simply aren't enough hours in the day, it may be time to take a step back and re-evaluate your situation. With the pressures of modern life it is easy to lose focus on the goals that are genuinely important to us. If this sounds like you, it is probably time to stop and take a closer look at how you really want to spend your time.

I invite you to start this right away. Commit now a time, perhaps away from your usual distractions when you can sit down and be alone with yourself and your thoughts. Then with pen and paper in hand, you can look at how you are spending your time now and how ideally you want to spend your time in the future. You need to discover your own motivation and turn it into a compelling reason to act.

Once you are clear about your own motivations, you will these as a constant reminder in order to even out the ups and downs. These reasons will help you through the tough times or when you feel it is not worth the effort.

When you have gained a clear idea of your goals for the future and how you wish to spend time you next need to look at how you are actually spending your time now. First of all, you should ask yourself the following questions.

Y. U 2022: What does my life both personally and professionally look like and feel like today?

Y. U 2022: What am I currently spending my time on?

Write down everything that comes to mind. Think about your work, who spend your time with your living environment and your income. Also, try to pinpoint the things that are missing from your life as these will hold the key to your using time more effectively in the future.

The lest way to discover where you spend your time is using a time log. A time log is a record of how you use your time, day in and day out. It is very important that you keep one so that you can see exactly where your time is spent.

If you this even for just one week, you will get a clear idea of how you really spend your time and will probably see some surprising results. Now, that you have clear idea of how you want to spend your time and how you really pass the hours, it is time to compare the two.

When do you this will most likely see huge differences between them. You will see that change is required. Sometimes big and somethimes small. Now you can begin to take steps to spending your time in a way that will make these changes come about. Start with the small things and set yourself realistic short-term goals. Basically, take it step by step. Continue to take small step towards your goals and later you can move onto some of the bigger changes may need to make.

3.4. CONCLUSION

The strategy of time management, which is something. I think most of us deal with on a daily basis. I have toddler at home and with the increasing number of opportunities that are coming our way, we are finding that is very important to maximize our time. Here are some things we do to help with time management.

1. **Don't waste time:** This seems rather obvious doesn't it? We used to waste a lot of time watching state, checking e-mail often. Keeping things in our feed that might be sort of amusing, but were just time suckers. We had to ruthlessly eliminate things that were pulling our off track.
2. **Carry a notebook:** I mentioned that I had started keeping a notebook with me at all times. So, for

example, if I have 15 minutes to wait at the doctor's office, I can begin to formulate a blog post or sketch some logo ideas.

3. **Keep a calender:** I used to just sort of keep a running list of things that I needed to do in my head and just get them done as quickly as possible. Now with work backing up I can no longer keep track of everything, nor can I give clients a feel for when I could begin their project unless I keep a calender in which I plan out projects, estimating the number of hours things will take. This goes a long way towards eliminating stress as well, I have a clear plan for getting everything accomplished on time.
4. **Work anywhere and everywhere:** We use online tools like g-mail, Google documents and Word Press so that we can work from any computer. We can turn on the computer and get some things accomplished.
5. **Break all tasks into small bits:** If we have even one minute, we sit down at the computer and do something. Every little thing we can do get us closer to finishing a task.
6. **Learn to say no:** That is a hard for us. . . really hard. We want to do everything. we want to help everyone that e-mails us and needs something designed, fixed, written, etc. But, we just can't saying no gets easier the more we do it.

In short, we can say that there had been a lot of discussion going around for the best strategy for effective time management strategy in world and in India. There could be numerous possible strategies and which could be followed for a better and effective results.

SELF-ASSESSMENT

1. Explain the strategy of time management in world.
2. Discuss the strategy of time management in India.

REFERENCES

E.L. (1987), College: *The Under Graduate Experience in America,* New York: Harper and Row.

Eming., J. (1977), *Writing as a Mode of Learning, College Composition and Competitions,* 28, 122-28.

Federiksen, N. (1984), "The Real Test Bias", *American Psychologist,* 39, 193-202.

Fulwier, T. (1982), "Writing An Act of Congition", in C.W. Griffen, *Teaching Writing in All Disciplines,* pp. 15-26, San Francisco: Jossey-Bass.

Griffin, C.W. (ed.) 1982, *Teaching Writing in all Disciplines.* San Francisco: Jossey-Bass.

Hollend, M.K. (1985), *Using Psychology* (3rd edn.) Boston: Little Brown.

White, E.M. (1985), *Teaching and Assessing Writing,* San Francisco: Jossey-Bass.

White, E.M. (1989), *Developing Successful Programs,* San Francisco: Jossey-Bass.

4 SKILLS OF TIME MANAGEMENT

"Good time management simply means deciding what you want to get out of life and efficiently pursuing these goals. Time management does not means being busy all the time it means using your time the way you want to use it which can include large doses of day dreaming and doing nothing. Good time management brings with it increased relaxation, less stress, more satisfaction and greater accomplishment."

—Dorothy Cuduback, Family Life Extension Speacialist

Content of This Chapter

Introduction, Time Management Skills in Agriculture, Time Management Skills in Industry, Time Management Skills in Services, Conclusion

4.1 INTRODUCTION

Too little time and too much to do is a common condition for many of us. Everyday demands or chores seem to engulf the day, leaving little time to pursue those things you enjoy. But, you do have choices about how you spend your time. Balancing what you need to do with what you want to do can lead happiness and success. Many of us, complain, "There just isn't enough time in the day!" But, the truth is that we have enough time to do what is important in our lives you can always make time for the people you value and for the activities worth doing. All you need do is become a master of how you use your time?

Turning time management skills into habits will take time but what better way to spend it? With the help of this chapter, you can learn valuable techniques for managing your time, your industry and your life. In this chapter, we shall discuss about the time management skills in agriculture, time management skills in industry and time management skills in services.

4.2 TIME MANAGEMENT SKILLS IN AGRICULTURE

Time is the most important resource you have, so it should be management well. Plan ahead as to how you will use your time. Your plan should be based on specific goals you want to achieve. Make sure the most important things are accomplished. Don't spend time on "busy work" activities. At the end of the day or week, look back to see if you accomplished the things you needed to.

1. **Why Time Management:** Keep a balance between your volunteer time, personal time, work time, etc. Accomplish priority items. Have free time wihtout feeling guilty. Gain a sense of accomplishment. Reduce stress.
2. **Managing Time in the Workplace:** According to Time Management Training, 50 per cent of management time is spent processing information and 50 per cent of that information is of no value.

(*i*) Prioritize your tasks.

(*ii*) Get the job done right the first time.

(*iii*) Do not waste time

(*iv*) Avoid procrastination.

Commodities and Products

This section provides information to help you assess value added market opportunities, investigate processing options and understand business and production issues for agricultural commodities and products. Information on the food industry and other markets and industries can be found in the "markets and industries" section.

Commodities and Products

1. **Agritourism:** Describes the act of visiting a working form or any agricultural, horticulture operation to enjoy, be educated or be involved in activities. Examples of agritourism are:
   - Farm tour for families and children
   - Day camps,
   - Hands-on-chores
   - Self-harvesting of produce
   - Buy or sleigh rides, and
   - Evernight stays in a bed and breakfast.

   Some people become involved in agritorism as a way of supplementing their income opportunity to educate the public and introduce people to farming, January 2009.

   Agritourism associations, resources and networks and other related organizations can provide benefits for farmers and ranchers wishing to diversify their operations. Such associations often provide information and resources and can helpful in three general ways. First, these associations can provide an advertising maintain websites that market attractions in a geographic area or map driving routes to participating farms, ranches and other agritourism sites. Second these groups can provide an opportunity to network, interact and learn from others who are involved in similar businesses. This enables farmers/ ranchers to build upon the experiences of others in similar ventures. Third, they provide information on trainings, conferences, trends and recent research.

Fee and lease pond fishing: On the water, there are no cars, no rush hour and no deadlines, just a chance to related conjunction with a rural bed and breakfast operation, a hunting lease venture or as a retreat centre, rural wedding or business meeting, a pond is a focal point for natural relaxation. This water resource is more than just a novel piece of landscape, it is on overlooked revenue genertors for agricultural landowners.

Many landowners across the United States have turned their farm pond or ponds into attractive to a number of different consumer types. These ponds are stocked and market fishing opportunities to parents who wish to have a quality experience with their your professionals who wish to get away with business clients, families, interested in a traditional reunion and as a local environmental educational resource for primary sources.

Game Birds: Game Birds are those birds that

have traditionally been wild or hunted but have been raised commercially for their meat, for egg production or for release in hunting preserves. Commonly raised game birds include gained fowl, partridges, peacocks, pheasants, pigeons and doves, quail or squab (a young pigeon), swans, wild turkeys and some ducks, such as mallards or wood ducks. Of these species, only pigeon, quail pigeon, quail, squab and wild turkey are native.

Hunting leases, nature based tourism, rural weddings, wine tours, business planning, establishment costs, acreage requirements for clay target shooting facilities, etc. are included in agritourism.

2. **Aquaculture**: For thousands of years, people have harvested the bounties of the sea and planted its "crops" as well. As demand for fish increases, farm-raised stocks will become more important to the food supply. The united nations reports that nearly half of the world's total food fish supply comes from aquaculture. World aquaculture is probably the fastest growing food-producing sector, yielding almost 60 million tons with a value of about $70 billion. Worldwide, more than 1 billion people rely on fish as an important source of animal protein, healthy lipids and essential micro-nutrients.

   Aquaculture is a catchall term that encompasses the production of what are generally referred to as the commercially important finfish and shellfish and crustaceans. A distinction can be made between "acquaculture and mariculture", or marineculture.

Aquaculture systems tend to be pond or confinment systems, and mariculture systems tend to be pen-type enclosures with open bodies of water, usually within the sea.

3. **Bio-mass:** Bio-mass is commonly cited as a renewable energy source. The term also is used by bio-mass to describe living dead carbon biological material that is part of the environment. Biomass is the renewable, living and recently dead plant matter whose cellulose, directly combusted or biologically, physically or chemically changed into an industrial bio-mass is processed into a "bio-product". Energy related bio-mass is processed into 'bio-fuel'. It should be noted that coal, oil and other fossil fuels were once bio-mass, but over time, that bio-mass was chemically and physically changed by geologic processes.

   This material is not considered bio-mass, since it is non-renewable and no longer part of the environment's carbon cycle. Organic matter can be formed or collected for bio-mass crops. This can be as simple as can, corn or wheat stalks, or collecting yard waste or industrial or recycled wood waste. It can be as complex as creating specialized aquatic environments for the production of higher aquatic plants.

   Any bio mass production strategy has several important hardles to overcome. First a simple economics of the system. An energy audit is necessary. This should look at the gained and the energy consumed by all aspects of collection, transportation and product including any depletion due to storage issues, and all associated costs and values. A engineering study, overall feasibility study and business plan should be describe the matter seasonality of production, agronomic and economic threats to the system, and similar.

When considering any bio-mass-utilization project of larger scope and scale, two-point factors or at least important considerations. The immediate availability of material, transportaiion cost. For example, limited acres of seasonally harvested switchgears continuous power generation for a municipality. Additionally, if the municipality must transportation costs that are excess of the value of the returned energy, even a few not be economically viable as a generation facility fuel. A good way to identify protential carefully look at the total infrastructure necessary to implement any bio-mass utilization develop risk avoidance and risk management plans that cover problem areas. Currently, there is considerable research in many promising areas of bio-mass utilization "green" biodegrable solid and fibrous plastics and coatings to various fuel chemicals. Much of this bio-mass is derived from tree and grass species, as well as the waste streams from construction farm and industrial production.

4. **Energy:** Energy is known as the bio-reactors, bio-refineries, enzymatic hydrolysis, bio-diesel, bio-mass, cellulosic ethanol, ethanol, manure digester biogas, solar power, wind energy.
5. **Fibre:** Fibres are class of materials that are continuous filaments or discrete an elongated pieces.

As they occur in nature, they are important constituents of living things, as well as non-living mineral materials. Natural and man-made fibres are, in turn, often used in the manufacture of other materials.

Fibres are classified in several ways. First of all, any fibre produced by plants, animals and geological process is considered natural fibres. Those composed of cellulose and lignin are considered vegetable or plant fibres. Some examples include the dietary fiber of vegetable foods, cotton for clothing, or hemp or flux of cordage. The fibres within and produced by animals may be far more complex with respect to their protein structures and functions. Some examples include insect and arachnid siks, animals tendon sinews and insulatory hair coating such as wool and mohair. Finally, there are some filamentous mineral fibres in nature, perhaps the most common are asbestos and some naturally occurring silica-based glass fibres.

Fibre uses are many and varied. Plant fibres may be used alone but more often are a constituent of a composite product. They may be woven into strands, compressed or 'felted' into mats, papers or films, or incorporated into composite material with organic fillers, metallic materials or plastics. Today due to concerns regarding "the renewability" and availability of resources and waste management, there is renewed interest in plant origin natural fibres. These cellulosic materials include cotton, jute, linen, hemp, flux, kenaf, cornstalk, ramie, soyabean and hemp.

Additionally, there are specialized markets for isolated dietary fibre that can be used as supplemental food product ingredient. For example, out fibre is rich in beta-glutan that clinical studies have showing significantly reduces. LDL and total cholesterol in the human body. More than 100 million Americans have elevated cholesterol levels. For ecample, 65 million who are "borderline high", (200-239, mg.1l), lifestyle modification such as diet can play a role in maintaining normal cholestrol levels, according to the National Institutes of Health National Cholestrol Eduction program. Partly due to these types of findings, soluble fibre was the first whole food for which the Food and Administration allowed a health claim.

6. **Forestry:** Natural and managed forests are one of the most important components of the earth's living and climatic systems. Around the world, forestry and the forest products industry are of major economic importance to rural livelihoods.

Forestry is the means by which press can be produced as a renewable resource for wood or bio-mass for direct timber sales, production of tress for ornamental plantings or woody material for composite products or for use us a combustion energy source. Integrated into forest management plans may be other resource management and asset generation or asset recovery options. These may involve revenue generation from hunting lease sales, government-sponsored conservation programes, tourism from winter sports access, syrup or mushroom production for food (production) products, educational activities and other strategies.

Forest resources, tree plantations and similar eco-systems usually are managed using scientific techniques. To re-forest a natural area or establish a plantation, selection of species and sub-species varieties, either in "pure" single species stands or mixed species systems, means selecting genetic stock with the proper micro-climatic adaptation and diesease resistance. Then, the forester must employ skill in the proper handling of seedlings, stand establishment and protection and management practices that include pruning and thining, controlled burns and managed extraction of the desired biomass of timber. A number of trade organizations, state and federal government agencies, university extension researchers and private consultants are available to assist with programme planning and problem solving.

7. **Fruits:** Fruits are defined as a product of vegetable growth edible to humans such as the developed ovary of a seed plant with its contents and accessory parts, which includes the pea, pod, nut, tomato, and pineapple. A fruit may also be the edible part of a plant developed from a flower with its accessorty parts, such as the peach, apple and banana. Oranges, apples, grapes and bananas are the most popular fruit.
8. **Grains and Oilseeds:** Grains are identified as cereals suitable as food for human beings. Oilseeds are those valuable for the oil content they produce.

9. **Livestock:** Livestock animals are defined as those used for meat production, accessory production, such as wool or warm castings, or those used for other human consumption, such as milk, cheese, honey, leather, etc.
10. **Nuts:** U.S. tree nut production in 2008 remained steady at 2 million tons, increasing 1 per cent from the previous year. Almond production set a new record high at 1.4 million tons, and walnut and maladamia nut production also increased. The total value of the tree nut crop slipped to $ 4.0 billion, down 7 per cent from 2007 (NASS).

    Tree nut consumption rose to 3.6 pounds per person in 2007. Americans ate more almonds and pistachios, but fewer hazelnuts, maladamias, pecans and walnuts. In general, the top three nut eaten in the United States are almonds, walnuts and pecans.
11. **Vegetables:** Fresh vegetable and melon production for 24 selected crops in 2007 totalled 494 million per cent from 2006. The value of the (total) 2007 crop was estimated at 10.9 billion dollars, a years ago. In terms of production, the three largest crops were onions, head lettuce and combined to account for 38 per cent of the total value when combined. California leader in fresh vegetable and melon production, accounting for 50 per cent of annual melon output. Production of the major vegetables used for processing increased 12 per cent to 17.8. Five of 11 main crops increased output, with tomatoes again leading the way.

Markets and Industries

1. **Energy**: The largest source of energy in the United States is fossil fuels, individual fossil fuels changed at different rates over the decades. But all the three major essential to meeting the nation's energy requirements. In 1949, fossil fuel consumption totalled 49 quadrillion British thermal units in 2005, the total was 86 quadrillion form of energy is nuclear power, which got its start in the United States in 1957. When Pennsylvania, nuclear electric power plant came on line. By 2005, the industry had extra 4 per cent of the nation's electrical output and 8 per cent of all energy used in the country energy is the renewable forms, which include conventional hydroelectric power, bio-mass and alcohol fuels, geothermal, solar and wind.
2. Food, Supply chain, fibre industry structure, pharmaceutical market trends, international markets, tourism and understanding markets are included in the market industries.

Value Added Agriculture

What is value-added Agriculture: Before, you start down the road to value added agriculture, you should understand where the road will lead you. Value-added a griculture is a movement that has created a life of its own. It is an idea that has the potential to change agriculture and rural America. However, we need to define what is valı'ə added agriculture?

Generally, there are five ways farmers have of adding value. For a more specific definition, we define value added agriculture using USDA definition.

However, to be successful in this movement we must look further into this concept of adding value. For example, there is a difference between capturing value and creating value. Regardless of whether you capture value or create value, the bottomline is that you get paid for providing value. If your business venture does not provide value to the system, there is no reason to expect a return. So the process of creating a successful business involves the search for providing value.

Providing value can be in the form of marketing a unique product, filling a market niche, simplifying the supply chain, providing a service, lowering costs, and many other ways. The more value you provide, the more returns you can extract from the marketplace.

Adding Value to Agricultural Products: Value added agriculture generates several billion dollars in economic impact for the state of Texas each year. In fact, the economic impact of adding value beyond the farm gate is usually several times the value of agricultural production at the farm gate alone.

Agricultural producers receive a much smaller portion of the consumer's dollar than do food processors, especially those who produce brand name. Capturing those additional dollars or adding value to farm or ranch products is a goal of many producers. Even for "commodity" products, such as beef, the farm-to-retail price spread indicates that those further up the supply chain earn much more than producers at the ranch or farm level. This leaflet defines value important, and provides guidelines for starting your own value added business.

What is "Value Added"?: "Value added" means adding value to a raw product by taking it to. At least, the next stage of production. This can be simple as retaining ownership of your calves and wintering them as on wheat pasture or placing them in a feedlot. Value can be added through membership in a cooperative that processes your products, such as cooperatives cotton gin. Or adding value may be as elaborate as going all the way to the consumer with a "case ready" food product. If you are considering a value added enter prise, there are two key questions to answer: 1. What is customer value? and 2. What creates a value added product?

What is Customer Value?: "Customer value" reflects the relationship between the benefits customers receive from and the price they pay for a product. The more benefits relative to the price, the higher the customer value. This does not necessarily mean that greater value results from a low price. The price of a particular product may be high, but if the associated benefits are high as well, the customers perceive value in the product. This interaction creates customer value and, thus the opportunity to add value to your product.

Creating customer value is critical in building a profitable and substantial business. However, one must bear in mind that it is the customer's perception of value, not the producers, that is critical. Consider the case of pre-conditioning calves. Does the cattle buyer perceive the pre-conditioning programme as adding value? That is will buyer pay more pre-conditioned calves (enough to cover the added cost) than for other calves? It is also important to recognize that different customers have different perceptions of added value. These perceptions correspond to their expectations of quality, service, convenience and selection.

What Creates Added Value?: "Value" is usually created by focusing on the benefits associated with the agribusiness product or service that arise from:

- **Quality:** Does the product or service meet or exceed customer expectations?
- **Functionality:** Does the product or service provide the function needed of it?
- **Form:** Is the product in a useful form?
- **Place:** Is the product in the right place at the right time?
- **Ease of possession:** Is the product easy for the customer to obtain?.

A product must have one or more of these qualities to generate additional value. Remember that a product is simply bundle of benefits, and that the more benefits there are the more customers will perceive the product as having value.

What's Driving Value Added?: Agribusiness, particularly the food sector is rapidly consolidating and increasingly responding to the changing tastes and preferences of consumers. Consumers have higher incomes than ever before. They are focusing more on convenience, quality, variety, service, health and social consiousness. They are also faced with the increasing value of (and demands on) their time. In a nutshell, consumers are more value conscious than ever.

The factors of rising disposable incomes and market fragmentation caused by retail consolidation exacerbate competition, but at the same time leave many markets to be exploited and create opportunities for producers to add value to their products.

Steps to Success in Value Added

Bulding a new business is difficult and takes hard work (nothing new for farmers and ranchers). But, for all the uncertainty, there are ways to craft a successful value added business strategy. The key factors in a detailed business plan are:

1. **Operations plan:** Flow of the business, quality and cost control.
2. **Personnel plan:** Needs, skills and training.
3. **Sales plan:** Including challenging but realistic goals.
4. **Management plan:** Evaluate strengths, weaknesses and resources.
5. **Investment and financial plan:** Cash flowing plan.

Beyond business planning and market research to get to know the customer, the essential elements for success in a value added business can be boiled down to four key ingredients for business managers:

(*i*) Adopt to market.

(*ii*) Be open to exploring new ideas.

(*iii*) Operate more as a resource manager than a producer.

(*iv*) Realize the importance of networking and the need to develop alliances.

These are difficult because they require a new vision of the farm or ranch. Managing resources and exploring new ideas means searching for new profit centres with your operation. That may seem tedious, but that is precisely what adding value is all about.

Business Skills

Communication Skills: Poor communication skills are oftened identified as one of the causes of a breakdown in the business development process. So, you must constantly work to improve your communications skills because they are very important for the success of your business venture. This is especially true in farmer-led-value-added business projects. By its very nature, farming tends to be a business where one person makes most of the decisions independently of others. So, farmers don't tend to see the need for communicating. However, in a value added business project with group (discussion) decision making, good communication skills are critical.

Effectively Communicating

1. **Effective Communications:** Effective communication is crucial for working successfully with others. It enables us to maintain relationships and accomplish tasks with both individuals and groups.
2. **Communicating Effectively:** Communication might be thought of as an "idea transplant".
3. **Developing Effective Communications:** Most Americans probably do not appreciate the importance of communication in their personal and work-day lives.

Conflict Management Skills: Conflict within a value added project committee or the board room of an operating business will not only divert away from important business issues but can also affect critical decisions relating to the viability of the business. However, conflict is a daily reality for everyone. Some conflicts are relatively minor and easy from others of greatest magnitude require a strategy for successful resolution or else they are tension and lasting enmity in the business. Knowing how to manage and resolve these are for the overall success of your value-added business.

Conflict is not necessarily bad. Properly managed, moderate does of conflict can be the root of change and allows people to learn and grow. It stimulates curiosity and in monotony and boredom. After conflict, closer unity may be established.

However, conflict can be harmful to your value added business and can divert time, from the goals of your business. In addition, prolonged·conflict can be injurious to a mental health. A step by step discussed for resolving business disputes.

Managing Conflicts: Individuals involved in a business may need assitance in resolving conflicts. So you are leadership role in managing and resolving these conflicts. Below are six steps are managing a business dispute For example, initiate dialouge, invole all parties, assimilate information, reinforce agreements, negotiate disagreements, and solidify agreements.

Decision-making Skills: The success of your value added business will be based on the decisions you make. The quality of your decisions is a function of how you go about making decisions. Are the decisions based on the proper weighing of facts and empirical evidence or are they based on optimistic expectations? Group decision making is important for the success of a value added business that is started and operated by a group of individuals. Examine various styles of group decision making in value added business projects.

Entrepreneurial Skills: Entrepreneurship is a skill that is at the heart of successful value added agricultural business development. In unleashes creativity and innovation in finding better ways to doing things. However, it is poorly understood by most people. For example, successful entrepreneurs are not plungers and risk takers. Although they may take risks, the risk are carefully quantified and compared to potential rewards. Entrepreneurial skills are essential for the success of your value added business. Firm resoures with exceptional entrepreneurial skills have a long term focus and are more to take advantage of emerging oppor-tunities.

Interpersonal Skills: Good inter-personal skills means how do you get along with people. Recent research indicates that a person's "emotional IQ"- the ability to relate to people is as important as a person's "Intelligence IQ". The art of getting along, the art of appreciation clash or coordinate, behaviour styles, tapping into your team's emotional intelligence are the criteria of interpersonal skills.

Management Skills: Building your skills for managing a value added project or business is an important endeavour. Regardless of whether you are managing a small project or a large company, individuals with good management skills are always in short supply. One of the first step in improving your management skills is to assess your managerial attitude. This will help indentify and assess how you respond to the changing nature and challenges associated with a dynamic business climate.

The role and structure of the farm business in modern agriculture is changing. It you are a value-added farmer, new ways of looking at your farm business helps you move from the perceptions and paradigms associated with the management of the traditional farm business to those of the farm business of the future.

Personal Management Skills: By improving your employee management skills, you can improve their productivity while increasing their satisfaction on the job. Although properly managing your employees takes time, it may save time and money associated with resolving employee problems in the future. The care and feeding of employees, human resouce planning, problem employmees, rules for your workers, learning to say what you mean to employees, when your employees battle-consider. Doing nothing, the knowledge coach, help your employees, fight illness, the time abusers.

Selling Skills: Contrary to popular opinion, new product do not "sell themselves". Even the best products need the help of skills sales people. Selling skills are at the heart of a successful marketing programme.

Stress Management Skills: Although a business may go through financial stress, its leaders often to go through emotional stress.

Both can be dangerous and affect the individuals involved. If, you are or one of your team members are having difficulty coping with a streesful business situation, you will find it of value to review "Managing emotional stress during a time of financial stress" and helping a business associate cope with emotional stress.

If you try to manage work, family and community responsibilities, you know the meaning of stress. Stress occurs when you, who should be thoroughly prepared can't quite get a handle on report you are supposed to present. Or, when you get call from a committee chairperson asking if you have confirmed next month's speaker yet, and that person has not returned your many calls. Learning about stress, its impact on your body and how to deal with its effects can help you manage your responsibilities.

What is Stress?

Medically speaking stress is the rate of wear and tear on your body caused by living. It is the physical, mental and chemical adjustments that your body makes in accordance to the circumstance of your life.

In other words, stress is response to what is happening around you. It is the process the body uses to keep balance and sustain life when various demands are made on you.

Some stress is necessary to motivate us and add spice to our lives. But, when the demands of your life exceed your resources, your experience too much stress which may result in damaging effects.

Stress can be good, as well as bad for you. It is like electricity. It can warm you and light up your life, or it can give you a fatal change. Regardless, stress is always with you. The important concept is learning how your body responds to the demands of stress. When stress becomes prolonged or particularly frustrating, it becomes harmful causing distress or "bad stress".

Recognizing the early signs of distress, and doing something about them, can make an important difference in the quality of your life and your ability to manage your responsibilities and that of organizations to which you have volunteered your time and energy.

Sources of Stress

Stress comes from a variety of sources, ranging from a sick

spouse to any angry co-worker. The sources of stress can be grouped into four major categories.

1. **Customary, anticipated life events:** These events represent the changes that take place throughout life: graduating from high school, marriage, returning to work after the birth of a child, telling someone you will chair an important committee, or being tapped to give a talk to a group of people.

   These events can be influenced, but not totally controlled by personal decisions. Normally, they cause a positive and stimulating form of stress. Symptoms of distress may be experienced when several events cluster into a short time period, or when you resist the changes represented by the events.

2. **Unexpected life events:** These events are the "tragedies" and "shocks" of life. Being involved in an accident, being the victim of a crime, the sudden death of a loved one, etc. An unexpected opportunity can also fall into the "shock" category.

   These stressors usually occur to you suddenly, without warning, and are not in your control. The stress symptoms that result are often sudden, and sometimes severe. Normally, however, such symptoms do not become chronic. With the passage of time, we heal and the symptoms are relieved.

3. **Progressive, accumulating events:** These represents the everyday strains of life. Especially stressful are unresolved conflicts in close relationships on going conflicts with a spouse, continuing parent child friction, long-term care for a disabled relative,

boredom with a career path, taking on too many outside activities, constant fitghting among factions in an organization to which you belong, etc. The symptoms of stress exhaustion resulting from these factors develop slowly. And, because they develop over time, symptoms are not easily relieved. The intensity of these pressures often seems to gain momentum and the "victims" feel increasingly worn out and unable to cope.

4. **Personal trait stress:** This is the self-imposed stress that is caused by perfectionsim, insecurity, lack of self-confidence and feelings of jealousy or inadequacy. It is the only source of stress over which you have significant control. Stress caused by low self-esteem impacts all daily situations and influences all interactions. Sufferers often become anxious warriers and are plagued by feelings of fear and disease. These symptoms can be chronic and lifelong unless the source of the stress-negative feelings about oneself is changed.

Health Problems

A single stressful event, even a really upsetting one, usually will not cause a great deal of physical or emotional damage. But, when several stressful events occurs in a short period of time called a stress pile-up anyone of a variety of unhealthy effects can be produced.

Damaging stress has been related to asthma, ulcers, cancer, headaches, heart dieases and stroke even to the common cold and other infectious diseases.

Learning more about stress and developing ways to manage it are positive health investment. There are many things that you can do to defend yourself against the effects of too much stress.

Steps for Reducing Stress

When stress occurs, it is important to recognize and deal with it. Following are some ways to handle stress. As you begin to understand more about how stress affects you as an individual, you will invent your ideas about how to help ease tension. Turn to physical activity: Remember, your body and mind work together. A regular routine of physical exercise will help to relieve the daily symptoms of stress.

Locate the source of your stress: You need to look inside yourself, as well as outside. Spending too much time analyzing your feelings may make them look bigger than they really are.

Share your concerns with others: It may help to talk to someone. Perhaps a friend, family, teacher or counsellor can help you see the problem in a different light.

Know your limits: It a problem is beyond your control and can not be changed at the moment, do not fight the situation.

Take care of yourself: Get enough rest and eat well, eat regular meals and snacks, reduce caffeine, consume more water, exercise regularly, limit your intake of alcohol and drugs.

Make time for fun: Balance work and community service with recreation by scheduling time strictly for yourself. Do something you really enjoy, whether it is bird watching, fishing, bowling, needle work, etc.

There is nothing you can do to totally eliminate stress

from your life you would not want that. Stress is important when it is under control. It keeps you alert and keeps you from being bored. However, when stress starts to have a negative effect on your life, it is important to determine the source of your stress and consider ways to lesson the impact on you.

1,500 Farmers Commit Suicide in India

Over 1,500 farmers in an Indian state committed suicide after being driven to debt by crop failure. It was reported today. The agricultural state of Chhattisgarh was bit by falling water levels. "The water level has gone down below 250 feet here. It is used to be at 40 feet a few years ago," Shatru Sahu, a villager in one of the districts, told down to Earth magazine.

"Most of the farmers here are indebted and only God can save the ones who do not have a bore well." Sahu lives in a district that recorded 206 farmers suicides last year. Police records for the district add that many deaths occur due to debt and economic distress. In another village nearby, Beturam Sahu who owned two acres of land was among those who committed suicide. His crop is yet to be harvested, but his son Lakhu left to take up a job as a manual labourer. His family must repay a debt of £ 400 and crop this year is poor. "The crop is so bad this year that we will not even be able to save any seeds," Lakhu's friend Santosh. There were no rains at all. That's why Lakhu left even before harvesting the crop. There is nothing left to harvest in his land this time. He is worried how he will repay this loans. "Farmer's suicides are increasing due to a vicious circle created by money-lenders. They lure farmers to take money but when the crops fail, they are left with no option other than death". Development should be for all. The government blames us for being against development. Forest area is depleting and dams are constructed without proper planning. Now we shall disscuss about the Time management skills in Industry.

4.3 TIME MANAGEMENT SKILLS IN INDUSTRY

Steering a Meeting as a Chairman

Meetings are an important tool to align and coordinate multiple people. Each meeting requires a chairman or chairwoman who stress this process in order to ensure that the meeting is held in an efficient way without wasting the participant's time. The following rules help you to become a meeting chairman.

1. **Confirm the objective of the meeting:** Everybody needs to be aligned on the purpose of the meeting at the beginning. This reduces unnecessary side discussions. Teams also work better when having a common goal. I therefore recommend starting each meeting with a greeting and the statement of the objectives for this specific meeting.
2. **Define key roles:** Every meeting requires three key roles to function.
   (1) The chairman the meeting and manges the time and the agenda. It is his/her responsibility to start and end the meeting on time.
   (2) The administrator takes the minutes and records decisions and action items. In the ideal case the administrator also follows-up on the action items to make sure that the responsible persons implement them. If there is a follow

up meeting the administrator reports on the implementation progress.

(3) The participants contribute to the meeting with their idea and also are responsible for the implementation of tasks. Never assign tasks to people who are not present at the meetings. If, the task itself cannot be completed by any of he participants assign someone to delegate it to the appopriate person. Since the participants are supposed to contribute with their thoughts it is important to reduce distractions. Don't allow people to use their laptops or mobile devices to check or write e-mails during the meeting.

3. **Summarize at the end of each agenda item**: Confirm all action items and decisions made at the end of each agenda item.This ensures that you can really close the item and helps the minute taker too. You might also ask the minute taker if he has any questions. The better the minutes are the less work you will have latter in checking them.

4. **Write and conform minutes during the meeting**: I have been a company that had two projectors with two screens in each meeting room. One screen was to share the presentation material related to the agenda. The second screen was usually reserved Box the minute taker and every participant conformed that the wording of the minutes correct. This procedure allows agreeing on the minutes during the meeting so that there is no necessity to send around drafts for conformation. The saves time to all participants and the implementation of

action and decisions starts immediately after the meeting.

If you do not have the space or budget for a such technically perfect solution you can also help yourself with a large display on the meeting table or by reading the wording of the minutes loudly at the end of each agenda item.

5. **Close the meeting on time:** As a general principle you should close each meeting on time, regardless if you are the chairman or a participant. As a chairman people will very soon know your habit and act in a way that in a way that allows finishing all items within the planned time. As a participant you can state that you have to go to the next meeting on that you shedueled a phone call. Finishing a meeting time is not only a good time saver but also a courtesy to all other participants who have busy schedule too.
6. **Properly close the meeting:** When the meeting come to an and properly close it. Thanks all participants for their contributions and conform the most important decisions and action items. If you know that the team requires another meeting on this project or topic immediately arrange the schedule for the next meeting. With everyone at the table it requires significantly less coordination effort. What usually might take-up to an hour or more will be completed within a few minutes.

How to Create a Good Meeting Agenda

A good agenda is a poweful tool to steer a meeting effectively. If you are in charge of organzing a meeting besides defining the schedule you will have to define the agenda. A good meeting agenda includes the following items:

1. Date and time
2. Meeting location
3. Participants and guests
4. Excused absentees
5. Optional: Dress code (e.g. for offsite meetings)
6. Agenda item name
7. Agenda item duration
8. Agenda item owners name.

Did you ever experience a discussion at the beginning of a meeting on who was to take the minutes? A very effective way to avoid such discussions is to already name the person who will take the minutes in the agenda which is distributed before the meeting. For regular meetings you might have an order so that it is everyone's turn in a while. Last but not least follow your agenda during the meeting.

No Meeting Without Agenda

Insist on having an agenda for each and every meeting (unless it is about personnel feedback). A meeting agenda should include information as the topic, the expected duration as well as the nature of the item (decision, information, action, etc.). It might also make sense to already define who will take the minutes. Also define the chairman of the meeting. If you are the one preparing agenda chances are high that you also will chair the meeting.

Reduce Meeting Duration

Meeting generally are scheduled for one hour. If, you have a busy schedule you might start to only after offer meetings with a duration of 30 minutes. You will realized that the attendants will be better prepared and also be more focused during the meeting.

This measure allows you to achieve the same in the half time. Of course, this does not work for all meetings but, if I applied regularly it can significantly contribute to free valuable time in your calender.

Opening a Conservation

The faster you come to the point the least the conversation will last. After a short warming up you might directly ask your counterpart "what can I do for you"?

Unwanted Visitors

Sometimes you might have to deal with unwanted visitors who came in spontaneously. There are a few rules on how to deal with them in a friendly manner but making sure that they will not steal too much of your time.

- Do not offer them something to drink
- Directly come to the point
- Chose techniques how to close a conversation.

Another possibility to immediately get rid of unwanted visitors is to agree on an appointment at another time or depending on their matter to reffer them to a colleague who might be able to help them too (or even better).

Schedule Meetings at Your Place

You have a choice to hold meetings at your place or someone else's one. If you have to visit someone at an external location you will esasily spend one hour or even more for getting there. Even within the same office building going to a meeting room or your colleagues office will take you a few minutes and significantly increase the risk of interruptions and distractions by other colleagues you will meet on your way. I know that there are limitations to schedule all in your place (customers, superiors, politeness, want to see the place of a new client, etc.) but keep this in mind when your schedule meeting. If you can shift only 5 percent of your meeting you will gain many extra hours per day.

You should not only plan your meetings but also explicitly plan the transit time to get there and back. This is especially true when you use an electronic calender whether other people in your network can also see if you are free or not. In case you do not plan the transit time will look free and other people might schedule an appointment although you are not yet back to the office yet.

Most Important Minutes of the Day

The most important minutes of a day are those when you plan your day. Before starting work you should be take a few minutes and check the tasks due, meetings, etc. and decide the priority and order for the day. You can plan you day in the evening of the previous day, in bed before standing up, when commuting, first thing at work, etc.

In general each minute you spend on your planning your day will pay off in higher efficiency and free time for other things.

The Daily Time Account

Every day has 24 hours, 1440 minutes or 86,400 seconds.

This is your daily time account and you decide how to make use of this valuable resource by retrieving minutes and seconds similar to a bank account. The big difference is that you cannot make savings because the next day will start with an opening balance of exactly 86,400 seconds again. Time that has not been used properly is vain.

This concept gives you use idea how important it is use our time in the right way since there are no savings nor overdrafts. You should keep this in mind when you set your goals and plan such day.

Set Yourself Time Limits

If you know, you have 8 hours for a task chances are high that you really will require 8 hours. In case, you set yourself a more anbitious target of, e.g., 6 hours you will probably also keep the time.

Giving yourself time pressure is a very powerful method to increase your speed and efficiency because you become more focused.

Determine Never to be Idle

Everyone can spend a lot of time just running idle and hanging around or just starring somewhere. This can happen at many occasions, whilst commuting or waiting for someone or just in between two tasks.

If you determine never to be idle to can significantly increase your productivity. A day has 1,440 minutes besides the time you sleep you can use every minute in a productive way. After you took the determination you will always look for some task or action. This does not only related to work but also applies to fun and leisure.

Identify and Change Bad Habits

Make a list of bad habits that are stealing your time, sabotaging your goals, and bloking your success. After, you do, work on them one at a time and systematically eliminate them from your life.

Quitting a bad habit leaves an empty space with the risk to go back again. A good way to eliminate a bad habit therefore is to replace it with a good habit. When changing a habit you will go through the classic emotional curve of change:

1. **Enthusiasm:** You might be in that phase just right now. You decided to change things in your life and you are full of excitement about what you all want to achieve.
2. **Rejection:** After the excitement has passed you start feeling the pain of changing the habit. At this stage you question your initial goals, if it is really worth going through this process, etc. Here is the highest danger for giving up. This is time where you need to allow yourself incentives and rewards each time you practice the positive habit instead of the negative one.
3. **Recovery:** After a while you will start feeling the progress of change and also see concrete benefits. Each day you will feel better about the change.
4. **Satisfation:** In the last stage the negative habit is fully replaced by the positive habit and feel good because you made it and because you also experience the full benefit of having changed. If you want you can allow yourself a small celebration with a special reward something you love to do but only can do from time to time.

If, you are fully aware of this change process it will be much easier to cope with the frustration during phase two. It will also help you a lot to get through this valley if you determine your rewards and incentives for positive behaviour in advance. Knowing this process you also understand why you should only attack one bad habit after the other. If you go for multiple bad habits at one time the rejection phase becomes very strong and you are very likel to give up the entire project achievement nothing but frustration and even higher hurdles to start again another time.

Focus on Motivation not Discipline

When I talk to other people on time management many tell me that they simply do not have the discipline to be effective. I think that discipline with regards to time management is a bad thing and it makes people fail early in their efforts to improve themselves.

If you try to have discipline you generally tend to try too much at once. It is often about changing habits and this is a difficult task requiring time. Then you feel that you are failing and accuse yourself that you simply lack discipline. This is a very negative feeling and it kills all motivation to go ahead. As a result often the entire improvement project is at stake and people simply give up. On the top of this the mental hurdle to start again get higher and higher with each failure.

So, my recommendation is- If you want to change yourself 'NEVER' use the word disciplince again! Changing your life and your habits is all about motivation and positive enforcement and rewards. Before, you start your personal development programme you write down the following:

1. Why do I want to change this?
2. What is motivating me?
3. What can be quick wins?
4. How can I reward myself? what reward can I give myself for achieving milstones and what will I reward myself with after accomplishment?

Then, you start with the quick wins. These should be easy to achieve and even if they only have small impact you should go for them. Achieving these quick wins will make you feel good and also hungry for more. Each time you have achieved something, you shall reward yourself. Use small rewards for small achievements and big rewards for large achievements.

After completion of the quick wins. You are ready to start a bit more challenging steps. However, it is important that you go step by step and don't try too much. When you don't manage to achieve a step, don't blame yourself. Resisting change an absolutely normal reaction. Analyse why you did not achieve your goal and try to find a better way. You might also increase the reward you will give yourself if you feel that the next step is more challenging to you than you initially anticipated. Keep your motivation high and NEVER blame yourself or others.

Start the big steps when you emotionally feel ready. It does not make sense if your mind tells you "I should" but everything in your body tells you "I don't want at all". In such a sense, I recommend to review your motivation and to ask yourself again why you want to achieve this objective. As a summary keep in mind you will achieve much more using positive motivation rather trying to have discipline. I think that many people who are known to have great discipline in reality were real artists in self-motivation rather than extremely strong in their mind.

Don't Fell Guilty: Avoid feeling quilty. We are all humans only and even the best practitioners of time management have phases where they do not manage to maintain control on their time. You have to realize that changing habits on time management requires time. Drawback therefore are normal and it is more productive to look forward and making it better the next time than creating emotional pain by feeling guilty. If you didn't do something at the time you assigned yourself, try to reschedule it instead of feeling guilty.

You Procrastinate
(Scheule Regular Meetings for the Whole Year)

When you know that you have regular meetings it is best to schedule them directly for a longer period in your calendar and to also send invitations to the other participants. This has the following benefits:

1. You don't have to coordinate the meeting each time.
2. It becomes a regular event.
3. Other participants will plan around it.

Of course, it might still happen that you will have to reschedule a meeting from time to time. But, since this usually is the reception, you will still have a major time saving compared to scheduling one by one.

Have a Daily Meeting with Your Assistant

If you have an assistant you should hold a daily meeting at a fixed time. It will become a habit where you discuss the following things:

1. The plan for the day.
2. Tasks to be completed during this day.
3. New appointment requests and conformations.
4. Business travel.
5. Follow-up requirements.
6. Requests to other people.

In the ideal case you come to the office much earlier so that you have checked your incoming mails first and are well prepared to define your requirements to the assistant.

A good option to keep yourself productive over the day is to also include time for a break and to relax into your schedule. You should create an appointment in your schedule and name it relax. During these minutes you can enjoy a drink, lookout of window or just drift. After the break you will resume your tasks with new energy.

Plan Time Buffers in Your Day

Do not fill every minutes of your day with appointments and tasks without buffers. There will always be new tasks coming up throughout the day as well as interruptions or delays.

It is wise to plan 30 per cent buffer throughout your day so that you have the time to react to such things without endangering your plan. In case you have spare time you can use it for conceptional work or to already complete tasks due later.

Telephone Hour

Reserve a certain fixed time per day where you make your phone calls. For outgoing calls you can pool them and do all your calls one after the other. For incoming calls people will learn that you are available at a certain time and start calling you during this windows. If you deal a lot with foreign countries don't forget to consider different time zones when scheduling you telephone hour.

Asking for a Return Call

When you ask someone to call you back, you should specify the following information:

- –The reason for the call
- –When you will be available
- –Your phone number

Even if the person has your phone number it makes to leave it, so that all information will be on one note or message, making it most convenient to call you for the other person.

How to Start Meetings on Time

Meeting that commence with delay are wasting all attendant's time. If you are the organizer of a meeting, you can use a few techniques to increase the probability that your meeting will start to time.

1. **Invitation:** State that the meeting will start sharp at the scheduled time. Make sure that all information such as building or meeting room name are on the invitation so that there are no excuses.
2. **Reminder:** Send a reminder to the participants about 30 minutes before the m...ting starts also confirming tnat the meeting commences sharp at the scheduled time.
3. **Running the meeting:** First, you must be thereon

time! close the door of the meeting room and start the meeting regardless of other people's absence. In case of too many people missing you can also call the meeting off. Make sure that the meeting terminates as scheduled. If people come late there is less time for the meeting itself. You might also mark the late comers in the meeting minutes if you find it useful.

4. **Credits:** If you can, establish a system where late comers have to pay into a central pot. This money shall hurt a little bit of you are late always. Regularly spend the money for the community on cake, coffee or other stuff. State these benefits are with regards from the late comers.

Eliminate the Urgent from Your to-do List

Urgent tasks create interruptions and distract you from your real goals. The urgent is focused on the short-term whereas the importatn things should be created to the achievement of your goals. If you regularly are confronted with urgent matters that suddenly pop-up, you first have to analyse the source of these urgent tasks.

1. **Procrastination:** One major source of urgent matters can be your own procrastination. Some people feel an excitement when they have to complete something on the last minute even if they had all to prepare things in advance.

   If this is true for you, there is a choice to be made. In case you are happy with this situation, don't change it, it will not work anyhow.

   If you feel bad about this most of the time, you have to apply techniques to manage your procrastination. In the first step you need a proper to-do list. Then you schedule time slots in your calender to work on the tasks you typically procrastinate. Even, if you cannot complete them during this time the progress make it easies to restart the next time. It is also important that you put away all possible distractions and also reward yourself once you completed the task.

2. **Other Colleagues:** If urgent tasks mainly come from other colleagues you need to openly address this. They keep interrupting you and reduce your overall productivity. This behaviour makes it impossible for you to plan your own tasks. Rather than blaming your colleague it is better to explain why these urgent matters are difficult to handle for you. When he understands your situation you comeup with a proposal on how you can even better support in case you receive the requests or information earlier.

   If this does not work at all and you have a feeling that your colleague does not care there might be no other way than using an urgent but not so important matter and let your colleague wait. Just make sure that it does not impact a customer.

3. **Your Boss:** If your boss permanently interrupts you with urgent tasks you need to improve your communication. Propose a regular meeting where you discuss upcoming tasks. This should help reducing the number of urgent items coming up suddenly. You also have to understand the difference between urgent and important. There

are tasks that might be urgent but not important. In general, I recommend giving the important task a higher priority than the urgent but unimportant task.

Change Your Mindset to Easily Connect with Other People

Everyday we have multiple opportunities to interact with other people. This includes people we already know but most of the times we are surrounded by people we do not know yet. Have you ever actively thought about how you approach people you don't know? Does is regularly happen to you that would like to talk to someone you don't know but you hesitate and miss the opportunity? A change in your mindset with regards to other people can make a huge difference in your approach.

I recently observed one thing that "Personal Development for Smart People" and found a simple but very effevtive advice on how set your mindset to be more open when meeting new people. One of his idea is to image that you already are connected to all other people. I tried to apply this idea for a few weeks and the results are amazing. You are connected makes you more friendly in the first place. It is probably common sense that people react in a nice way and both feel good.

But, it also is amazing how much easier it becomes to approach totally new people. Discusion with other people started in a very natural and open way a human touch.

You also have to be aware that this approach does not become a habit immediately. It takes a few weeks until you automatically apply it to every person you meet. But, I can assure you that it is worth going for it. It does not cost money or hours of preparation just a though to be connected already before you start talking.

Take Notes and Review them Everyday

One of the first things to learn is time management is to write things down even if you have a good memory. Scientific research showed that we remember much more things when we write them down. According to Buddeley's model of working memory our memory consists of a phonological loop, a visual and an episodic loop. These loops represent short-time memory and it seems that they reinforce each other. This means that the probability to remember something is much higher if you write it down enven if you don't need the notes later.

The second reason for taking notes is that you free your mind. Permanently reminding yourself that you don't have to forget this or that simply causes stress. Once you wrote down all items you can focus your mind on achieving the task you are currently working on.

I therefore recommend having a note pad with you where you takes meeting notes, reminders or where you can do brain storming. Taking it with allows you to also turn idle time into productive time regardless where you are. Althogh, I strongly believe that there is no alternative to having an A4 note pad, so that you are quick and also have sufficient space. On top of the paper you might also use an electronic help such as evernote in case you travel a lot. It allows you to take quick notes by voice, picture or text through your mobile phone and automatically synchronizes it with PC at work or at home.

It is absolutely mandatory that you plan a fixed time to review your notes once a day. The best time to do this is when you plan your day. During this time you transfer tasks into you to do list update your calendar and schedule other activities related to your notes.

Sleeping on the Plane

Long distance flights are often at night. Although these flights are a great opportunity to get a little bit of sleep, I know many people that they cannot sleep on the plane. This is a collection of a few items that help falling asleep in a plane.

1. **Fall a sleep during take-off:** Did you ever notice that many people fall asleep during take-off and landing of the plane? The air inside the plane gets recycled without adding fresh air at these times, so that the oxygen level in dropping. This sudden drop makes us feel asleep. This means that you should plan to start sleeping during take-off. Although you are not allowed to decline your seat you should get into a comfrotable position and close your eyes once the plane starts moving away from its parking position.
2. **Use earplugs:** You might not always realize it since the sound is very stable but it is very loud inside a plane. You have the sound of the motor of the air-conditioning and the air outside in addition to all kind of noises made by other passengers and the staff. The easier way to reduce the noise level is to use earplugs. He head phones will noise reduction function are a great option if you don't find them too large.
3. **Use the eye-shield:** Use an eye-sheild to protect from the bright light and the constant movements taking place in a plane at all times.

4. **Tell the purser you want to sleep:** Once you are sleeping you don't want to wake-up just because they are serving some meal or drinks. Let the puser know early that you don't want to be disturbed and that you are ready to skip a meal in case you are sleeping. Some airlines even often stickers to indicate this wish for night flights.
5. **Don't check the inflight entertainment programme:** More and more planes personal in flight entertainment systems in each seat including the economy class. Having a choice of a few dozen movies and games you will certainly find something interseting. If you want to sleep on the plane you therefore better don't even look at the programme. Once you start watching a movie it probably will take you more time to fall asleep.
6. **Reserve a comfortable seat:** In first or business class it does not matters so much which seat you are in. If you fly economy class you should my to get a seat in front of a wall or the emergency exit since it provides more space. When I want to sleep on the plane, usually I get a window seat. You can put the pillow into the window and win a few additional centimeters of space.
7. **Wear clothes to relax:** Wear loose clothes if you want to sleep on the plane. Use trousers without a belt. Since, it is cold in high attitude you should also take something warm with you. It is hard to sleep, when you are freezing.

10. Essential Time Management Skills

Have you ever started the day with great ambitions and

then realized at the end that you didn't get anything done? It happens to everyone, but it happens to some people more often than others.

Time management allows you to have a higher degree of control over what you do in a day, in a week or a month. Time management skills can help you spend the hours you have on what is most important to you.

Organizational skills are easier for some people than others. For instance all time management advice includes some form of writing down what you want to accomplish. For man people, this is easy and natural. Other people have difficulty creating lists and following through on them. It's a list brain/right brain thing and has to do with whether your brain favours logic and structure or creative and unstructured thinking. Time management requires discipline. If you are not prepared to be disciplined, you are not going to be a very good manager of your own time. Here's a top-10 list of time management techniques that I have employed myself. Notice that I didn't call them "best practices". However, they do work for me and can work for you as well.

1. **Create a list of things to do each morning:** If you don't keep track of what you want to accomplish. You are not going to have a chance for effective time management. Create to-do list at the begining of each day or at the end of the prior day. The list can include business and personal items and can be put on paper, you work station, PDA, etc. Refer to the list several times during the day. For example, if you have 10 minutes before a meeting, glance at your list. There might be e-mail you wanted to send that would only take 10 minutes.

When you complete each item, check it off. If, you are like me, you derive satisfaction from being able to check off an item as complete.

2. **Write down all follow-up items on your list:** To keep track of new things that come up during the day, place them on your daily list. If your list is full and the activity can be completed (or the next day), place it on your list for a day or two out. Have you ever wondered why people tell you they will do something and then don't follow through? It's because they don't write it down. When I was a manager. I would often talk to people about we needed to complete. I trusted their memory. If they didn't bring a pencil and a paper, I gave them so they could write down what needed to be done and the due date.
3. **Carry forward unfinished, work and follow up:** Now you have a list of work for the day, and you have added new items for follow up during the day. What do you do with the things you haven't completed at the end of the day? You carry them forward and add them to your list for tomorrow. But don't be procrastination. You don't want to carry an expanding list of activities from day-to-day. If the activity is important, get it done. If it's not important, follow up with the person who expecting something from you and explain that the work hasn't been completed.
4. **Keep track of due dates:** Use your list to keep track to due dates. This includes commitment to work colleagues and friends. My experience is that people miss due dates more often than the hit

them. If you are not clear, ask when an activity needs to be completed, write it down, and then use time management skills to make sure they work is done on time. If you can't meet the commitment, communication that in a timely manner.

5. **Create a list of priorities for this month and next:** I know many people make lists for today. How many make high-level lists of the things they need to do this month and next? Unless you have a transactional job where your time frames are always short-term, you need to stop at the beginning of each month and determine what you want to accomplish. These lists are obviously at a high level, but again, they keep you focused on what you want to accomplish. As the month progress, start adding items to your list for the next month.
6. **Keep track of longer term reminders:** Your things to-do list isn't going to help you for follow up you will need to remember in the distant future. For stance you may tell a colleague that you will follow up with him to check progress in two months. You need to have a keep track of this followup and to remind yourself two months in the future.
7. **Keep a clean desk:** I never knew of a good time manager who worked in a pigsty. In fact, it usually follows that people who have cluttered offices or cubicles aren't very good time managers. You can be a good time manager when you spend a lot of time looking for stuff in a cluttered work environment.

8. **Keep all of your current work in one area:** Over time, you may work on many separate activities and initiatives. Keep your things organized. I always keep all of my curremt work papers in one area, where I can get them easily. When I am finished with a project, I move the folder elsewhere.
9. **Purge files and documents you no longer need:** Here's that one might startle you. For the past 10 years. I have had one file drawer where I keep all my papers from completed work initiatives. I keep adding new work folders to the front of the drawer, and when the answer gets full, I throw out files from the back end. In other words, I never keep more files than can fit in one drawer.
10. **Back-up online files and purge:** I have a similar philosophy about online documents. I would guess that 95 per cent of what you have online in your work files probably has shelf life of three months or less. I periodcally back-up my files to CD (or disk) and then go through and quickly delete all the older junk I don't need anymore.

4.4. TIME MANAGEMENT SKILLS IN SERVICES

What is Power Your Learning?

Learning the process we go through to acquire new knowledge, skills, attitudes or values. We tend to think of learning only in relation to formal study but we are learning all the time through our experience. We all know that everybody is different and that some of us appear more effective at leraning than others.

You probably can't remember how you learnt but it

almost certaibly wasn't in a class. You did it through curiosity, making sense of trial and error determination and learning from your experience. As adults we sometimes forget about some of these apparently "unconscious" aspects of the learning process. Understanding these hidden skills will help you be a more effective learner in all aspects of your life.

Never before have time management skills been as important as they are now. Life tool for most of us. In the private sector, ask any working mother or a college student work for an education. And in the business sector, ask any business owner trying to juggle at the one time.

With improved time management skills we can make the shift from reactive to pro-active and have the time to work towards them. It's no secret that those of us who can manage get more things done.

When one has the time to give priority to the issues in our daily business on private live attention, the stress levels drop and we are able to manage our resources in a more effective.

Here's 21 ways to dramatically your time management skills:

1. Be decisive.
2. Set clear goals and objectives.
3. Set a daily work plan, the night before.
4. Prioritise tasks using A-B-C-D then reprioritize a task using 1-2-3 to identify.
5 Separate the urgent from the important.
6. Use the law of enforced efficiency, what is the highest value use of your time?
7. Use the 80/20 rule to improve your time

management skills by identifying the tasks greatest benefit and do those first.

8. Develop stamina and high energy through regular exercise and diet.
9. Develop single handling skills to concentrate on one task at a time.
10. Eat the ugly toad first, do the hardest thing first up.
11. Organize your work space by using the acronym TRAF: Toss-Refer-Action-File.
12. Use travel time to listen to educationaals CD's and prepare work schedules.
13. Develop expertise in key tasks through practise and repetition.
14. Work in real time, at a fast tempo and develop an ongoing sense of urgency.
15. Time management skills generally improve automatically when you learn to make (do not) proper decision.
16. Re-engineer work processes, map them out and identify what needs to be done and reducing the number of steps by 30 per cent.
17. Reinvent yourself once a year. Identify what you need to do to become more productive only constant in life is change.
18. Ask yourself the following on a regular basis- knowing what I know right now, would same way.
19. Set priorities, identify what tasks you can procrastinate on that is, the lower prior 80 per

cent of tasks that have less value and only contribute 20 per cent of the productivity.

20. Decide to work to live, not live to work. This means working towards a balance life of time on down time and the quality of time at work for the aim.
21. Be intensely, 21 ways to improve your time management skills. Implement just a way ahead of the pack.

Time Management Let's You Organize Your Life and Get Things Done

Having a "to-do" list as long as your arm will be likely to make you feel overwhelm over all productivity on a daily basis. This will definitely not help you gain any ground a success and get closer to accomplishing your goals some studies have shown that they can only have about seven tasks "in the hopper" at once. However, this comes with a does not refer to multitasking! In fact, some recent studies have indicated that multitude the most efficient way for many people to work.

Keeping a "to-do" list about seven tasks at a time will ensure that list gets smaller everyday. Each day take a few minutes to outline the tasks you need today. Prioritize those tasks, beginning with the task that will get you closer to can wait should appear closer to the bottom of the list, and be done when there is some of your energies should be focused on completing those tasks that will get you closer want out of life.

But some thought into how you work best. A morning person may out to a accomplish of the mental or physical tasks early in the day, when energy is best. Those afternoon choose to start off with smaller bites out of the list.

Effective time management strategies are critical if you expect to get anything done, at a time, until you complete it. If you do this, you will see. your "to-do" list get shortest means you are closer to achieving success, and this is one way to actually measure you daily basis. Watching that abundant life get closer and closer each day can reinforce you positive attitude and that's a real receipe for achieving success.

3 Sure fire ways to Learn Time Management Skills

May people have this erroneous that if they possess an organizer and list down all the things that they need to accomplish in a day, they will be able to finish all their tasks. However, accomplishing tasks require more than just organizing skills you should also develop your time management skills.

Usually, learning time management skills can be a pretty tedious especially if you do it alone. Time management requires a lot of discipline, and most people are not disciplined enough to follow the schedules that they made for themselves. Most of the time, they fall into the pit of procrastination, ending-up tried and stressed.

You can avoid making this mistake by following these three guaranted ways to make time management an easier task. By utilizing these tips, you will realize that learning time management skills can also be fun!

1. **Learn time-management skills with friend**: If you are an expert procrastination and newable when it comes to time management, then it would be pretty difficult for you to adjust your schedule at

by yourself. But what are friends for, if not to help you out in your direct need? Finding a buddy who will act as your alarm clock whenever you have tasks that need to be accomplished can help you in your quest of learning time management skills. You can also return the favour to your friend, so that both of you get to learn in the process.

2. **Have an accountibility partner:** If you cannot work with a friend because you always end-up not finishing anything, you might want to try having an accounting partner. Your accountability partner will serve as both your mentor and motivator when it comes to learning time management skills and goal setting. Keep in mind though that your accountability buddy will not do the work for you, he or she will only provide you with assistance in finishing your tasks and achieving your goals.
3. **Be flexible:** Flexibility means being able to handle different kinds of taks in a quick manner. Learning how to breeze through your duties without affecting the quality of your work is one sure fire way to learn how to manage your time.

Once you have utilize these three tips in managing time, you will be well on your wall to accomplishing your tasks and achieving your goals.

"Time is life, If we can manage our time means we are controlling our life, if we can't manage our time it will not manage us."

Developing your time management skills requires a certain amount of discipline, and if discipline is something that is now to you, you will have to develop these new skills as you go along. However, most of these skills are quite easy to grasp so you will quickly adopt them and they will become natural for you.

Perhaps the most important of these skills is the ability to plan your day. Of course, you will also need to plan in the longer term, but to be truly effective with your time need to make the best possible use of the time each day offers.

If you can plan your day well, while being open and willing to deal with any new situations that arise, you will have developed two of the most important time management skills.

The basic ingredient for effective daily planning is a time plan for each and everyday. This may seem like a chore, however it need only take about five or ten minutes to do. That's not long is it? When you do it is up to you. You can do it at night before you go to bed, or first thing in the morning. I find morning the best as your mind is fresh after a good night's sleep.

It is important to make a commitment to planning out your day before it starts. Those 5-10 minutes will give you clarity about your actions for the day so you are more likely to be highly productive, and feel less stress and pressure.

For the most part, your time plan will help you be effective with your time. However, life is, unpredictable so situations will arise that you did not account for in your time plan. Learning how to deal with these situations effectively is another important time-management skills when this happens, encourage you to stay calm and not flustered. Instead, take a minute to ask yourself what the best course of action is, and listen to answers that come.

How to Make to-do Lists Work for You

To-do lists are effective time management tools but only if the, Here are six strategies for making your to-do lists work hard for everyone.

1. **Keep it simple:** Whether you use a computer based to-do list or a paper tablet, its too complex, you won't use it. . . guaranteed. I keep my to-do list tablet. I list "major" tasks to be accomplished, with big sure each one. A major task is not necessarily one that takes a long time.
2. **Limit yourself:** Small papers tablets work well, because there's a limit to how much page? I stick to a maximum of 10 tasks, all of which can be account week of when I list them.
3. **Set a due date and stick to it:** Due dates help prioritize what you do and when. Do not work on which you write them down. Jot down the due date beside each the order of their deadlines.
4. **Use a dark marker to reinforce your feeling of accomplish:** Cross off sub-steps as you complete them with a regular pen. Use cross off the major tasks. Boy, does it feel good!
5. **Redo the list every workday:** Do it every evening. This gives you a clean idea of what you have end of the next day.
6. **Add pop-ups to your list:** When something pop up during the day that has to be attended important phone call, add it to your to-do list even if you

have cross it off. To-do lists not only tell you what you have to-do, you are using your time well.

Top 10 Time Management Mistakes

1. **Keeping too many things in your head:** A common mistake to keep track of all the things you need to do and places you needed.
2. **Doing grabs your attention next:** When you are doing task, how do you choose what to do next?
3. **Not spending enough time on your top priorities:** If you task the day, but don't accomplish the things that really matter to you. You must time on low priority items.
4. Doing very efficiently that which need not be done at all: Time management consultants this is one of the worst ways you can waste your time, you don't even realize you are doing it.
5. **Poor Planning:** You have probably heard the saying "If you favour poor planning is one of the main reasons projects fail, fall behind schedule. Lack of planning leads to inadequate preperation, unexpected problems.
6. **Working in a disorganized and distractive work environment:** You have too much control over your work environment, there are things that distractions and clutter from your desk.
7. **Attempting to do too much:** In time management the work condition of having too much work, more work, than you can normally have the result of external circumstances such as a big deadline a co-worker's rest but it is often self-inflicted.

8. **Always saying yes:** Saying yes 'to request' for your time is practice. In fact, better you are in managing your time and your projects, you will be choosen to handle important that need to be completed of care.
9. **Not managing your inflows:** Work flow management is one knowledge work that traditional forms of time management have been use adequately.
10. **Confusing activity with productivity:** This final mistake is mismatch between the lower tactical levels of time management and the where goals, vision and purpose come into play.

4.5. CONCLUSION

"We all have time to either spend or waste and it is our decision what to do with it. But once passed, it is gone forever."
—Bruce Lee

Every individual on earth has the same amount of time 60 seconds in a minute, 60 minutes in an hour, 1,440 minutes in a day, or 86,400 seconds in a day, and 5,25,600 minutes in a year. While a vast majority of people and every sector confesses faltering to come to grips with it, extremely few can claim to have made the most of it. How is it that they gave it all done? it's because they have managed a way to figure out how to manage their time effectively.

Time management is more than just managing time. It is about controlling the use of the most valuable and undervalued resource. It is managing oneself in relation to time. It is setting priorities and taking charge of the situation and time utilization. It means changing those habits or activities that cause waste of time. It is being willing to adopt habits and methods to make maximum use of time.

With good time management skills one is in control of one's time, stress and energy levels. One can maintain balance between one's work and personal life. One finds enough flexibility to respond to surprises or new opportunities. It is not how much time one has, but rather the way one uses it. The bottom line is well one manages time.

"Internationally Known Authority" on Time Management Dr Alec Mackenzie in his book. The time trap argues the very idea of time management is a misnomer because one really can be managed: Financial capital, physical capital, human capital, information and time. While each of the first four can be augmented, reduced, tranferred on otherwise controlled. Time cannot be manipulated.

Dr. Mackenzie contends that when it comes to time, one can only manage oneself in relation to it. One cannot control time us one can control other resources—one can only control how one uses it. In the world in which we live, time cannot be replaced or re-created. It is therefore not for us to choose whether we spend or save time but to choose only how we spend it

SELF-ASSESSMENT

1. Examine the time management skills in agriculture.
2. Duscuss the time management skills in Industry.
3. Describe the time management skills in Service.

REFERENCES

Taking Control of Your Time, Boston: Harvard School Press, 2005.

Time Management: Increase Your Personal Productivity and Effectiveness, Boston: Harvard Business school, press, 2005.

Allen David, *Ready for Anything: 52 Productivity for Work and Life,* London: Viking Penguin, 2003.

Covey Stephen, R. Roger, A. Meril and A. Rebecca Merill *First Things First,* New York Simon and Schuster, 1994.

5

Time Management for Everyone

"You can't manage time, it just is. So "time management" is a mislalled problem, which has little chance of being an effective approach what you really manage is your activity during time, and defining outcomes and physical actions is the core process required to manage what you do".

—David Allen

"Time is really the only capital that any human being has, and the only thing he can't afford to lose".

— Thomas Adison

"Better three hours too soon than a minute too late to."

—Shakespeare

Content of this Chapter

Introduction, Time Management: The Big Picture, Time Management for Everyone, Conclusion

5.1. INTRODUCTION

Time management skills are your abilities to regonize and solve personal time management problems. The goal of these time management lessons is to show you what you can do to improve those skills.

With good time management skills you are in control of your time and your life, of your stress and energy levels. You make progress at work. You are able to maintain balance between your work, personal and family lives. You have enough flexibility to respond to surprises or new opportunities.

All time management skills are learnable. More than likely you will see much improvement from simply becoming aware of the essence and causes of common personal time management problems. With this time management lessons, you can see better which time management techniques are most relevant for your situation. Just get started with them. Many of your problems gradually disappear. If you already know to how you should be managing your time, but still you don't do it, don't give up. What you may be overlooking is the psychological side of your time management skills, psychological obstacles behind your personality. It's depending on your personal situation. Such obstacles may be the primary reason why you procrastinate, have difficulties saying no, delegating, or making time management decisions. The psychological component of your time management skills can alos be dealt with. The time management skills information below will point at a relevant solution for your situation. Now we shall discuss about the time management of big picture.

5.2. TIME MANAGEMENT: THE BIG PICTURE

Some people are natural time manageres. You know them. These are the people who never let their toast burn, who never leave a pile of clothes wrinkling in the dryer, who never leave their children stranded at a day care while the after hours charges accumulated. Other people have to work at time management. If you fall into this second category, there are some general guidelines for managing your time.

1. **Take responsibility for your choices:** This guideline is most important, You have chosen to be here. Law school is an enormous commitment of time and money. For many of you, law school is detour off of a successful career path, others of you have moved run just yourselves but your families to a new place and a new life in the Twin Cities. You have already made the big choice to be here. Time management just means following through on the smaller choices it takes everyday to succeed. Succeeding in law school "DOES NOT" mean you have to spend every minute studying. It does mean that when you choose not to study, you recognize that decision as a conscious choice.
2. **Be accountable to yourself for meeting your goals:** This guideline goes hand in hand with the first. You take responsibility, you pay the price for your choices. Imagine you have set the goal of outlining personal jusrisdiction over the weekend. You planned to want Friday, night, but a friend invites you a movie. You can go to the movie, but you have to pay the price. The "price" does not have to onerous, it can be simple spending Saturday afternoon in the library so that you get your outline done. The "price" should not be failing to complete the outline.

3. **A principle from budgeting pay your bills first:** Many people pay their bills these did by automatic withdrawals. That way, they know they have met their obligations before start spending the extra. Time management works the same way. Certain time is spoken for each day. That may include class time, a job, child care time, etc. Reading, outlining and time to complete legal writing assignments need to take priority right after the scheduled obligations. "TREAT STUDYING LIKE AN APPOINMENT". Put on your calender, just like a bill you must pay on a regular basis. That way, when the friend invite you that movie on Friday night, you will know clearly that you ARE MAKING A CHOICE, either to forgo your appointment with your civil procedure outline (and 'reschedule' it for later in the weekend) or to say not your friend and follow the original plan.
4. **Also from budgeting plan for emergencies:** Financial planners everywhere tell people to set aside a 'rainy day' fund. You need to treat your time the same way. DO NOT 'SCHEDULE EVERY MINUTE'. Leave some slack in your schedule for a flat tire, a sick child, an assignment that ended up taking twice as long as you thought it would. If the emergency doesn't happen, then you have the happy choice of using that extra time to go ahead in school or to kick back and enjoy the benefits of your new efficient lifestyle. Whatever you choose is fine, just make it a conscious choice.
5. **And a tip from dieting-save dessert for last:** Again, being a law student does not mean you

have to spend every moment studying. And sometimes a social opportunity arises that is just too good to pass up (yes, this can happen, even to law students). But in general, save the fun for last. See guideling No. 3. Pay your bills, eat the healthy balanced meals. DO YOUR HOME WORK. Then, if you have money, calories, or time left over by all means enjoy yourself. In fact, you will undoubtedly enjoy yourself more if you are no burdened with the guit of knowing you have left important tasks unfinished.

6. **Set realistic goals:** Outlining personal jurisdiction may be a realistic goal for a weekend. Outlining classes and completing your legal writing memo probably is not. No one starts a fitness regime by running a marathon. People who set unrealistic goals for themselves usually end-up discouraged, defeated and unlikely to keep trying. There will be times you won't make your goal, but you will come closer and have a greater chance of success if you keep those goals realistic. Over time, success at each small goal will add up achieving your ultimate goal success in law school.

Misconceptions About Time

There are several misconcepts which we all have about time. They affect everyone including those persons who may be quite successful and effective. Here are some of the misconceptions identified by Dr. Mackenzie.

(*i*) **"Time management is simple"**: According to Mackenzie the concept of time management is simple-all it requires is common sense. While it is true, that the concept is the self-discipline required to practice effective management is not easy.

(*ii*) **Work is best performed under pressure:** Psychological studies this to be no more than an excuse for procrastination. One does not work well under pressure only does the best one can under the circumstances. Pressure and challenge must not be confused. Lara's performance when the West Indies team is in trouble has more to do with application and determination rather than pressure.

(*iii*) **I do not have the time:** The effective worker or manager often gets more work done in the earlier hours of the morning than most laggrda get done in the whole day. He then no longer has to work against tight deadline and under stress which contributes to heart problems and not usually the ultimate reduction of time on this earth.

(*iv*) **Time management might be good for some kinds of work but my job is creative:** Time management is not about routine. It is about self-discipline. Lack of discipline prevents one from being great instead of simply good.

(*v*) **Time management takes away the fun and freedom of spontaneity:** Spontaneity is working under stress, forgetting appointments, making constant excuses and apologies to be fun? would it not be much more fun if by better organization one had one or two more hours everyday to spend with the family, to play games, read a good book, plan for tomorrow and the day and week after or just relax?

Symptoms of Poor Time management

Poor time management shows up by way of one or a combination of typical perceptible sysmptoms. Managers would do well to look for and reflect on whether they are subject to any of those symptoms with a view to take necessar corrective actions.

The following are some of the indicators of poor time management.

1. Constant rushing (e.g. between meetings or tasks).
2. Frequent delays (e.g. in attending meetings, meetings deadlines).
3. Low productivity, energy and motivation (e.g. I can't seem to get worked up about anything).
4. Frustration (e.g. 'oh', things just don't move ahead).
5. Impatience (e.g. 'where the hell is that information I have asked him for?').
6. Chronic vacillation between alternatives (e.g. "which-ever option I choose it is going to put me at a big disadvantage, I don't know which way to jump").
7. Difficulty setting and achieving goals: (e.g. I am not sure what is expected of me).

Why do/will I have so little time?

1. Management by crisis	• Paper work
2. Lack of planning	• Poor communication
3. Incomplete information	• Poorly organized meetings
4. Personal organization	• Leaving tasks unfinishing

5. Attempting too much
6. Inability to say no
7. Responsibility unclear
8. Ineffective delegation
9. Inadequate staff and resources

- Inadequate controls
- Lack of self-discipline
- Socializing
- Drop-in visitors
- Telephone interruptions

The Eleven Time Thieves

Dr. Donald E. Wetmore ("Time Thieves: The 11 Biggest Time-wasters Revealed") lists out the eleven 'inconsiderate troupe' of eleven thieves that gang up to steal some of the precious time away from productive use of managers.

1. **Poor planning:** Failure to see the value of planning and getting impatient to get something done are the causes of poor planning. Absence of a plan of action is likely to trigger off a false start, resulting in unproductive time utilization on the critical path of the task being understaken. Consequently, the managers might not find enough time for completing the task.
2. **Crisis management:** Most often, crisis management is an offspring of lack of prioritization of tasks. As a result of the inability to distinguish between the urgent, the important and the necessary tasks, unimportant tasks are likely to get done first at the cost of important tasks. Consequently, the managers are not likely to find enouth time to get around to the important things.
3. **Procrastination:** It is easy to put off tasks if they are not due right away. The trouble is tasks pile-

up and can force managers to run into a time crunch later. Procrastination is generally triggered off by the fear of failure success, perfectionism, wanting to do it all or incorrect priorities. It is a virtue to want to do a good job. But some people become so anxious about getting a job done perfectly that they never complete it. Managers should examine whether their effort to get the job perfectly are really improving things or preventing them from getting the job done.

4. **Interruptions:** Interruptions and distractions arise due to lack of planning, poor concentration over environment. They are unnecessary thieves of a manager's time and come in many forms-drop-in visitors, telephone, e-mails, unscheduled meetings, poor communications and confused chain of authority, etc. Managers should be less willing to automatically give away their time just because they demand it. They should learn to distraction if they are to get work done. They should work in areas they are less likely to be disturbed and tell people when they are busy and cannot be disturbed.
5. **Not delegating:** Wanting-to-do-all by oneself is yet another thief that could left the managers lose control. They feel that employees can never do anything as well as they can. They fear that something will go wrong if someone else takes over a job. They lack time for long-range planning because they are bogged down in day-to-day operations.
6. **Unnecessary meetings:** If a meeting is held without

a specific agenda and nothing productive comes out of it, clearly that meeting was unnecessary. Obviously, such meetings are thieves as the time is wasted and things just do not get started.

7. **The "shuffling blues"**: Managers often waste much time because of disorganization. Keeping things that they need in a specific place, eliminating clutter, making sure that they have all the materials or information that they need before starting on the task and following a day-planner on schedule will keep the "shuffling blues" away at the work place.
8. **Poor physical setup**: Not having the things that the managers need frequently within easy reach and having a lot of the things that they seldom require close by results in wastage of a lot of time, wearing out the carpet, retrieving what they frequently need. And of course, as they pass others they will often pull them aside to steal some of their time.
9. **Poor networking:** Quality relationships with employees and others can be a substantial time-saver as they open doors for the managers with all kinds of opportunities. Failing to develop a good network base will cause them to waste time creating what they might have had through their network.
10. **Bad attitude:** Nothing sinks a day more effectively than having a poor attitude. It causes the managers to dwell on the problems and not the solution and makes it possible to throw the day way. When they

are burdening others with their problems and complaints they are forefitting their valuable time.

11. **Negative people:** Being surrounded by negative people could means the managers are spending a lot of their listening to them but getting nothing much or purposeful from them. Obviously, avoiding such people will help the managers to minimize wasted hours and get some of their productive time back.

How much time do your spend such day on the following time stealers?:

1. Watching TV
2. Reading newspapers/Magazines excessively
3. Idle chat, gossip and telephonic talk
4. Opening and sorting mail
5. Returning telephone calls
6. Meetings
7. Paying bills
8. Day-dreaming
9. Fretting over personal problems
10. Caught in traffic snarls
11. Planning how to change things
12. Waiting for things to happen
13. Taking naps
14. Eating snacks between meals
15. Drinking
16. Smoking
17. Shopping
18. Wagering money.

Monochronic and Polychronic Views of Time

Just as a person's overall personality is made-up of and reprensented by his or her traits, a person's time personality is made up of a series of time styles—monochronic or polychronic. It is expected that a person's awareness of the monochronic/polychronic side of personal time style affects his or her overall approach to time use, perceptions of time pressure and the amounts and order of time spent on tasks. This, in turn, affects his or her personal efficiency.

Monochronic approach to time management is essentially objective and lays emphasis on promptness, speed, brevity and punctuality. It is a very efficient and focused way to manage work and life. Monochronic time manageres are those who thrive on detailed planning and organization. They refer to focus on one task at a time and they follow a schedule from which they don't like to deviate. They tend to get upset by distractions or interruptions and are inclined to put new tasks off until a later date, when they can be worked into the schedule.

Polychronic approach to time management is subjective and lays emphasis on inspiration, imgination flexibility, intuition, and dedication. Trust, bonding pleasure and quality of life influence more strongly the decisions of a person who 'ticks' in polychronic time. Polychronic time managers prefer to have many projects under way simultaneously, enjoy changing from activity and are unflustered by distractions and interruptions. Unlike their monochronic, counterparts, polychronic managers believe they perform well under pressure.

Monochronic Managers	Polychronic Managers
1. Do one thing at a time	Do many things at once.
2. Concentrate well	Are highly distractible and subject to interruptions.
3. Take time seriously	Consider time commitments and objective to be achieved, high possible
4. Low context, need information	High context, have information
5. Are committed to the job	Are committed to the people
6. Adhere religiously to plans	Change plans often and easily
7. Are concerned with not disturbing	Are more concerned with
8. Seldom borrow or lead	Other closeness than privacy
9. Emphasize promptness	Base promtness on the relationship
10. Are accustomed to short-term relationships	Strong tendency to build lifetime relationships

Clearly, monochronic approach is better suited for dealing with routine and predictable task, while polychronic approach is better suited in dealing with such as creating a new concept or resolving an argument. Conflict arises when managers apply a monochronic style to a situation that demands polychronic time, or managers prefer polychronic style while the situation warrants the use monochronic style.

So how do the managers cope with a healthy need for subjective, polychronic, self-imposed time and at the same time fit in with the monochronic and objective time measures? The only way managers can figure out which method works best in a given situation is based on sound reasoning and acumen.

How can Yet an Extra Hour Out of Each Day?

Here, are some tips to help you squeeze those extra minutes out of your day. Of course, you can adapt these so that they will fit in with your situation.

1. Get up earlier.
2. Watch less TV (I mean how many law and order spin offs one need to watch?).
3. Avoid allowing others to waste your time.
4. If you don't have to drive to work, use that time to study or plan. If you do drive to work listen to motivational tape on the way to work instead of that mindless talk.
5. Organize your work, do it systematically.
6. Make creative use of lunch time.
7. Dlegate authority if possible.
8. Spend less time on unimportant phone calls.
9. Think first, and then do the task.
10. Do what you dream about doing, instead of just dreaming about it.
11. Work hardest when you are the most mentally alert.
12. Eliminate activities that make the smallest contribution to your life.
13. Always do the toughest jobs first?
14. Before each major act task, "Is this really necessary?"

15. Choose interesting and constructive literature for spare time reading.
16. Learn how to sleep. Sleep soundly, then work refreshed.
17. Skip deserts.
18. Stop smoking.
19. Write notes or letters while waiting for others.
20. Always carry an envelope with paper in it and a few stamps.
21. Combine tasks that are done in the same area.
22. Be promp for all opportunities.
23. Lay out your clothes the night before.
24. Call on specialists to do work that you do efficiently.
25. Learn to read more rapidly.
26. Take a nap after dinner. Then take a shower. Begin the evening hours relaxed and refreshed.
27. Avoid interruptions.
28. Avoid making a big production out of tiny tasks.
29. Search out job shortcuts.
30. Know your limitations.
31. Work to your full capacity. I know it's tough to break bad habits. However, it is necessary to make sacrifices so that your business can be successful.

Elements of Effective Time Management

Time goes by the same rate no matter what one does. One cannot speed it up or slow it down. Unlike the other resources that one manages, there is no way to control time. The best one can do is take charge of oneself in the framework of time, investing oneself in those things that matter most in one's life.

Effective time management requires reducing the impact of the time stealers and increasing the effectiveness of a manager getting the things done that need to be done. The following are the important elements that combine to enable a manager eliminate distractions, interruptions and inefficiencies in the work process to make the most of time management.

(A) Evaluating How Time is Used

The first step of effective time management is identifying how a manager is using his time. This can be done by.

(*i*) **Activity time log:** The first to managing time better is to find out how managers are currently spending their time. Keeping a time log is a very effective way to do this. Through an activity time log, managers can make a list of the activities or tasks that they spend time on. The very act of measuring is often enough to raise their unconscious habits into their consciousness, where they then have a chance to scrutinize and change them. Time log requires that managers track all the tasks including the routine tasks such as commuting, reading a newspaper, eating and attending etc- in a systematic way and the successive sequence from the start, through the end of the day.

(*ii*) **Goal setting:** Why is goal setting so important in time management? From the time management perspective, a person's life is a sequence of big and small choices and decisions. It is those choices that a person really manages, not the flow of time. A key difference between successful and unsuccessful manager is the quality and practality of the goals they set for themselves. Goals state clearly the measurable and specific results to be accomplished by the managers and the time frame to attain them.

Goal setting is the wisdom that comes from practical experience that helps manager direct their conscious and subconscious decisions towards success. The process of setting goals helps manager choose where they want to go in personal and professional life. By being aware of precisely what they want to achieve, they know the efforts required for it. Goals helping in monitoring the day-to-day activities and ensure the activities are progressing in the right direction.

(*iii*) **Defining priorities:** Prioritizing means " taking conscious control of one's choices and deciding to spend time on the activities that are important and valuable, and less time on the ones that are not. . . ." The importance of prioritizing tasks or activities is best driven home by the popular 'pebbles and jar' parable.

One day, an expert in time management was speaking to a group of managers. As he stood in front of the group of high-powered over-achievers he said, "okay, time for a quiz" and he pulled out a gallon, wide-mouth mason jar and set it on the table in front of him. He also produced about a dozen first-sized rocks and carefully placed them, one at a time, into the jar. When the jar was filled to the top and no more rocks would fit inside, he asked "Is this jar full?" Everyone yelled, 'Yes'

Probably not, one of them answered

"Good", he replied, he reached under the table and brought out a bucket of sand. He started dumping the sand in the jar and it went into all of the spaces left between the rocks and the gravel. Once more he asked the question, "Is this jar full?"

"No !" the audience shouted.

Once again he said, "Good". Then he grabbed a pitcher of water and began to pour it in until the jar was filled to the brim. Then he looked at the spectators he asked, "what is the point of this illustration?" one eager beaver raised his hand and said, "The point is, no matter how full your schedule is, if you try really hard you can always fit some more things in it!"

"No", the speaker replied, that not the point. The truth this illustration teaches us is, "if you don't put the big rocks in first, you will never get them in at all. "What are the big rocks in your life, time with loved ones, your faith, your education, your dreams, a worthy cause, teaching or mentoring others?

(*iv*) **Scheduling activities:** After identifying the activities and prioritizing them, it is time to create a schedule. When scheduling, it is important to plan to weekly schedule as well as a daily schedule. The weekly schedule is important for the overall success of the activities and tasks, but it is the daily planning that will help one to track one's progress and determine whether or not one is on schedule.

Managers should try using significant project milestones in their weekly planning but for daily planning break each milestones down into the necessary components and plan the completion of those components on a daily basis. It is helpful to keep one's schedule in an appointment book or electronic organizer, but for purposes of planning one can use a scheduling grid as follows:

How we waste Time

1. Lack of Discipline	• Inability to say "No"
2. Indecisiveness	• Poor delegation skills
3. Personal disorganization	• Day dreaming
4. Procrastination	• Worry

Time Waste — Caused by others

1. Telephone Interruptions	• Unscheduled Meetings
2. Drop-in-visitors	• Poor Communications
	• Confused chain of authority

5.3. TIME MANAGEMENT FOR EVERYONE

1. Time Management for Working Women

Time Management: Making Time Your Friend

(*i*) **Establish your purpose (mission) for life:** Ask yourself "what am I living for?" What do I want my life to count for by the time I am 30?" What will I have want to have accomplished? Write them down. A happy woman is one who knows where she is going.

(*ii*) **Establish your goals:** Keeping your purpose in mind, establish the lifetime measurable goals: five year goals, goals for the coming year, one week, one month, three, six, nine and twelve month goals. Be realistic and make your goals measurable, so you will have a sense of accomplishment when you have reached them. Don't have too many goals or you will frustrated if you don't reach them.

(*iii*) **Establish your priorities:** List the things that you have to do each week. Also list the things that you would like to do including some time for yourself. Think through which activities are most important. Ask yourself if each activity is necessary? Are there responsibilities that can be delegated to others? Remember that "the good is often the greatest enemy of the best."

(*iv*) **Make time to plan:** Do yearly, seasonal and weekly planning. Evaluate if you are really accomplishing the goals that are important to you. Remember that a little planning saves your time in the long-run.

(*v*) **Have a flexible weekly schedule:** In planning leave ample space for interruptions. Be flexible, your schedule is to help you and not to run you. The purpose is not to cram two days itno one. The purpose is to learn to life happily with time, to relax, to have the sense of satisfaction that your life is in control and you are accomplishing daily the things that are the most important to you. At first, you may find it helpful to keep track of how long it takes you to do certain chores so that you can plan more realistically for the coming weeks. Buy and use a yearly, monthly and weekly planner. Take it with you wherever you go. Keep your addresses and phone numbers in the same book.

(*vi*) **Live one day at a time:** List 3 or 4 things that you would like to accomplish that day and number them according to priority. Tackle your top priority item first. Don't plan too much or you will be sure to be frustrated.

(*vii*) **Time robbers:** Be careful about "time robbers" – too much talking on the phone, television, Internet, sleeping, crafts, window shopping, etc. Learn to say "no". Be selective in what you do.

2. Time Management for House Wife

Personal Growth through Time Management

Managing your time is all about being focused. If you look at the Pareto Principal: the 80:20 rule states that 80 percent of efforts that are not time managed or unfocused generates only 20 percent of the desired output. However, 80 percent of the desired output. However, 80 percent of the desired output can be generated using only 20 percent of a well time managed effort. It is designed to show you how much you can accomplish with time management.

Many people view time management as making lists, appointments and task output. While all those are basics of time management. It also goes much further. The basic skill of making a to-do list can be fine tuned to make a more produtive and helpful list to accomplish more than you intended.

Another meaningful part of time management is

intelligence and discipline the more knowledge you are about a task the quicker you can get it done. For example, if you learn how to write list posts quickly, you can cut posting time in half just with experience.

Life management is the same principal, everything you to do can help you manage your life, short-cuts to work, how to maximize your gas mileage, budgeting, etc. Are all skills that can help you accomplish more things in less stress. Being balanced and happy is more important that just time management. Many people fail to see this and think that in order to. be good at time management you have to be doing something all the time. Relaxing should be on your list, some see relaxing as a negative time management exercise, but it is not about being busy, it is about getting results.

The six areas to try to improve are physical, social, intellectual, career, emotional and spiritual.

The physical aspect involves having a healthy body, less stress and fatigue.

The intellectual aspect involves learning and other mental growth activities.

The social aspect involves developing personal or intimate relations and being an active contributor to society. The career aspect involves appropriate feelings and desires and mainfesting them.

The spiritual aspect involves a personal quest for meaning.

You don't have to 'plan' for every area, but analysing and determining. What areas you are neglecting in your life can be very helpful. If you are not happy with your health, you need to assign some time each day to help that, be it taking a day off, or just a cat nap or working out at lunch.

One good exercise is to make and review goals on a regular basis. This includes both short-term and long-term goals in each of the six areas. You can make this take easier by having the list printed and within easy reach to review when needed.

Determining your best time to work may be a trial and error process, knowing when not to work is sometimes as important as knowing when to work. Another tip to help personal growth and not just production is learning to say no. This is a tough one for me that I am constantly working on.

Setting up rewards for getting something done is a great motivator, watching a lifetime movie in exchange for making 3 posts a day is a good one for me. Also procrastinating is a morale killer, try to get the task done, it can be that bad and you will end-up feeling worse about not getting it done that you would feel just doing it.

Positive attitudes and positive thinking help to keep you going, keeping a journal and list of accomplishments can help greatly as well. These are just some of the things you can do to do more than just manage your time. Time management is not just getting things done it is the art of building a happier and healthy life. What are some of your life goals and steps you would like to change?

What are you Really Living for?

Create a value-based time management plan. "I wish, I would spent more time at the office." History has never recorded these as anyone's last words. I am fairly sure it never will. "I wish, I would spent more time with my family" is a much more likely deathbed sentiment. List the three life that mean the most to you. Taken together, they might be your reason for living.

Here's how American's completed that list in a recent national survey. The number listed next to each item indicates the percentage of people surveyed who listed it among their top three priorities. (So obviously the numbers add-up to more than 100 per cent).

Priority	Percentage
1. Family life	68 per cent
2. Spiritual life	46 per cent
3. Health	44 per cent
4. Financial situation	25 per cent
5. Job	23 per cent
6. Romantic life	18 per cent
7. Leisure time	14 per cent
8. Home	11 per cent

Got your list? Good. Now next to each of the three note the amount of time you spend on it each week shocked?

If you aren't spending large chunks of time on the three elements you have listed as the most important priorities in your life there are three possible explanations.

1. Important things don't necessarily require a lot of time.
2. You are mistaken about your priorities.
3. You are n't putting your time where your priorities are.

1. Does the Way You Spend Your Time Truly Reflect Your Values?

The Myth of 'Quality Time'.

Two strong social forces combined to move Harriet Nelson and June Cleaver out of the kitchen and into the workforce.

First, we began to require two salaries to keep up with our increasing material expectations. In 1985, less than 2 percent of American homes had on players in them, and only about 7percent had answering machines. These are our new necessities.

At the same time, women began giving public experssion to the notion that being just a housewife didn't allow them to develop fully or to take their place as equal partners with men sin society. They didn't just need jobs, they wanted careers. As more and more farmer stay-at-home moms took jobs outside the home the myth of the super woman developed. "You can have it all" translated into "You must do it all"!

2. Time Management for Kids

Time management is an organizational concept traditionally associated with adults and the workplace. The experts tells us that more efficient use of time means greater productivity. So organizations encourage individuals to prioritise, plan ahead and make the most of the time that they have at work.

It is important that working parents are good managers of time so they can meet the demands of children and partners, keep a boss happy or a business a float while maintaining some personal time. Sound planning helps us to lead a balanced life because it increase the use of discretionary time at our disposal.

Time management is not just for adults. Kids also benefit by putting some basic management techniques into practice.

In the early years of school you can help kids to become organized by displaying in a simple chart which outlines special activities for each day. Encourage children to refer to the chart each morning and plan ahead. For instance, if, Tuesday is library day they can pack their borrowing bag and any books to be returned.

As children learn basic time concepts such as weeks and months give them a calender to place on their bedroom wall. They can cross off the days or countdown until special events such as birthdays or the end of term. They can also use a calender to plan each day including their after school activities.

As children progress to upper end of primary school more complex management and planning skills are needed, particularly to deal with home work. In fact, year six teachers include some time management in their programs as they know that children with good organizational skills are more likely to cope with secondary school where they have multiple teachers who all set homework.

Parents can help upper primary and secondary students better manage their time in the following ways:

1. **Provide your child with a student diary:** You may convert an old exercise book into a diary or buy one designed for young students. Encourage children to place important events such as after school activities and daily home work in their

diaries. My eleven year old son sits with my wife adn I each Sunday night as we compare our diaries for the coming week.

2. **Teach your child to break complex:** Homework tasks such as projects into smaller jobs and then plan out the work. If a project is due in tco weeks, work out what needs to be done and work backwards from the due date.
3. **Encourage children to measure the time they spend on:** home-work and encourage them to work efficiently and quickly. It is a common for students to think they have spent hours doing home work when really they have frittered much of their time away sharpening pencils, arranging books or playing games on the computer. Sometimes establishing a set time such as thirty miutes is an effective way of encouraging kids to work quickly.
4. **Help children to prioritise their work if they are busy:** When teaching year six I used to encourage children to categorize their homework as either important. Urgent or Both. Important meant that the task needed considerable attention to detail or research before it could be completed, while urgent meant that it was due soon, usually the next day. If a student gave work a category B for Both then it was panic stations as they had a great deal of work to do in a short time. The point of this exercise was help students get on top of their work rather than leave it until the last possible moment.
5. A valuable time management technique for adults

and children is to establish a routine that suits individual physical requirements as well as schedules. My son is a night owl who can work really productively after dark wheras I have a daughter who tends to crash when the sun goes down. Both children have different homework routines that reflect their physiological differences.

Time management for children is primarily about self-management. I am not suggesting that children abandon their wonderful sense of spontaneity and slavishly regulate their days, however some basic planning strategies can help them deal with their loud.

4. Time Management for Student

As a student there are some basic principles of time Management that you can apply.

1. **Identify "Best Time" for Studying:** Everyone has high and low periods of attention and concentration. Are you a "morning person" or a "night person". Use your power times to study, use the down times for routines such as laundry and errands.
2. **Study Difficult Subject First:** When you are fresh, you can process information more quickly and save time as a result.
3. **Use Distributed Learning and Practice**: Study in shorter time blocks with short breaks between. This keeps you from getting fatigued and "wasting time". This type of studying is efficient because while you are taking a break, the brain is still processing the information.

4. **Make Sure the Surroundings are Conducive to Studying:** This will allow you to reduce disractions which can "waste time". If there are times in the residence halls or your apartment when you know there will be noise and commotion, use that time for mindless tasks.
5. **Make Room for Entertainment and Relaxation:** College is more than studying. You need to have a social life, yet, you need to have a balance in your life.
6. **Make Sure you have Time to Sleep and Eat Properly**: Sleep is often an activity (or lack of activity) that students use as their time management "bank". When they need a few extra hours for studying on socializing, they withdraw a few hours of sleep. Doing this makes the time they spend studying less effective because they will need a couple hours of clock time to get an hour of productive time. This is not good way to manage yourself in relation to time.
7. **Try to Combine Activities**: Use the "Two Fer" Concept. If you are spending time at the laund-romat, bring your psychology notes to study. If you are waiting in line for tickets to the REM concert, bring your biology flashcards to memorize.
8. **Important Things to Remember With Time management for College Students:** To all college students, one of the main differences of high school students from them is the eagerness to successfully handle their own time. If you start educating yourself with time management, you have a great advantage over other college students.

Parents are not always there to discipline you about being on time and the responsibilities of keeping a schedule. They are not at all times available to scold when you are about to go to school rate.

Time management is not neccessary just to create a good name at a future job, but it is as well requirement for a disciplined and orderly future. The anwer to successful time management is being able to become your self's supervisor.

1. **Keep your lasting objectives within your reach:** Make a plan to reach your objectives. You know where you are. You think of the possible ways that you can take to your destination.
2. **List all the things that you know:** Use a timetable to record your class schedules, social activities, and pastimes. When a future event is postponed or is reset for the next month, put it in a blank space in your timetable.
3. **Decide the things you want to do tomorrow before the day ends:** You can use a to do record for your everyday activities. Set the planned activities into their proper time and consider the rest of record.
4. **Make your plan work:** Sometimes, it is simpler to finish a work and directly deal with what we believe is a disruption. Still, there are time disruption progreses into rich clients. Follow your plan. If somethings require your consideration, put it into your timetable or if you think it is an emergency and needs urgent attention, ensure you reschedule your present task.

5. **Do the things that seems to be difficult for you:** Once the difficult task is done, the rest of your task will seem easier for you. But, if the difficult task is the one that stops you from starting, then begin with something simpler to encourage yourself that you can do it afterwards.
6. **Break things down the unreasonable:** Separating big homework into tiny parts will make it simpler to include them into your timetable. Also, you can pick your achievements as you complete each stage. It is more pleasing to think about what you have finished successfully that it is to worry over the things left for you to finish.
7. **Rules were made to be changed:** Give yourself time to become flexible. Allow yourself to deal with disruptions in your timetable. Also, designate time to do the task, make some time to enjoy yourself as well. Plan for leisure activities and think of them as essential ingredients of your day it can provide you with something to work on and study seriously and with priorities.
8. **Keep in mind, tomorrow is always there to welcome you:** Like other skills and abilities, it takes times to know how to correctly handle your time. Even the most proficient in time management has days when they do not properly meet their scheduled plans.

If you have failed once, it is not a reason for you to give up on time management. What you can do is to collect the pieces and begin a new schedule the following day. Check your timetable at the end of the week to know the things that work for you and did not work.

Just make sure to follow your timetable always to have a great time management in each day of your college life.

5. Time Management for Ph.D. Student

Time management for research training is linked to matching an emotional commitment to a project with a neccessary rythm of work. There are three main variations in the nature of all research training which require attentive management to evolve with a defined overlap into each other.

Doing a Ph.D.. should be fun, rewarding and be seen as a privilege. It's the only time in your life that you can spend 100 percent of your working time learning to do research, finding out new things, having freedom to pursue new areas and getting paid for it, without any administrative or other responsibilities. Those who stick it out to do so because despite the relatively poor pay, long hours and lack of security, it is all we want to do because of intellectual satisfaction it brings, the excitement of discovery, the freedom to make your own work schedule, the apportunities for travel, the pleasure of being in an international community of like-minded people and the possibility that we might actually help the human condition.

1. **Choose a supervisor whose work you admire:** Find out first what they have done and are doing and search to see how productive they are) located in a department or institute with good infrastructure (equipment, patient samples, seminar series, etc.),

and who has enough grant funding not to limit your project too muh.

2. **Get involved and take responsibility for your project:** This is probably the most important transition from the Honours Year. To be successful research you need to develop strong skills in independent and effective thinking, critical analysis, problem solving and time management. The only way to develop these skills is to take responsibility for your project. You need to immense yourself in your research and exercise your mind with every experimental plan and every experimental outcome, including failures, rather than looking around for people to blame. If you simply follow directions and close the door behind you at the end of the day you will never progress in research tenacity is essential.

3. **Work hard:** Don't think you can get away with a 168 hours week. You will need to work long days all week, and for part of most weekends. That gets you to closer to a 50-60 hour week, which is what you need if you want a successful career in academia. If research is your passion, this is actually easy to-do, and if it isn't your passion, then you are probably in the wrong field. You should be going to work because you want to not because you have to of course. Ultimately, the number of hours doesn't matter the only thing that matters is productivity, but unless you are a genius and very organized and very lucky, you will need to work this hard to get out enough good papers to make a good start in a scientific career.

The extra hours are the cause, not consequence of success.

4. **Play hard**: Take some weekends off, and reasonable holidays so, you don't burn out. But if your work is very dependent on people around you, don't plan to work over Christmas and New Year and then take your holidays when your colleagues are all hard at work. On the other hand, if you are totally autonomous and not using equipment that is liable to break down, the holiday season is a great time to work in place, and without competition for equipment.
5. **Read literature**: Both in your immediate area, and around it, both the current and the past. You can't possibly make original contributions to the literature unless you know what is already is there. See it is a challenge put an interesting paper on your supervisor's desk before they put it on yours! The best time to read paper is between experiments or in the evenings or weekends. Use this as an opportunity to spark thought-provoking scientific discussions. Your supervisor will be busy, but should always make time for these discussion.
   - Furthermore plan your days and weeks very carefully.
   - Keep a good lab book and write it up every-day.
   - Be creative.
   - Be active, not passive, in your approach to research.
   - Try to keep a three-part portfolio of sub-

projects that are 'safe' moderately safe and challenging.

- Go to as many seminars as you can and all of them in your general area.
- Make the most of any opportunities to attend a conference or workshop.
- Take a notepad and write down the action items when you meet your supervisor.
- Practise your writing in any way you can.
- Buy yourself a lap-top if you can possibly afford it.
- Make the most of any opportunities to talk about your work.
- Appreciate the most bio-medical research is very expensive and is mostly funded by taxpayer's money and private donations.
- Look ahead.
- Set yourself deadline and try to keep them.
- Plan to work abroad at some point.
- Think very early and very carefully about what you plan to do after Ph.D.
- Start collabarations.
- Talks to sales reps.
- Look for opportunities to write small grants.
- Joint professional societies.
- Take courses.
- Get involved in institute or department events.
- Work out if you are a good collaborator, or more suited to working alone.

– Ultimately to be a successful research scientist, you need to be at least four of the following:

(*i*) Extremely motivated,

(*ii*) Creative,

(*iii*) Very smart,

(*iv*) Very hard working,

(*v*) Very skillful in the lab,

(*vi*) Very lucky.

6. Time Management for Entrepreneur

It is often said that you should not put off till tomorrow what you can do today. Unfortunately for business owners, such immediately of action isn't always possible. Juggling priorities becomes on essential skill.

We operate for business, all based Birmingham, Ala: Amchex collection services, Legal Locator Nation Wide, and two furniture bsinesses, Happy Rents and Mr. King Furniture. All are fast growing. In 1994, and 2005, the four companies had total sales of about $20 million.

In 1992 and 2004, we are honoured as Alabama's top Blue Chip Enterprise Initiative designee. The programme sponsored by connecticut Mutual Life Insurance Co., the U.S. Chamber of Commerce, and Nation's Business recognizes small business that have overcome tough challenges and emerged stronger. (The challenge we face was adjusting to the momentous business impact of the 1996 federal tax code overhaw.)

Our success is in large measure a result of knowing how to respond to demands on our time. As, we have learned at time management seminars, such demands can be broken down into four categories:

1. **Important and urgent:** These demands are easy to assess. When a pipe bursts and water pours into your basement, there is little doubt about how you should be focusing your energies.
2. **Less important but urgents:** These are problems that require immediate action to keep a business running smoothly. An example is arranging back-up when a receptionist calls in sick or a truck breaks down.
3. **Less important and not urgent:** This is where most of us spend waste too much time. There are many businesses tasks that can be delegated. Such as the initial screening of job applications, you don't have to read every resume and routine bookkeeping chores.
4. **Important but Not Urgent:** This category covers endless payoffs. Planning is one example. There are tasks that make the most difference in how a company functions, yet a lack of urgency makes it easy to never get around to them.
5. **Prioritizing:** The prioritize business people often error by not giving those tasks that are important but not urgent, "high enough priority". Here are some of the things we do that have the biggest impact on your four companies.
6. **Weekly planning:** It's our highest priority. The two of us set aside half a day each week for a walk of six to eight miles. This is when we review what out goals are, what were doing to attain those goals, and what we are going to do in the future. By being away from our desks, we avoid interruptions and feel more creative.

7. **Visits to other successful companies:** It's easy to say, you don't have time for business trips because of your workload, but we have learned a number of important lessons including the time value of hiring the best people available and allowing them to work without interference, by visiting other successful companies.
8. **Being active in trade associations and in the community:** Trade associations meetings and conventions offer a wealth of information, ideas and contacts. Community services offer the opportunity to meet community leaders, improve quality of life, and enhance your own name recognition and list of contacts.
9. **Staying in touch with clients:** By doing so, we know what they want and need. That, in turn means we plan better and spend less time putting out brush fires.

Fundamental to effective time management is asking and re asking yourself these questions: "Is this how I am supposed to be spending my time?" Is there something more important. I could be doing? When the answer to this question is "no". You are maximizing your time potential and have your priorities in the right order.

7. Time Management for Producer

The need to achieve organic growth has led many agencies to raise producer goals and provide more incentives for new business production. They also have reviewed their sales process and what producers can do to be more productive. As a result, new sales approach is emerging which is helping producers gain and sales time and use that time more effectively. Following this approach means changing old ways and old habits, but the result can be dramatic. The key to this new approach is good time. management, which requires delegating, planning, qualifying and self-analysis.

1. **Delegating:** Top producers spend at least 30% of their time in new business sales acitivites. Many producers miss this mark because they spend too much time in other acitivites such as servicing customers or marketing accounts. People who fail to delegate usually believe that no one else is capable of doing the work or that coustomers will not accept anyone else. In fact, most agencies have experienced people who can handle these tasks well. And customers can be easily transitioned to work with these staff members once producers make the decision to delegate.

   Producers usually grow their books by initially working on smaller accounts and gradually selling larger accounts. Once the book reaches a large size, a producer's sales time becomes limited. To create more sales time, producers need to give up accounts to someone else in the agency. Larger accounts can be assigned to new producers whose salaries can be offset by the newly assigned accounts. Many agencies require their producers to shed accounts each year as part of the sales process.

2. **Planning:** Many producers will work on any size account and any class of business. Other producers targets accounts by size, niche and their fit with agency carriers. They pass on accounts that are too small or do not fit their profile of a desirable

account. Once the target account has been determined producers plan their prospecting activities to identify and research those accounts. Top producers devlop a list of key accounts, but they also have key centres of influence and referral sources. They gain prospects, not by taking call-in referrals, but by soliciting leads from their referral sources and current clients or by becoming active in civic organizations.

Producers who are most effective also plan their week's calls, constantly filing their calendars with sales appointments a week or two ahead. They also plan meetings with their service staff who benefit by knowing. When their producers will be available for questions and updates.

3. **Qualifying:** Producers who are good qualifiers ask questions designed to determine the prospect's fit with their target account. They want to find out, for example, whether the client is interested in the high quality products and services that the agency, offers, or if the only consideration is price. But, they also want to determine the client's interest in buying from them. If the client does qualify, the producer will want to determine whether the client will actually commit to buying. If certain conditions are met either in product or price, will the client agree to "fire" the current agent? If the producers does not get this commitment, the producer moves on to the next prospect.

Effective producers take responsibility for their part of the submission process. They take time with the prospect to gather information necessary to complete the application and follow-up the quickly to ask for additional information. In doing so, they have the many hours the service staff spend trying to construct applications with little information. They can also feel confident that carrier under writers will be able to work on the complete submission, rather than begin their own follow- up for missing information.

4. **Self-analysis:** Top producers understand that sales effectiveness comes from their own efforts to improve, so they review their sales, plans, their hit ratios, their led sources and their sales calls to see. What they can learn and where they can make improvements. They discuss sales calls with their managers or their peers and ask for feedback. They are students of sales who work at improving their are core sales skill, such as listening, questioning, positioning and closing. Their enthusiasm for their craft and their resulting success keeps them motivated.

8. Time Management for Professionals

Time management is a very important skill to master not only for our professional lives, but also for our personal well-being. Effective use of time enable us to work more productively, lower stress levels, and have more time to do the things we need and enjoy doing. Here are ten tips that will help your time management.

1. **Orgnize your work area:** File things where you will find them, not where you think they belong according to a category. Think "Where would. I find this?"

2. **Commit to a particular allotment of time for each project:** Allowing yourself an hour a day for taking an action on a new project will keep your momentum going without being overwhelming or boring.
3. **Do your most difficult work when you are in your peak performance state:** If you are an early morning person, do that extra-effort needed project first thing in the morning. It late evening hours are more your speed, save that high energy project for that time.
4. **Perform less demanding work at the time of day when you are most likely to be in a slump:** If mind-afternoon is your body's sluggish time, save your mindless tasks and other less improtant to-do for this time. The point is to get what you need done without wasting whatever time you have available to you at any given time.
5. **Schedule your phone calls around your peak performance levels:** You want to give your customers clients your very best attention and this requires energy and enthusiasm.
6. **Place your phone voice-mail mode at strategic times of the day:** Voice-mail is wonderful for those times when you are either feeling sluggish, want some quiet time, or just want to get a project done, you can access your messages later and return calls on a priority basis.
7. **Let others in your home (office know when you don't want to be disturbed):** Constant interruptions are annoying and distracting they are also

time zappers. Letting people know when it's ok to interrupt and when it's not is crucial to time management.

8. **Prioritize your day:** Everything's not an earth-sharttering emergency! Someone else's perception of a priority does not mean it is so to you. Discern what needs your attention immediately, what can be delegated, and what can be addressed later.
9. **Delagate:** Everything that needs to be done does not have to be done by you. Delegating to another person can save you, a lot of time in mandare tasking.
10. **Instead of a to-do list, create a goal for the day:** Throw out the to-do list that never gets done, causes you stress and frustration, and makes you feel like a failure. Instead, set yourself a single goal for the day.

9. Time Management For Teacher

At times, teaching can be overwhelming. You have stacks of papers to grade, conferences to attend, grades to calculate, e-mail to respond to and if, there is any time left teach. So much to do and so little time in which to accomplish it. Included herein are teacher tested ideas on how to save time without sacrificing the quality of your teaching.

Before instituting a time management plan, however you need to spend a few days simply observing and reflecting. Keep a notepad hereby. When you find yourself using your time in efficiently to it down. For example, do you spend a considerable amount of time explaninig to student what they need to do in order to makeup missed assignments? If your time taken up filling, e-mailing, phone-calls, disruptions, copying materials, taking attendance, repeating, directions? See, where your 'time leaks' are and then find a way to plug them. You may be surprised at the activites, that are soaking up your valuable time.

1. **Organization of the teacher:** Organization is the cornerstone of time management. A big time-waster, according to many teachers, is 'hunting and gathering'. That is looking for that missing lesson plan, collecting tools and equipment from students after completion of a project, searching out that IEP that was due yesterday, procuring books for a unit. Effective time managers are masters of organization. A place of everything and everything in its place is their motto.
2. **Used a daily planner:** Keep all your do list there. or, keep one clalendar handy and write everything on it that you need to accomplish. Some teachers keep a planner on their desk at all times. Some use large desk calendars. Whichever you prefer use it.
3. **Do not try to accomplish difficult tasks when you are tried:** Save those for your peak periods.
4. **Do not waste class time by calling out student's names in order to take roll:** One student one at work take roll.
5. **At the beginning of year, assign each student a number which corresponds to the numbers in your roll book:** Instruct students to put their

numbers on their papers. Then, when you collect the papers. Simply one student has put them in numerical order.

6. **If you have never tried "grade book' you may like it:** It can save your time by tallying grades, curving grades, allowing you to print the grades for a particular student, quickly seeing what assignments a particular student is missing, etc. Some are better than others.
7. Make transperiencies for directions to tasks.
8. Put out of storage all material that you will be distributing that day a place it in one area.
9. Create a list of classroom routines and procedures that will make the day flow smoothly.
10. Don't reinvent the wheel. There are literally thousands of lessons, units and thematic plans and interdisciplinary plans available on the internet. Go to search engine. Such as Google and type in keywords. It is a storehouse of terrific information for teachers.

10. Time Management for Leadership

Time in the organization is constant and irreversible. Nothing can be substituted for time. Worse, once wasted, it can never be recognized. Leaders have numerous demands on their limited time. Time keeps getting away and they have trouble controlling it. No matter what their position, they cannot stop time, they can-not slow it down, nor can they speed it up. Thus, time needs to be effectively managed to be effective.

On the other hand, you can become such a time fanatic

convert by building time management spread-sheets, creating priority folders and lists, colour coding tasks, and separating paper work into priority piles that you start to waste more time managing it to deeply.

What most people actually to do is analyse how they spend their time and implement a few time saving methods that will gain them the most time. The following are the examples of some of the biggest time wasters:

1. Worrying about it and putting it off, which leads to indecision.
2. Creating inefficiently by implementing first instead of analysing list.
3. Procrastinating.
4. Crisis management.
5. Unanticipated interruptions that do not pay off.
6. Unnecessary errors.
7. Poor organization.
8. Failing to delegate.
9. Ineffective meetings.
10. Poor planning.
11. Lacking priorities.
12. Micro managing by failing to let others perform and grow.

The following are examples of time savers:

1. Managing the decision-making process, not the decisions.
2. Concentrating on doing only one task at a time.
3. Throwing undeed things away.
4. Using checklist and to-do lists.

5. Adjusting priorities as a result of new tasks.
6. Keeping things simple.
7. Setting aside for reflection.
8. Knowing when to stop a task, policy or procedure.
9. Getting rid of busy work.
10. Not wasting other peoples time.
11. Establishing daily, short-term, mid-term and long-term priorities.
12. Maintaning accurate calendars, abside by them.

11. Time Management for Professors

'Remember', Benjamin Franklin once said, "Time is money". Most of us complain that we have too little time, yet experts estimate that the average person wastes up to two hours per day. If your office desk is messy, you have trouble locating things, frequently miss deadlines or important appointments, or often fell unprepared, you may have time management issues. There are four suggested strategies for time management.

1. **Set goals:** You need to carefully look at the professional and personal aspects of your life. What do you wish to accomplish in your career? Family? Finances? With your physical well-being? Set both long-term goals, and shorter, easily attainable goals that will move you forward. Be sure the goals you set are not only realistic, but that they are truly 'your' goals. Plan to reassess these goals periodically perhaps put a reminder on your early calendar to review them.
2. **Set priorities:** Look at your responsibilities and ask:

- What is the purpose of this job?
- What are the expectations?
- What are the priorities and deadlines?
- What are the measures of success?
- What are the acceptable costs?

3. **Develop a plan:** When working on your plan, think of it as really two plans—a "to-do list" and an "action plan". On the 'to-do list', list the tasks that need to be accomplished in their simplest units. Prioritize the list, and then re-order it. Try tackling the hardest task or the one you least like to do list. You may find you work best with a 'to-do list' for each day, each week or each month whichever methods works best for you stick with it, and try to refrain from carrying tasks over from the previous list.

   An action plan is a list of related tasks that are needed to achieve a goal. "For example, an action plan for getting a post-residency position might include: write to prospective groups in the area you want to target, line-up letters of recommendation from faculty, apply for a license in the state in which your want to work.

4. **Resources and delegation:** It's simple fact you don't have to do it all alone! In fact, you can accomplish with help. Be sure that you communicate clearly the importance of the task, the timeline and the benefits to the individual who will help you. Treat people well and they will be more likely to help you a second time.

In short, we can say that feeling healthy, getting

adequate sleep and making time for exercise. Acknowledging these priorities allows you to experience productive study time that leads to an enjoyable educational experience. Effective time management programs require you to establish priorities that will help you accomplish your goals.

12. Time Management for Farmer

Learning to control events, attitudes and responses day-in and day-out will help you manage those hectic, stressful time.

Perhaps you have noticed that some farmers crumble under the pressures of events that you find easy to handle or perhaps you have wondered how other farmers can go on inspite of the stress load they carry.

Control Events

To reduce the pile-up of too many stressful events at one time. Farmers can control some situations.

Stress Management for Farmer

1. Plan ahead. Don't procrastinate. Replace warn machinery parts during the off season.
2. Before the harvest discuss who can be available to run for parts, care for cattle, etc.
3. Set priorities about what has to be done today what can wait until tomorrow.
4. Plan your time. Say no extra commitments that you do not have time far.
5. Simplify your life. If possible, reduce your financial dependence on others.

6. Postpone stressful events within your control such us elective surgery.

Control Attitudes

How farm family members view situations is a key factor in creating or eliminating unwanted stress.

1. See the big picture: "I am glad that tire blew here rather than on that next hill".
2. List all the stresses you now have, change those you can accept the rest.
3. Shift from worrying to problem solving.
4. Turn your crises into challenges
5. Notice what you have accomplished rather than what you failed to do.
6. Set realistic goals expectations daily. Give up trying to be perfect.

Control Responses

1. **Relax:** Whether you are walking, driving or phoning, do it slowly and relax.
2. **Turn in your body:** Notice any early signs of stress and let them go.
3. **Take care of your body:** Exercise regularly and eat well-balanced meals.
4. Avoid smoking cigarattes.
5. Shake away tension as you work by vigorously shaking each of your climbs.
6. Take a break.
7. **Think positive thoughts:** "I will succeed".
8. Look for the human in evening you do.

9. Balance your work.
10. **Get help when you need it:** There are times when all of us can be benefit from professional help.

Furthermore farmer can manage four categories of time management:

1. Set Goals
2. Set Priorities
3. To-Do List
4. Develop a Plan.

13. Time Management for Software

Time panic is an "award winning" application for tracking time spend at the computer. If you need to keep track of the work, you do and when you do it and want to stay on top of tracking projects or your business, then 'Time Panic' is the ideal solution.

1. Improve your efficiency at work.
2. Keep on top of all your projects.
3. Keep an overview of all your priorities.
4. See where the time is going in your day.
5. See which projects/clients consume the most time.

Time is one of the most important assets you have. Learn to manage it and you will get more done, stay on top of your deadlines, improve efficiency and boost your productivity.

All of which can be achieved without having to spend more time at work. In fact, this time tracking tool can help you get the same amount of work in less time.

Let time panic put you back in control of your working and private life.

Features of Time Panic for Windows

Time management software has a vast number of features designed to make it easier your time. Whether you need to keep track of time because you charge for it simply was personal productivity. Time panic is the time management software you are looking for.

Time Tracking Features

1. Automatic logging of start time and end time.
2. Continuous display of your current working time in the task bar.
3. Day view and year view.
4. Commenting and categorization of activities by project, type and collaboration type.
5. Sub-projects.
6. Easy differentiation between chargeable and non-chargeable tasks.
7. Configuration of image buttons as activity templates. Hence just one mouse click to start a new activity and to stop the previous one at the same time.
8. Tacking of public holidays and days off (annual leave, sick level, flex time).
9. Specification of planned working hours and planned breaks.
10. Calculation of overtime.
11. Ease of adding or changing time tracking data later on.

12. Printable reports.
13. Export in an excel-compatible format.
14. Custom flags for activities and days that can be used as filter criteria in reports.
15. Configurable formats for date, time and duration.
16. Sharing of projects and work types.
17. Filters for reports, search functions.
18. Support for hibernation and stand by mode.
19. User defined key board short-cuts.
20. Reminder with automatic pause detection.

General Features

1. Multi-level undo and redo.
2. Auto save of all changes.
3. Can run in the notification area. It then display your current working time in the tool tip of the tray icon.
4. Set up and detail users guide. Upgrade from any previous version.
5. Unicode and XML support.
6. Demo-data.
7. Runs on USB drives.

Available Language

1. English
2. German
3. French.

14. Time Management for Family

Family Time Management: Tips for Daily Living

Juggling a family, a career and a relationship with our significant other can be a challennge for a family with two children ourselves, a husband in a demanding career, and being a work at home. Here is a list of tips for daily living that can help manage your time and may help make things a little less hectic.

1. Keep it simple, give two choices instead of asking "What do you want?"
2. Set limits on things like T.V., video games and phone chatter . . . for everyone in the household.
3. Make adjustments when you have to, you can't be everywhere at once.
4. Don't forget to consider your travel time, prep time, clean-up time, waiting time.
5. Deal with things as they happen (the mail came, sort it now instead of waiting until later also eliminates clutter that you would have to clean-up later).
6. Get involved in a car pool to get kids where they need to go, school, soccer, baseball, football . . . sharing these.
7. Follow routines and schedules, such as getting up at the same time and leaving at the same time daily . . .create a pattern (routine get home, do your home work, 30 minutes to watch TV/play game/read, dinner get a bath, quiet time, bed time).
8. Plan a head for holidays and weekends with activities and things to do. These are most chaotic times, even if you do something spontaneous instead at least you had a plan ready you can always use the plan for the following weekend.

9. The goal is to get it done, not make it perfect.
10. Have a menu plan to save loads of kitchen and shopping time and leave more time for talking and enjoying the evening together.
11. Give everyone their own alarm clock instead of being the "mom clock" and explain the consequences of not being up and ready to leave a time.
12. Minimize distractions (putting video games and T.V in cabinets that close does wonders in a house hold).
13. Set your priorities and adjust as needed, they can change monthly, weekly, daily.
14. Keep a to do list, things that need to be done, including time for yourself.
15. Have a family/household meeting to communicate each other goals and needs for the current time frame.
16. Likewise for the family time, set aside 30 minutes each day that eveyone is focused on doing something together . . .anything at all.
17. Follow a daily patterns or routine so that everyone is on the same page and knows what to expect.
18. Multi-task, put away the dishes while you are on the phone, or dust the electronics while you are waiting for a file to download.
19. Make room in the family budget for small outings like a trips to the movies or a day at the zoo once a month to get everyone out and about and having fun together.
20. Finally, remember that bed time, and not just for

the kids, set one for yourself too so you can good nights sleep.

(**Note**—Use/put proper photograph in 5.3 from Internet.)

5.4. CONCLUSION

Here, we discussed about the big-picture of time management. Furthermore, we can say that the concept of time management is not limited area. But, in Modern time, Time management is everywhere likewise time management for working woman, housewife, kids, student, Ph. D. student, entrepreneur, producer, professionals, Teacher, leadership, professors, farmer, soft-ware and family, etc.

Now that we have come towards the end of the book, we have realized that how our time gets wasted because we never thought of managing time in an effective manner. It is said that "time and tide waits for none". So our attempts would be to make the best use of time and prevent others from wasting our time too.

This chapter winds up all our observations on time management in this book. It summarizes as to what causes us to waste our time and suggests soulutions to save time as much as possible. It also offers tips to make the best use of time.

As with all the precious resources, "Time is a scarce resource." The wisdom lies in making the of it. Horace Mann says

"Lost, yesterday,
Somewhere between sunrise and sunset,
Two golden hours,
Each set with sixty diamond minutes,

No reward is offered,
For they are gone forever.

TIME TIPS

1. Count all your time as time to be used and make every attempt to get satisfaction out of every moment.
2. Find something to enjoy in whatever you do.
3. Try to be an optimist and seek out the good in your life.
4. Find ways to build on your sucesses.
5. Stop regretting your failures and start learning from your mistakes.
6. Remind yourself, "There is always enough time for the important things". If it is important, you should be able to make time to do it.
7. Continually look at ways of freeing up your time.
8. Examine your old habits and search for ways to change them.
9. Try to use waiting time review notes problems.
10. Keep a paper or a calender with you to jot down the things you have to do yourself.
11. Examine and revise your lifetime goals on a monthly basis and be sure to include progress towards those goals on a daily basis.
12. Put-up reminders in your home or office your goals.
13. Always keep those long-term goals in mind.
14. Plan your day each morning on the night before and set priorities for yourself.

15. Maintain and develop a list of specific things to be done each day, set your priorities and then get the most important ones done as soon in the early part of the day as you can. Evaluate your progress at the end of the day briefly.
16. Look ahead in your month and try to anticipate what is going to happen so you can better schedule your time.
17. Do first things first.
18. Have a confidence in yourself and in your judgement of priorities and stick to them no matter what.
19. When you catch yourself procrastinating ask yourself, "What am I avoiding?"
20. Find time to concentrate on high priority activities.
21. Put your efforts in areas that provide long-term benefits.
22. Be sure and set deadline for yourself whenever possible.
23. Delegate responsibilities when ever possible.
24. Ask for advice when needed.
25. Push yourself and be persistent, especially when you know you are doing well.
26. 80 percent of "crisis management" events are preventable.
27. One hour of planning will save 10 hours of doing.

SELF-ASSESSMENT

1. Describe the big picture of time management.

2. Discuss the time management for any five sector/ for everyone.
3. Examine the time tips in brief.

REFERENCES

Amos, Julie- Ann, *Making the Most of Your Time*, Oxford: How to Books Ltd., 1999.

Boehme-Ann, J., *Planning Successful Meetings and Events: A Take Charge Assistant Book*, New York: AMACOM Books, 1999.

Dobson, Ann, *Managing Meetings: How to Prepare for Them, How to Run Them, and How to Follow up the Results*: Oxford: How Books Ltd., 1994.

Mackenzie, R. Alec, *The Time Trap*, New York: AMACOM, 1997.

Mina, Eli, *The Business Meetings Sourcebook: A Practical Guide to Better Meetings and Shared Decision Making*, New York: AMACOM Books, 2002.

Rogak, Lisa, *Smart Guide to Managing Your Time*, New York: John Wiley and Sons, Inc., 1999.

6

Time Management for Goal Setting

"Effective goal setting begins and ends with time management. You must be able to balance your time in the best way possible in order to achieve your goals."

– Prof. Pearson

"Goal setting is another powerful process helping you think about your ideal future, and to motivate yourself to turn this ideal vision of the future into your reality one day soon."

– Prof. Black Berry

Content of this Chapter

Introduction, Time Management for Student Goal Setting, Effective Time Manangement Tips, Techniques. Tools and Strategies, Goal Setting Management skills and Time Management, Importance of Goal Setting and Time Management, Conclusion

6.1. INTRODUCTION

Why is personal goal setting so important in personal time management? From the time management perspective, your life is a sequence of big and small choices and decisions that you really manage, not the flow of time.

Personal goal setting is the wisdom that comes out of a lot of practical experience and psychology research to help you direct your conscious and subconscious decisions towards success, building up your motivation to achieve your personal or business goals.

Generally essential goal setting guidelines an effective expression of the important goal setting guideline is that you should set 'SMART' goals. What the SMART goal setting guidelines actually mean is that your goals should be—

1. Specific
2. Measurable
3. Attainable
4. Rewarding
5. Timely

1. Specific

With a specific goal you can clearly see that what it is you want to achieve, and you have specific standards for achievement. In making your goal specific it is important that you actually write them, which is crucial in all good setting guidelines. The more specific is your goal, the more realistic is your success and the shorter is path to it.

When you work on making your goal specific, your programme your subconscious mind to work for you. Then your feelings and thoughts will lead you to your goal instead of pointing at the obstacles. To make your goals specific you also need to work out the other components of SMART goal setting guidelines below.

2. Measurable

For a goal to be measurable you need a way to measure the progress and some specific criteria that will tell you when you can stop and the goal is achieved. Feeling the progress is very important for you to stay motivated and enjoy the process of achieving the goal.

3. Attainable

An attainable goal is a good for which you see a realistic path to achievement and reasonable adds that you get there. This does not mean that the lower you aim the more likely you reach success. It is well known that goals are work best have a challenge in them. They are chosen as ambitious as possible, but still reachable. Then they will give you more motivation and sense of achievement.

4. Rewarding

A goal is rewarding when you have clear reasons why you want to reach that goal. This is one more place where it is important that the goal is really yours. Have your specific reasons and expected reward in writing. If, possible even with some visual pictures.

Imagine how you are going to feel when the goal is finally reached. This will ensure that the goal is realy worth achieving. Then, every time you get stuck and don't feel motivated enough, read your reasons and look at the pictures. This is a known and very powerful practical technique of how to get through difficult moments and cannot quit.

5. Timely

The fifth requirement of the 'SMART' goal setting

guidelines is that your goal should have a specific time limit. This is also very important for your subconscious mind. Besides, time is the price you pay for the reward from achieving a goal. Setting the deadline will protect you from paying higher price than the goal is worth. This is also your protection from procrastination and perfectionism.

6.2. TIME MANAGEMENT FOR GOAL SETTING

When you are a student, one of the last things you have on your mind is setting goals, it feels like you just want to have fun all the time.

1. Review Weekly

Each week you should set aside one hour here you make sure that you are keeping up to date in your goals and this time can be used to set tasks for the next week. Make this on a day when you have some free time and you can relax, once this is done you are set for the rest of the week.

2. Set Time Quota Goals

Set a goal that you will do all your homework on a certain day of the week. That way you save the time it takes going back and forth between homework, you get in homework mode making you more effective also.

3. Stop Watching TV

Do you know how much an average person watches TV? Hours per day. Now that might not sound too drastic. But let us say that you watch 4 hours per day, that's 2 months of constant time, no sleeping that you use-up per year. Now I know lots more important and fun things. I could do with that time. Get assignment in earlier, increase my income, etc.

4. Set Goals per Subject, But not Too Many

Set different goals per subject depending on what you want to achieve and how good you are at the subject. Do not set too many though as you will feel overwhelmed.

5 Follow a Good System

By following a good system goal setting for student you can minimize the amount of the on setting and achieving the goal and spend more time doing what you love best.

Now the problem is, how do we set those goals and successfully achieve them?

Starting is always the hardest. Just thinking about your goal and thinking that you already have it is the easiest, because you are not taking steps. To start taking steps, in the evening for yourself write a task that you have to do the following day. Start with 10 push ups. Next evening you increase the step but surely, you will complete your goal.

Put yourself, because if you will not push yourself you have to remember that nobody make a decision and commit to it. Taking baby steps will help you get started. With time will become a giant step and soon your goal will be complete. When your goal will be complete, you feel good about the results that your getting and would want to do more.

How to Reach any Goal

Have you ever had a dream or an idea that you were really excited about, but was so big, it stopped you dead in your tracks? Those big, lofty goals are a necessary ingredient to success, yet so many of us let them weigh us down instead of propel us on. The absolute key to attaining any goal, and especially those big, lofty ones, is focus. Take one step at a time, and focus mainly on the present.

But how exactly does one go about focusing manily on the present? It's true that, at the same time, it's important to know (and, therefore, focus on) on your ultimate goal. I equate it like this.

Let's say you are about to like up a small mountain (a large hill, really). You know where you want to go to the top of the mountain (your goal) and focus but you can't see it yet. Still, you know it is there. There is no doubt in your mind that the top exists. Your first focus is on the larger goal of the top of the mountain. So what is the next step?

The next step is to take a step your focus instantly comes back to the details the first step, then the next, and so on. Your eyes scan the path for any obstacles, but you know you can easily overcome them, because your focus is in the present and on the current steps you are taking, your goal is stell there, it's just not the centre of your current focus.

Have you ever been so absorbed in what you are doing that time files by? This is an example of present moment focus. If you concentrate on the step at hand, you will very soon find yourself at the end result! You got there, not by concentrating on the goal, not by anguishing over the goal, not by stressing out about it, but by your clear and consistent focus in the present moment.

The paradox of attaining a goal or manifesting a big

dream is that you must want your goal so much, and be willing to let it go. In other words, your focus must not create an unhealthy attachment to the outcome (the ulimate goal). You always know when you are detrimentally attached to your goal or dream, because a negative emotion will be present when you think if your goal (like hopelessness, despair, anger, guilt, blame, etc.) Any negative emotiion linked to a goal is telling you that you must change your perspective and look at it from the society.

So, when you think of a current goal, allow yourself to know that your goal it is possible there for you. Then, turn your focus on the present moment and the next small step that get you heading purposefully in the best direction to your goal. Remember, it's simply the steps that lead to the top!

How to Find a Reason to Set Goals in Your Life

You have chosen some life changing goals, weeded out the unrealistic ones, and turned the others into achievable ones. Just remember that writing down your goals is your first step. The second step is to take action to pursue them.

Have you ever seen people make new year's resolutions but they never reach their goal? The haven't given themselves a reason to do so. Goals give you a direction, but if you can't think of a good reason to pursue a goal, chances are good that you won't, no matter how important it may be.

People have all sorts of reason to pursue a change in their lives. Maybe they are sick of the rut they are in and have decided they are going to get out of this rut as soon as possible. Maybe they have lost a job or are about to lose one. May be they are just tired of barely scraping by and want a better for themselves. Maybe they want to finally live life on their terms and have no limits.

Whatever the case, people who take action have a reason. Once you have a reason to change, you will take action. If you don't have reason, so you probably won't change. It's simple as that.

The only reasons that matter are the ones you choose for yourself. If you find a personal reason for achieving a goal, you greatly increase the odds that you will reach it. It's easy to write down a goal, but it's much harder to stay motivated to keep working towards it.

A more effective way to achieve your goal is visualize them or day dream about them. You don't just write down and read your goals. Your image just yourself achieving your goals and visualize yourself living them. The more you can see your goals in your imagination, the more exiciting your goals will appear, helping you towards achieving it.

Visualization helps you see what you want before you even get it. The same principle goals. The more you see them, the more you will find yourself wanting them, and the more action everday to move one step closer to reaching them.

Create a Personal Strategic Plan

"Success is not an accident. It begins with a well-conceived plan". You can and will achieve more in the next year that you have in the past ten with a disciplined Personal Strategic Plan.

Personal strategic planning is a disciplined thought process, which produces fundamental decisions and action that shape and guide who you are, where you are going, what you do, and how, when and why you do it. All of this is done with a focus on the future.

The purpose of personal strategic planning is to help you:

(*i*) provide direction, meaning and purpose for your life.

(*ii*) make decisions that positively affect your future.

(*iii*) focus on your energies on what's most important.

(*iv*) achieve the greatest results in the shortest period of time.

(*v*) significantly increase your level of performance.

(*vi*) enjoy more time, money, balance and freedom.

(*vii*) eliminate uncertainty, anxiety, doubt and fear.

(*viii*) leverage your skills more effectively

(*ix*) enhance your quality of life, and overall peace of mind.

(*x*) Be more, do more and ultimately to have more from life.

Personal strategic planning is based on the premise that life will not go according to plan, if you do not have a plan.

(A) Successful plan must include the following:

1. **Personal Philosophy**: Every person has a personal philosophy, consisting of some rules, adopted from one's parents, culture, religion, acquaintance and so on.

   Generally, speaking this rules, as a body are not well thought out and contain a wealth of inconsistencises and contradictions.

2. **Legacy Statement:** Your legacy serves as your life's defining statement. It serves a twofold purpose. First it provides an overarching framework for all mission statements and goals to follow.

   Second it answers the question, "What do I want to be remembered for?"

3. **Mission Statement:** A mission statement is a declaration of who you are, why you exist and what you intend to accomplish. In business, the organizational mission answers the big question: "what is our business?" In personal planning the question is "what is my life's business?". In both cases, the answer must define the reason for being.

4. **Core Values:** Our values acts our compass, guiding us through life's terrain are certain way of knowing that you are living in accordance with your values is by defining guidelines and measurement for value centered living.

5. **Code of Ethics:** Words quietly influence our attitudes and opinions. Codes of conduct, personal creeds, and pledges all reflect an effort to make sense of things to organize behaviour, and to better understand ourselves.

6. **Lifetime Objectives:** Your objectives should be written with in the framework of your legacy and mission statements. The key to any personal strategic plan is to visualize your desired outcomes in advance. Be sure to write and re-write your life-time objectives as affirmations of the future you are working to realize.

7. **Goals:** The key in writing your goals is to make them measurable, specific and time bound.

   Goals needs to be written for each of the ten critical areas of life to include: Personal, Health, Recreation, Family, Friends, Community, Career, Financial, Household and Spiritual.

8. **Personal Board of Directors:** A personal board will aceelerate your progress by providing both wisdom and support for the attainment of a specific purpose.

9. **Maintenance and Performance Check-Ups:** On a monthly basis, you should pause to evaluate your performance. What progress have you made? Where have your been challenged? What do you need to differently or more of? It is also important to step back and consider whether any of your goals are unachievable.

10. **Personal Reason Why:** You won't become successful until and unless you identify, support and empower your reasons why. Your why's provide fuel for achievement, and are the reasons behind all action and inaction.

    The hallmark of all high achievers is a burning why. They know what they want, how and when they will achieve it, but most importantly they know why they want to become successful at achieving their goals.

    You can significantly increase the odds of success, if you know who you are, what you want, where you are going, how you will get there, and what you will do once you arrive.

    The best way to predict your future is to create

it. Therefore, a well-defined personal strategic plan, properly executed, is your meal ticket to success.

Daily Goal Setting and Self-Improvement

In this world, in which we live, it is easy to become stagnant, to be comfortable where we are. This leads to lazy, lower quality lives that get boring quickly. You may find yourself stuck in a rut, comfortable, but bored and getting nowwhere. Have you considered setting goals for yourself? Most of us make goals around the new year that we forget a week later.

Daily goal setting is an excellent way to improve yourself on a consistent basis. When you wake-up in the morning, what thoughts usually run through your mind? What you want to breakfast, or five more minutes, or what you have to deal with today? What if instead it was, "what small thing can I do today to better myself?"

When people picture daily goal setting, it usually involves writing something down. That can be can important step, but it certainly is not the only one. Once you have written your goal, set it in a place you will see it. One day it might be a task you want to complete or working hard to keep your temper with your family.

Perhaps the goal you choose is not something you can complete in one day. Those are called long-term goals, but they must be divided up into manageable, daily goal setting options. It might be a goal to lose weigh, to save money or finish reading that book. These are fine goals, but they must be broken down if they are to be accomplished. What will you do this very day to help you reach your goal of losing weight? It could be healthy breakfast today, an apple for a snack instead of pizza, and no dessert. These are short-term, achievable goals you can visualize taking you to your larger goal. Taking a long-term goal apart is essential in making personal progress.

Daily goal setting is for everyone who wants to continually work on becoming a better person. At the end of day, assess what progress you have made. May be slipped and lost could not resist that scoop of icecream. It's not end. There is always tomorrow. Here, the idea to have a time frame in mind for reaching long-term goals.

Goals: The 6 Universal Laws of Successful Goal Achievement

1. **The Law of Purpose:** Have a strong and clear reason for wanting to hit the goal that you set. This strong reason will keep you going when you are tested.
2. **The Law of Delayed Gratification:** Put off all non-essential gratifying pursuits until your goal is accomplished. You do not want to diffuse your focus. You want to consolidate your ambition by pointing at the successful achievement of your goal.
3. **The Law of Strategic Planning:** Strategically map-out the steps that are necessary for the accomplishment of your goal. Plan in advance what you intend to do in order to hit your goal. Layout a plan for taking the most direct route to completing your objectives.
4. **The Law of Consistent Effort:** Take consistent action towards hitting your goals. Do not back off. Keep a steady approach with your work ethic. As

you remain consistent you will gain momentum. Positive momentum will increase the ease with which you hit your goal.

5. **The Law of Positive Association:** Your association can help or hurt you. If you foster friendships with people who react negatively to you pursuing your goals you open the door to them hindering you. Their opinion and comments can affect you negatively. When you spend time with positive supportive people to opposite is true. You are inspired and uplifted in their presence. You do more because you feel better about yourself as result of being interacting with them.
6. **The Law of Accountability:** When you have an accountability partner your results are multiplied. You get a two advantages. You have someone who supports you and gives you feedback. You also have an added reason for doing the needy reason why you want to do what you set out to is because you said you would. You are a person that you would do it. It is hard to go back on your word. If you tell another person going to do something you usually try with all of your strength to do it.

6.3 EFFECTIVE TIME MANGEMENT TIPS TECHNIQUES AND STRATEGIES

Goal setting is a process that helps you get clear on what you want, make an action plan to help you get there, launch into action, and persist until you reach your destination or find a better one.

This process can significantly increase your probability

of success and achieving what you want. Research studies show a direct link between goal setting and enhanced performance in sports and business.

Earl Nightingale put it this way, "People with goals succeed because they know where they are going. It's as simple as that."

Why Personal Goal Setting Works

Texas oil Billionaire H.L. Hunt once said that there are only two ingredients necessary for success. The first is that you have to decide exactly what it is that you want.

This is where he believed many stumble. They never decide what it is that they really want.

They may think they want something from time to time, usually something generic and vague like "being rich" or "a better job", but it's just a fleeting thought, they never truly get clear on what these things really mean.

Hunt said that once you have decided what it is that you want, the second ingredient is to determine the price you have to pay to get what you want, and then resolve to pay that price by establishing your priorities and getting to work.

Many who get past the first ingredient never apply the second one. They don't understand that you have to pay the price in full before you can claim your prize.

You can think of goal setting as a process that helps you to decide exactly what it is that you want, and then to systematically pay the price in order to get it. It is a process that helps you focus your time and energy on your targets through careful and deleberate planning.

What is a Goal

A goal is a well-defined target that gives you clarity, direction, motivation and focus. Goals are tools that help you in five main ways:

(*i*) Make a positive change in your life.

(*ii*) Form a new habit or change an existing habit.

(*iii*) Improve or develop a skill, talent, or ability.

(*iv*) Realize a dream or other important outcome.

(*v*) Improve your performance on a task or activity.

We hear a lot of talk about how important it is to have goals. Goals give you a roadmap to your future. They provide something to strive for some point in the future to reach. But, what exactly is a goal, and how do you know when you have achieved it?

Someone expert has to defined that a goal as a specific, intended result of a strategy. So lets examine it a little more closely.

First, the definition tells us that a goal is specific. When you set your goals, you want to be a specific as possible. Setting goals is a focus your attention on what you want in the future. If you are not specific, you will never know where you are going. It would be like trying to follow a map that has no street names. You would have an idea of where you wanted to go, but no real way of knowing how to get there.

An example of a goal would be "I want to go back to school and get a Bachelors Degree in English." This is very specific. It's not just stating. I want to go back to school. It's stating exactly what type of degree you want to obtain. Think about it, if you just use I want to go back to school as your goal, there are still many unanswered questions.

Like which classes should you take, and where you do you want to go to school? If you state that you want a degree in English, you will able to plan which classes to take, and it may narrow down your search for a school, as only certain schools offer degrees in English.

Next, the definition says that a goal is an intended result of a strategy. When you set a goal, keep in mind that it is a result not a step in the process. The process is the strategy.

Looking at our example above of going back to school getting a degree in Engish is a result. But, there must be a strategy. You aren't just going to walk on to a college campus and be awarded a degree in English. You must develop a strategy to deal with things like which school to attend, how to pay for school, and how many classes to take at one time.

The end result the goal is a degree in English. The strategy is all the steps it will take to get there. Also a Degree is a pretty big goal. You can break that down into smaller goals. For example, you could say, "I want to finish 4 clases by the end of the year." That is a specific result. But, it is a smaller goal than obtaining the degree.

Setting smaller goals that lead up to the larger goal is a great way to progress through your plan. It gives you steps to look forward to that you can celebrate along the way to the larger goal.

Another important aspect of setting a goal is having a plan or strategy to achieve that goal. Writing down your goal also makes the goal more powerful. It has been proven that when people write things down, they are more likely to focus on them and achieve their goals.

Think about where you want to be in the next five years. What kind of work do you see yourself doing? Is it related to the kind of work you are currently doing? If you do not know what you would like to do, and feel like you can't picture yourself in five years. Start smaller ask yourself, what you would be doing if money were no object. If you did not have to work for a living what would you do? Examine your answer to that question. Is there some small part of that passion that you could develop into a career? Once you have an answer to those questions, think about what you could do today to begin moving toward that future. If doesn't have to be a big step, it could be as small as researching a degree, a company, an occupation.

Goal Setting: Why Should I set Goals?

The fact is that goal setting works! Research studies have shown a direct link between goals and enhanced performance in both sports and business. Earl Nightingale put it this way, "people with goals succeed because they know where they are going. It's as simple as that."

Top Reasons to Set Goals

1. **Goals can give you a target to aim for:** Dr. Maxwell Maltz, author of the classic Psycho-Cybernetics, said that human beings have a built in goal seeking "Success mechanism" that is part of the subconscious mind. This success mechanism is constantly searching for ways to help us reach our targets and find answers to our problems. According to Maltz, we work and feel better when our success mechanism is fully engaged going after clear targets.

All we have to do use this mechanism is to give it a target. Without one, our success mechanism lies dormant, or worse, pursues targets we didn't consciously choose.

Goals provide your success mechanism with clear targets of your own choosing based on what is most for you.

2. **Goals can help you concentrate your time and effort:** One important reason goal setters achieve such out-standing results is that they have learned how to focus and concentrate their time, energy and resources on a single objective, even if it is just for a few hours at a time. Their concentrated power can produce results that are much greater than those achievable through the diffused and unfocused energy many people use to get through their days.

   A clear example of the power of the concentration and focusing of energy can be seen in a simple magnifying glass. The light from the sun arrives at the earth as diffused energy.

   We know the energy is there because we can feel the heat from sunlight on our skin. When this diffused energy is concentrated through a magnifying glass, and then focused on a specific point, it can easily burn a piece of paper or wood. The same amount of energy that in one instance could only produce a very slight increase in temperature, when focused can start a fire.

   Another example is the laser beam, when all the light waves from a given source are concentrated so that they are all in phase, we end-up with a laser beam. When a laser beam is focused on a given target, the results can be astounding: the light waves from a powerful laser beam can easily cut through a thick piece of metal. When we focus and concentrate our time, energy and resources, we can similarly cut through many of the challenges and obstacles that are standing in our way.

One major time management challenge we are facing today is that there are more things available for us to do than anyone could possibly attempt, let alone accomplish, in an entire lifetime. If we are not careful, it is very easy to diffuse our time and energy with many different trivial pursuits, aimless distractions, and general busyness.

Goals provide a way to focus and concentrate your time and energy into carefully chosen targets that are designed to make significant positive impacts in your life.

3. **Goals can provide motivation, persistence and desire:** Most significant accomplishments are riddled with obstacles, struggles and failures. It is estimated that Thomas Edison failed over one thousand times before he finally discovered a way to make the light bulb work. It is very rare for something important to be accomplished successfully on the very first try.

If you want to achieve anything significant, it is likely that you will struggle and fail many times before you finally reach your target. High achievers keep picking themselves up after each fall and continue working steadily toward their targets until they finally reach their goal. Struggle and failure are often part of the price you have to pay for high achievement.

As you can see, any major accomplishment requires motivation and persistence. Where does this motivation come from? It comes from your desire and purpose, from the reasons why you want to accomplish it?

It's been said that a person with a big enough "why" can been almost any "what" or "how", "when your" "why" is big enough, you find a way to reach your targets, even if you have to struggle and try many different things to get there.

One of the main reasons people give up so easily in the face of failure is that they lose sight of their "why". Goals can help you remember your "big why" when you need to pick yourself up and keep going in the face of adversity.

4. **Goals can help you establish priorities:** You will many forks in the road between where you are now and where you want to be. Instead of just going with the flow and letting the "current" or other people's interests determine where you end up, you have to consciously decide which way to go.

   Goals and missions, visions and dreams that inspire them, provide a natural framework to help you identify and establish your priorities and make the "right" choices based on the long-term view of what is most important to you.

5. **Goals can provide a roadmap to take you from**

where you are to where you want to be: A well crafted strategy with an accompanying set of intermediate goals provides a frame work to reach for away targets. One of the best ways to deal with large or seemingly "impossible" tasks is to break them up into a series of intermediate achievable steps and get to work on each piece. As Brian Tracy likes to say, "By the yard it's hard, but inch by inch it's a inch!"

Your intermediate goals give you valuable feedback: they tell you whether you are making progress or not, and can warn you if you are getting off course.

In almost any endevour, you will need to make adjustments to your plans and overall strategy as you learn from your mistakes, face and overcome obstacles and experience unexpected setbacks. As the old adage states, "No plan survives first contact with the battelfield." Your strategy will also need to change and adapt based on the situations and circumstances you experience.

Note that in all the five reasons above, I say that goals can help you in various ways. In order for goals to help you, they have to be the right kind of goals and you have to use them in the right way.

Top Six Reasons People Don't Set Goals

Experts estimate that only 5-10 percent of people bother to think about their goals on a regular basis,and only 1 percent to 3 percent have clear written goals. If goal setting is such a powerful tool, why don't more people use it?

1. **They don't have a good reason to set goals:** Goals can help you get what you want, but they won't

help you figure out what that is! You have to be clear about what you really want before you can use goals to help you get it.

2. **They don't know about it**: Another reason people don't set goals is that they don't realize the power and value of goal setting as a tool for success and high achievement. Maybe they were never introduced to goal setting. After all, it is not something usually taught in our school or college system. If you don't know abuot a tool, you can't use it.
3. **They don't know how to use it**: Many people think they have goals, but what they really have are just wishes. You ask them what their goals are and they say something vague and generic like "I want to be rich", "I want a better job", or "I want to be healthy". Those are good dreams to have, but they are not goals.

   Other say that they tried goal setting and concluded that it doesn't work. They tell you something like "I tried setting a New Year's resolution a few years back, but I didn't even last a week?" What they don't realize is that most New Year's resolutions are merely vague wishes, not real goals. People almost never write them down or prepare a plan foı achieving them.

   Imagine someone trying to use a power drill without knowing that you have to plug it in, and then telling you that power drills don't work! Goal setting is a tool that helps you achieve what you want step by step, but you need to know how to use it properly or you won't get anything from it.

4. **Fear:** Fear is a powerful emotion that can help us in many circumstances, but can also be destructive and paralyzing in others. Goal setting often requires us to overcome several deep-rooted fears: fear of failure, fear of rejuction and fear of the unknown. Failing to overcome these fears leads to mediocre goals that produce mediocre results, or worse, to not setting goals at all.
5. **They feel too busy and disorganized:** A common reason people don't set goals is that they are too busy and disorganized to even consider taking on new challenges. They reject the nation at a subconscious level and come up with excuse after excuse of why they can't get goals right now.

    They just can't fool themselves into believing that they well be able to achieve their goals when they already feel stressed and overwhelmed just trying to cope with their current demands.

    One common excuse is "I will set goals some day when things settle down a bit and I get more time", but they never end-up finding the time. You have to make time for goal setting.
6. **They get overwhemled:** Many people get inspired to try goal setting because they read about it or hear it on the news. They want to be more successful and achieve better results, and they understand that goal setting can help them.

A large number of them fall into a common trap that quickly leads to overwhelm and frustration, and they often end-up abandoning goal setting before they even get started.

The trap 'I am talking about is trying to set a large number of goals for every aspect of their life. They grab a piece of paper, write the word "Goals" on it and then struggle to come-up with anything to put down. They are trying to juggle in their mind everything they want in all the different areas of their life before committing to any one thing. No wonder they can't find it. Or they may comeup with too many goals for everything from health, fitness, spouse, kids, community, spiritual, learning, career, money, toys . . . and quickly realize there is not way they can handle it.

Think of goal setting as a muscle. Like any muscle, the more you use it, the stranger it gets, but you have to be gradual about it. What would happen if you go into the gym and try to bench press too much weight? You would strain or tear your chest muscles. To get stronger, muscles need gradual increases in resistence.

Goal setting is the same way, you have to start small and gradually build-up. New goal setters should limit themselves to one small. "Warm-up" goal that they can pursue from beginning to end in a matter of a few weeks or months. After completing their first goal, they can increase the resistance by pursuing one or two larger goals.

Eventually, most people can simultaneously pursue one or two large goals in every important part of their life without feeling overwhelmed.

They just have to get there gradually to avoid straining their goal setting "muscles".

Why Manage Your Time?

I would like to tell you that you only have so much of it

and it shouldn't be wasted, but I won't. There's a much more important reason it will increase your productivity by making more time available to do more work. Increasing your productivity will lead to adding more value to your organization and that will make you more successful.

1. **How Do You Spend Your Time:** Most of us don't really know how we spend our time each day. We think we do, but we tend to forget, or don't realize in the first place, the time wasters in our workdays. Things like distractions, Visitors, ·interruptions, lack of focus and disorganization.

   In order to identify these time wasters you must keep a work-diary of each task or activity you perform during your workdays for one week. Why a full week five whole days you ask? Because it will take five days too see trends in your daily habits and activities. In order to manage your time, you must document your time wasters and that takes being diligent and honest in your entries. You should use a simple form with columns for time of day, activity description, and amount of time for the activity. Make entries as activities are completed instead of waiting until the end of the day.

   When you have completed your entries for the entire five days, categorize each activity by whether it added value to your job and your objectives, or wasted time. Add up the wasted time activities to see how much actual work time you lose each week. This will be an eye-opener and should motivate you to use time management techniques in your daily life.

2. **Planning: the to-do list:** When you are going to have to plan your days and the best way to do that is with a to-do list. Using some 'best practice' techniques with your list will help you get the most out of it. You must first know what your goals and objectives are. What will add value to your organization in the near and long term? Knowing your goals and objectives will help you prioritize your activities.

   Begin by listing the tasks and activities for the next day on a sheet of paper. Next, assign a priority code to each one. You can use ABC code as follows. A priorities are important and urgent. B priorities are important but not urgent and C priorities are urgent but not important. A, B, and C priorities is to substitute these three words: must, should and would. In other words, and A priority is something you must do, a B priority is something you should do and C priority is something you could do.

3. **Working the list:** Work the items by priority and begin with the first priority A item. Work your fist item until it's finished. Then, and only then, should you go on to the next item, and so on. Working this way will keep you on focus to complete the most important activities first keep you from "bouncing" from item to item, wasting time and you will gain satisfaction upon completion of each subsequent item.

   Be flexible when working your list. There will be times when new and unplanned, extremely urgent, A priorties will pop-up and need to be addressed. There will also be occasions when an item take more time than expected to complete. Take these occurrences in stride by completing them as soon as possible and then get back to working your original list.

4. **Planning for the next day:** Review your list at the end of the day. Mark the completed items off the list (with great satisfaction). Carry over items not completed to your next day's list. Check your calender and add items due tomorrow to your list, also add tasks assigned since yesterday and then prioritize this new list before leaving for the day. Planning at the end of the day will give you a sense of how productive your day has been and will allow you to begin the next day on task 1 day.
5. **Signs of overload and what to do:** From time to time we find ourselves with more work to do than there's time in the day addressed in the short run by working additional time to complete the tasks. However, persists it can lead to an overload condition where urgent, important A priority work do organization can afford to be in this condition very long without getting in trouble with other stakeholders.

Warning signs of overload include: not getting all A priority items done each day, and it is not getting to B and C priorities at all and more items than usual carried over each day.

One solution to overload is to go to your supervisor and ask if you are using the correct and, in light of the overload condition do you need to reprioritize so that the most important get done each day. You will usually get some good advice on which items are the "hotted" supervisor.

6. **Handling interruptions:** Interruptions are a reality in the workplace and cannot completely be eliminated. So we minimize their effect on our productivity. Some common interruptions are: the telephone, mail, and work in visitors.

   The telephone interruptions can be eliminated during intense work sessions by simply your work line. However, that extreme solution is usually a bit overkill. If you take a call, your goal communicate the information that is necessary in the most efficient amount of time and Easier said than done in most cases you say? Dr. Dru Scott has some excellent tips on conservations in her book and tapes. How to put more time in your life.

   E-mail and even snail mail can be distraction to completion of a task. It's very temptation you are doing to check the e-mail just into your inbox after the "ding" alerted you of new the office snail mail arrives in your in box. You may be similarly tempted to start reading sorting through it. In any of these cases you will be distracted from the focus needed to-do list.

   You don't have an infinite amount of time in your life. So why not use it wisely? Doing great satisfaction of completing your work as planned, and it will help you to be a more organize person allowing you to be more valuable to your organization and therefore success.

6.4. GOAL SETTING MANAGEMENT SKILLS AND TIME MANAGEMENT

Time management skills are your abilities to recognize and solve personal time management problems. The goal of these time management lessons is to show you what you can do improve those skills.

With good time management skills you are in control of your time and your life, of your stress and energy levels. You make progress at work, you are able to maintain balance between your work. Personal and family lives. You have enough flexibility to respond to surprises or new opportunities.

All time management skills are learnable. More than likely you will see much improvement from simply becoming aware of the essence and cause of common personal time management problems with these time management lessons, you can see better which time management techniques are most relevant for your situation.

Just get started with them. Many of your problems gradually disappear. If you already know how you should be managing your time, but you still don't do it, don't give up. What you may be overlooking is the psychological side of your time management skills, psychological obstacles hidden behind your personality.

Depending on your personal sitution, such obstacles may be the primary reason why you procrastinate, have difficulties saying no, delegating, or making time management desisions.

The psychological component of your time management skills can also be dealt with. The time management skills information below will point at a relevant solution for your situation.

How to Avoid Procrastination

Ability to beat procrastination and laziness is among the most important time management skills to learn. Identify your causes of procrastination and start sighting it now. The essence of procrastination is very well reflected in this quote by Bernard Meltzer: "Hard work is often the easy work you did not do at the proper time."

Have you ever seen your most important task being put off until later and then later and later, while you are getting busy with many not so important activities? Did you hope that you may have more time and better mood in the future to start the task and do it properly? Does an approaching deadline mean a crisis for you? Do you keep hesitating every time you make a decision.

If you often see yourself in such low productivity situations then there is a big chance that your life got under control of the procrastination habit. And those situations are only the most explicit symptoms.

What is it?

A basic definition of procrastination is putting off the things that you should be doing now. This happens with all of us time after time.

Yet, what makes a big difference for your success is your ability to recognize procrastination reasons and expressions in their different forms, and to promptly take them under control, before this bad habit steals your opportunities, damages your career and pride, or destroys your relationships. So why do not you do it now?

Causes of Procrastination

What are typical reasons why you procrastinate? Here are a few of the most common situations to consider in your anti-procrastination efforts.

It can be as simple as

- Waiting for the right mood.
- Waiting for the right time.

Then look at the way you organize your work. You may notice other reasons for procrastination like.

(*i*) lack of clear goals.

(*ii*) Under estimating the difficulty of the tasks.

(*iii*) Under estimating the time required to complete the tasks.

(*iv*) Unclear standards for the task outcomes.

(*v*) Feeling as the tasks are imposed on you from outside.

(*vi*) Too ambiguous tasks.

And there are also many connections with:

(*i*) Underdeveloped decision-making skills.

(*ii*) Fear of failure or fear of success.

(*iii*) Perfectionism.

Career Goal Setting and Career Choice Tips

One of the toughest issues in career choice and career goal setting and planning is identifying what is it you want. Even when it seems that know what you want, you may still have doubts on if your career choice is right. Reaching clarity in those issues may be the most important thing you can do in your career planning and goal setting.

Here are a few career goal setting guidelines that can help. Most people even very successful ones, have some periods in their career path, when they seem unsure about their career choice and goals. It is totally human to feel that way. Often, such periods just come and go. For example, they come when you face some overwhelming obstacles on your way. It is all over as soon as you get through the obstacles. That situation by itself is not a problem of choosing career, only a test of your perserverance.

But what if those doubt persist, if they always live somewhere in the background of your thoughts? If it just does not feel right? If this is the case, then it is time to look more carefully at your career choice and occupational goals and objectives.

In most cases the answers are inside you, though not that easy to find. Yet, you can see a much clearer picture of your ideal job or career choice as soon as free yourself from certain psychological traps.

The psychological blocks easily hide in your thinking, they often have quite deep roots, and you cannot just switch them off. And letting them stay hidden and ignored is a big mistake that can cost you career satisfaction and life happiness.

Barbara Sher, a well-known therapist and career counselor, has been digging dipping into those psychological blocks in career choice and career goal setting with many of her clients. What she found is that in most cases the clients were "locked in an internal battle and didn't even know it. "Yet, as soon as those inner conflicts are uncovered and understood, it is relatively easy to take care of them. Barbara Sher has identified the typical inner conflict scenarios, such as "On the wrong track and moving fast", "I have lost my big dream", or I want too many things, just to name a few of the many.

Finally, after you clarify what it is you want, in your career goal setting and planning you can use, for writing job objectives and goals.

Goal Setting and Your Subconscious Mind

To understand better how personal goal setting works, it is good to have a simple picture of how your mind is functioning. You can think of your mind being built of two parts: conscious and subconscious minds. Conscious mind is responsible for your current awareness and decision making. It is only around 12 percent of your mind. The other 88 percent is your subconscious mind.

Subconcious mind is where you have your personality, where all your feelings and thoughts come from your memory, with all your perosnal values, beliefs, and habits, is also there.

You have quite good and direct control over your conscious mind. It takes more effort and sophistication to direct and reprogramme your subconscious mind, this is where smart personal goal setting techniques and guidelines are particularly helpful.

Did you know? You go through 120 minutes of natural mind-programming every single day of your life? Whether you like it or not? You would better make sure you are not programming yourself negatively during this time!

Top Four Secrets Revealed in ProgrammeYour Mind for Success in Record Time

1. The daily, nature-included 120 minutes "window of opportunity", "mind programming time, when you can programme your mind for absolutely anything you want . . . easily, effortlessly, painlessly and . . .instantly! This is the greatest and most ancient mind-programming secret of all times to be revealed!
2. Your self-improvement chart! with critical segments and dangerous points identified for you!
3. The Amazing Mind-Programming Magic Questions: Ask yourself these questions and your mind will start programming itself for anything you want easily and . . .Automatically!
4. How to Build your own self-improvement, mind Programming 'Magic Lamp'! This is the only self improvement technique on the face of this earth that yields instant changes and amazing results! Period!

Top Seven Uses of Programme Your Mind for Success in Record Time

1. Lose excess weight, look and feel great!
2. Real success and achievement!
3. Nuke bad habits like smoking, drinking, nail biting, etc.
4. Accelerated learning and stronger memory retention!
5. Master sports skills!
6. Have super self-confidence and motivation!

7. Transform your children into real super kids!

6.5. IMPORTANCE OF GOAL SETTING AND TIME MANAGEMENT

Effective goal setting begins and ends with time-management. You must be able to balance your time in the best way possible in order to achieve your goals. Most of us fail to achieve goals because we "lack the time". That is why this section needed to be included in this guide.

The concept of time management has been in existence for more than 100 year believe it or not. Unfortunately the term 'time management' creates a false impression of what a person is able to do.

Time can't be managend, time is uncontrollable and we can only manage ourselves and our use of time. That is all that can be done. Time management is actually self-management.

For effective time management we need the ability to paln, delegate, organize, direct and control every aspect of our lives just to find 30 minutes a day that is devoted to something productive that is just for us.

There are Common Time Wasters Which Need to be Identified

In order for a time management process to work it is important to know what aspects of our personal management need to be improved. Otherwise what is the point in trying?

Below you will find some of the most frequent reasons for reducing effectiveness in and around our lives. You might want to check the ones which are causing to be the major obstacles to your own time management. These are referred to as your time stealers.

Identifying Your Time Stealers

1. Interruptions for example the telephone or TV (these are also distractions)
2. Interruptions for example, guests.
3. Meetings.
4. Tasks you should have had else do for you.
5. Procrastination and indecision.
6. Acting without total information.
7. Dealing with other people's issues or problems.
8. Some sort of personal crisis, for example, family member is sick or injured.
9. Unclear communication.
10. Inadequate knowledge.
11. Unclear objectives and priorities.
12. Lack of planning.
13. Stress, anxiety and fatigue.
14. Inability to say "No" to anybody with a request.
15. Personal disorganization.

There are quite a few isn't there? Fortunately, there are strategies you can use to manage your time in a better way and be more in control and reduce stress, but you can analyze your time and see how you may be both the cause and the solution to your time challenges. Below, we will look at time management issues in more detail.

1. **Shifting priorities and crisis management:** Management guru Peter Drucker says that "crisis management is actually the form of management preferred by most managers". What is ironic is that actions taken before the crisis could have prevented it in the first place.

2. **The telephone:** Have you ever had one of those days when you just had to answer the phone with "grand centralisation, how can I help you?" The telephone can be our greatest communication tool can be our biggest enemy to effectiveness if you don't know how to control it's hold over you.
3. **Lack of priorities:** This is probably the biggest and most important time waster. It affects all we do both professionally. Thos who accomplish the most in a day know exactly what the want to accomplish beforehand, just ask Donal Trump.

   Unfortunately too many of us think that goals and objectives are yearly things and not daily considerations. These results in too much time spent on the major things and not on the things which are important to our lives.
4. **Attempting too much:** Many people today feel that they have to accomplish everything yesterday and don't give themselves enough time to do things properly. This leads only to half finished projects and no feeling of achievement as all things are done in a hurry and appear rushed to others.
5. **Drop in visitors:** The five deadliest words that rob your time are "Have you got a minute?" Everyone does it, colleagues, the boss, your peers, and your family and friends. Knowing how to deal with interruptions is one of the best skills you can learn.
6. **Ineffective delegation:** Good delegation is considered a key skill in both managers and leaders of homes and work.

   The best managers have an ability to delegate

work to staff and family members to ensure it is done correctly. This is probably the best way of building a team moral and reducing your own workload at the same time.

The general rule is this: if one of your people around you can do it 80 percent as well as you can and then delegate it.

7. **Procrastination:** The biggest thief of time is not decision making but decision avoidance. By reducing the amount of procrastinating you do, you can substantically increase the amount of active time available to you.
8. **The inability to say "No"!:** The general rule is, if people can dump their work or problems on to your shoulders they will do it.

   Some of the most stressed people around lack the skill to "just say no" for fear of upsetting people. Get over it because these people can do it for you.
9. **Meetings:** Studies have shown that average professional person spends about 17 hours a week in meetings and about 6 hours in the planning time and untold hours in the follow up.

Manage Your Time Better

There are many ways we can manage our time. I have listed some strategies you can use to manage your time in a better and more efficieent manner. They are noted below:

1. **Always define your goals as clearly as possible:** Do you find you are not doing what to do just because your goals have not been set properly yet?

One of the factors which make successful and happy people stand out is their ability to work out what they want to achieve and have written goals which they can review them constantly.

You long-term goals should impact on your daily activities and be included on your "to-do" list. Without a goal or objective people tend to just drift off personally and professionally.

2. **Analyse your use of time:** Are you spending enough time on the projects which although may not be urgent now but are things that you need to do develop yourself or your career?

   If you are constantly asking yourself "what can I do to make things easier for me right now?" it will help you to focus on "important tasks" and stop reaching to task which seem urgent but carry no importance towards your goals.

3. **Have a plan:** How can you achieve your gaols without a plan? I don't even think that is possible. Most people know what they want but have no plan to achieve it except by sheer hard work. What's the point in doing hard work when you don't know how to apply it/

   Yearly plan should be reviewed daily and reset as your achievements are met. Successul people makes lists constantly. It enables them to stay on top of priorities and enable them to remain flexible to changing priorities. This should be done for both personal and business goals.

4. **Action plan analysis:** Problems will always happen when you set a plan. The value of a good plan

is to identify them early and seek out solutions immediately.

Good time management enables you a measure the progress towards your goals because "what you can measure, you can control!"

Always try to be productive in the achievement of successfully managing your time.

Time management is not a hard subject to understand, but unless you are committed to building better time management techniques into your daily routine you will achieve partial results and end-up right back where you started.

You have to commit to managing your time better and remember to include time for yourself.

By setting goals, eliminating time wasters and doing this everyday, you may find you will have extra time in the work to spend on those people and activities most important to you.

Importance of Goal Setting for Students

When you are a student, one of the last things you have on your mind is setting goals, it feels like you just want to have fun all the time. Well by following these tips, you can get the best of both worlds.

1. *Review Weekly*

Each week you should set aside one hour here you make sure that you are keeping up to date in your goals and this time can be used to set tasks for the next week. Make this on a day when you have some free time and you can relax, once this is done you are set for the rest of the week.

2. *Set Time Quota Goals*

Set a goal that you will do your homework on a certain day of the week. That way you save the time is takes going back and forth between homework, you get in homework mode making you more effective also.

3. *Stop Watching TV*

Do you know how much an average person watches TV ? hours per day. Now that might not sound too drastic. But let us say that you watch 4 hours per day, that's 2 months of constant time, no sleeping that you use up per year. Now I know lots more important and fun things, I could do with that time. Get assignments in earlier, increase my income, etc.

4. *Set Goals per Subject, But not too Many*

Set different goals per subject depending on what you want to achieve and how good you are at the subject. Do not set too many through as you will feel overwhelmed.

5. *Follow a Good System*

By following a good system goal setting for students you can minimize the amount of the on setting and achiveing the goal and spend more time doing what you love best.

Importance of Goal Setting in Business

Accountability has been a word attached to goals for a long time. Is this not something that we can accomplish on your own? What is the big to do about it?

Well, if we sit down and recall each goal that we set out to accomplish all the little ones on up to the larger than life goals.

But there must be clearly defined goals that, at the end of the day is rewarding clearly set the goals for your business. Think about where you would an envision your business to be in six months. Do not keep yourself from even looking beyond that, how about two years or even further, how about five years?

It is an organized way to pur your goals on a schedule time frame. This will make it a reality to see the process beginning to take a real start to see it written down. Always be careful with this process as it is the foundation to an important realization. The internet is a helpful tool as well, although there is a lot of misinformation out there. In short, take your time and research your subject thoroughly first.

It is a really good idea is to break your goals into small manageable chunks. You might start by concurring your goals in increments, monthly and daily goals. By doing it in this manner gives you the confidence you need to defect the next trek-up the mountain at your place. It is easy to forget that we can run up that mountain without taking the time for some training first. Stay the original plan, remain focused because that victory line becomes more visible.

Consisteney helps to give you that positive outlook on your long-term goals, first your six month goal and once you have reached those then that one year goal maker is already half way there, all that hard work in the beginning will be your motivation to push for your next achievement.

Accomplishing your daily goals will be like adding fuel to your ambitions, desires and motivation, always treasure each victory and each success.

Hold on to your straightforward aspirations and stick with it. Because if you surround yourself with those that believe in you, your goals and your ambitions, you are sure to succeed in your goals. Set-up challenging but reasonable goals for yourself. Keep in mind that with each goal a measurement is incorporated.

To succeed in any area of your life, be it business or personal, you must start with a goal. Your ability to set and achieve goals will provide you a sense of direction and is the first step in becoming successful.

People say that you only have to work hard to get where you want to be in life. Well that's true but you can't get to where you want to be if you don't know where you are going.

Does that make sense? You can't set out to go to a restaurant and not know where it's located. Just because you know where you want to go doesn't mean that you can locate it. Sure, you could drive around for hours looking for it but why make it hard on yourself. By doing some preliminary work before you set out on your journey. You could save yourself time, money and energy.

Goals enable you to control the direction of your life and they allow the things that are happening around you to be self-directed or positive rather than random or negative. Keep in mind that you can't control what has happened in your past but you can decide whether your future controls you or whether you control it.

By learning to set goals you will become more confident. Working toward goals will raise your self-esteem and, self-respect. As you move toward setting then accomplishing your goals, you will have a tremendous feeling of personal pride and accomplishment.

Importance of Goal Setting for Entrepreneur

Setting and achieving goals is where success happens! We often get struck at the beginning of the process with assessing our situation and setting goals without following through to completion. Setting goals without achieving them equals failure.

Failure can be defined as simply missing the mark, not achieving goals set. If you don't set any goals for yorself, you could say have succeeded because you didn't fail. We are striving animals. Setting and achieving goals is the mainstay of purposeful living. The successful entrepreneur mindset uses goal directed thinking in every aspect of designing and running a business.

Effective goal setting happens when we choose goals that we believe we can truly achieve. We keep those goals ever in front of us, never losing sight of where we want to go in life. The ground work for effective goal setting starts with this crucial components.

Keys to Effective Goal Setting

1. **Have a vision:** Start with a fully detailed vision for yourself and your business. Without a vivid image of how your business will look in the future, you will not be able to set all of your daily, weekly and monthly goals that will proper your business beyond your imaginagion into reality.
2. **Know your passions:** Often the problem with goals isn't in setting them but being motivated actually achieve the goals, you have set up. Think about really gets you fired up. I am not talking about simply your direct sales company but rather what drives your dreams. Your passions need to

be able to get behind your list of goals and fuel the fire that makes you ACT. Goal setting without action is what . . .simply a diversion from the actual "work" of making things happen.

3. **Be brutally honest:** Setting goals means being honest with yourself and others. Living a life fully and achieving your goals required complete honesty. Look deep inside yourself. Know your strength and weaknesses. Don't pretend to have skills or talents that simply exist within you. It is a major waste of your time and energy to strive to be someone else. Your vision, passion and gifts that exists within you will carry you toward your goals. As "To thine own self be true".
4. **Set goals that are yours to achieve:** Your goals must be literally 'your goals'. It is possible for you to be passionate about someone else's goals. For you to achieve the before you, you must believe deep within yourself that the goals are working toward where you want to go. Don't take on goals for yourself that were designed by someone life and your vision then set goals that you will walk through fire to achieve.
5. **Live a life of action:** Remember to spend less time on setting your goals than action motion. If you have a tendency to get stuck in the 'planning' stage of goal setting, the setting smaller achievable goals each day that you make a priority to reach before there your goal is three home parties a week then set a goal that is yours to achieve within.

6.6 CONCLUSION

The whole point of setting a goal is to help you bridge the gap between where you are and where you want to be. If you set goals and work toward them diligently, you can have all the things you want. People who set and achieve their goals are people who have decided what they want, committed themselves to going after it, and haven't let anything stand in their way, short of violating the rights of others.

A proper goal gives you all the incentive you need to grow in your awareness of being a perfect expression of an infinite power, designed for excellence and abundance. As you become more welcoming and aware of your relationship with God, and of all the potential that's been built into you, you will function more effectively in harmony with the laws of the universe. Living in synch with all of this will yield results, you have never dreamed possible. They say that awareness is curative. It gives deep meaning to life because it spells the end of your robotic existence, no more walking in the deep ruts formed by your harmful programming and counter productive life.

SELF-ASSESSMENT

1. What is goal setting?
2. What is the importance of goal setting?
3. Discuss the effective time management tips, techniques and strategies.
4. Examine the importance of goal setting for businessman and entrepeneur.

REFERENCES

Goal Setting and Achievement, Walter J. Wadsworth, Info@Achieve Max.Com

Goals and Goal Setting, Larrie A. Rouillard, Achieve Max.Com

Goal Setting, Susan B. Wilson, Achieve Max.Com

Magic of Believing, Claude M. Bristol.

The Magic Lamp, Keith Ellis/Achieve Max.Com

Make Success Measurable, Douglas K. Smith.

Simple Steps to Impossible Dreams, Steven K. Scott, Achieve Max.Com

Index